G.I. JOE

BEST OF WORST OF

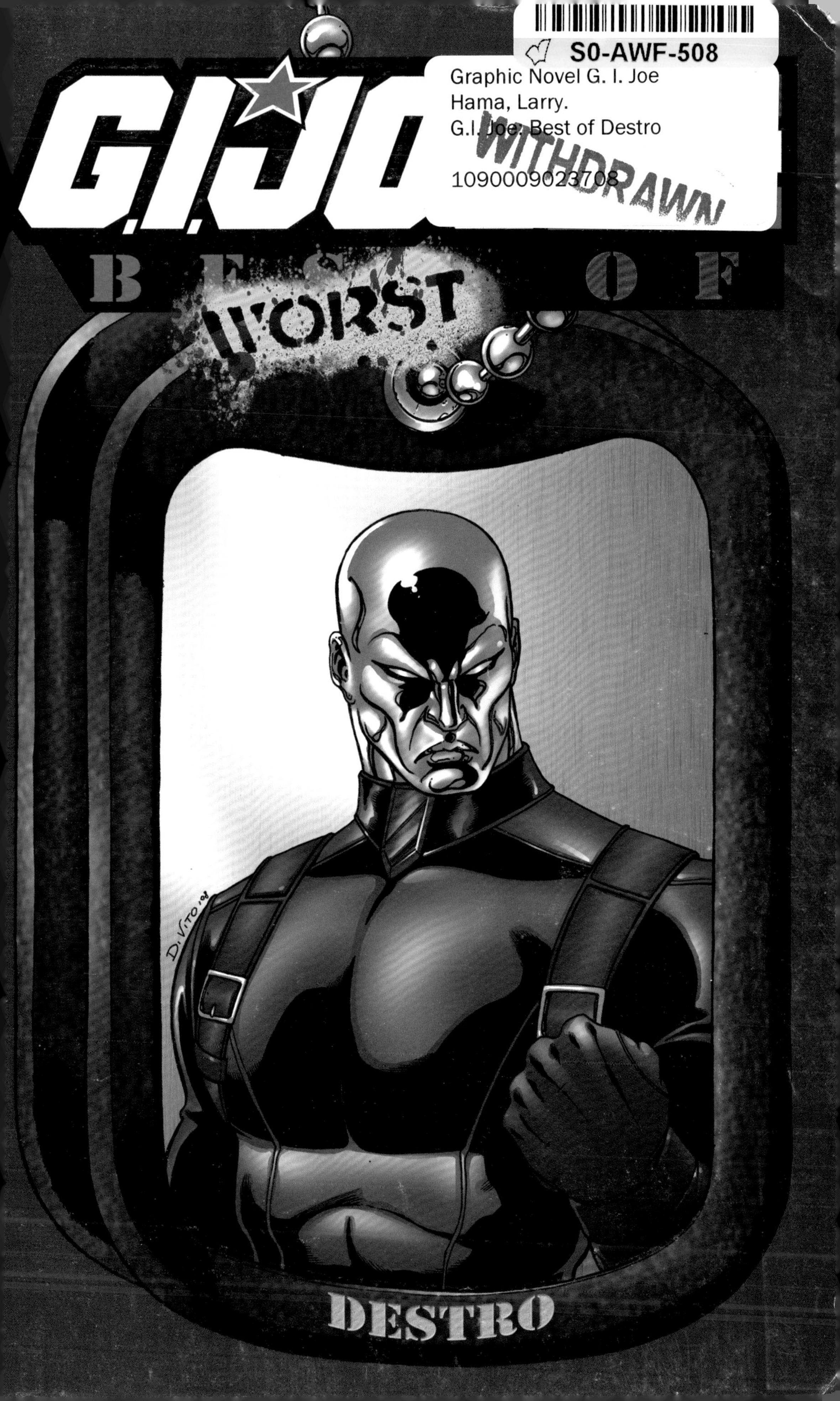
D. VITO '08

DESTRO

ISBN: 978-160010-448-0

12 11 10 09   1 2 3 4

www.idwpublishing.com

Special thanks to Hasbro's Aaron Archer, Michael Kelly,
Amie Lozanski, Ed Lane, Michael Provost, Michael Richie,
Sarah Baskin, Samantha Lomow, Joe Furfaro, and Michael
Verrecchia for their invaluable assistance.

Additional thanks to Dan Buckley, David Bogart, and Jeff
Youngquist at Marvel Entertainment for their assistance in
acquiring the re-colored pages presented in this collection.

Originally published by Marvel Comics as G.I. JOE: A REAL AMERICAN HERO Issues #11, 14, 33, 57, 78, and 87.

IDW Publishing
Operations:
Ted Adams, Chief Executive Officer
Greg Goldstein, Chief Operating Officer
Matthew Ruzicka, CPA, Chief Financial Officer
Alan Payne, VP of Sales
Lorelei Bunjes, Dir. of Digital Services
AnnaMaria White, Marketing & PR Manager
Marci Hubbard, Executive Assistant
Alonzo Simon, Shipping Manager

Editorial:
Chris Ryall, Publisher/Editor-in-Chief
Scott Dunbier, Editor, Special Projects
Andy Schmidt, Senior Editor
Justin Eisinger, Editor
Kris Oprisko, Editor/Foreign Lic.
Denton J. Tipton, Editor
Tom Waltz, Editor
Mariah Huehner, Associate Editor

Design:
Robbie Robbins, EVP/Sr. Graphic Artist
Ben Templesmith, Artist/Designer
Neil Uyetake, Art Director
Chris Mowry, Graphic Artist
Amauri Osorio, Graphic Artist
Gilberto Lozcano, Production Assistant

All stories written by
Larry Hama

Collection Edits by **Justin Eisinger** & **Mariah Huehner**
Collection Design by **Chris Mowry**
Collection Production by **Amauri Osorio**

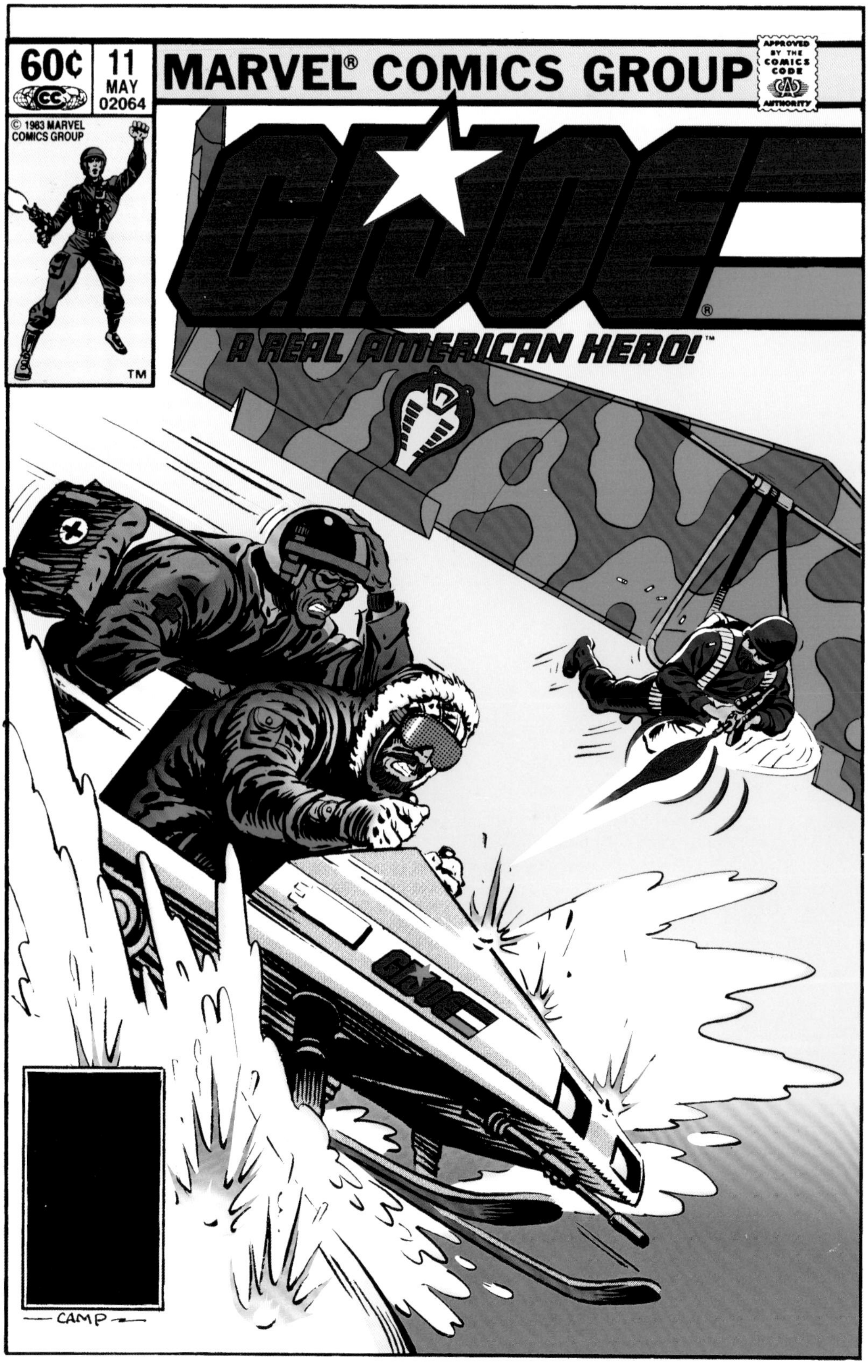

60¢
11
MAY
02064
MARVEL® COMICS GROUP
APPROVED BY THE COMICS CODE AUTHORITY
© 1983 MARVEL COMICS GROUP
TM
G.I. JOE®
A REAL AMERICAN HERO!™
G.I. JOE
CAMP

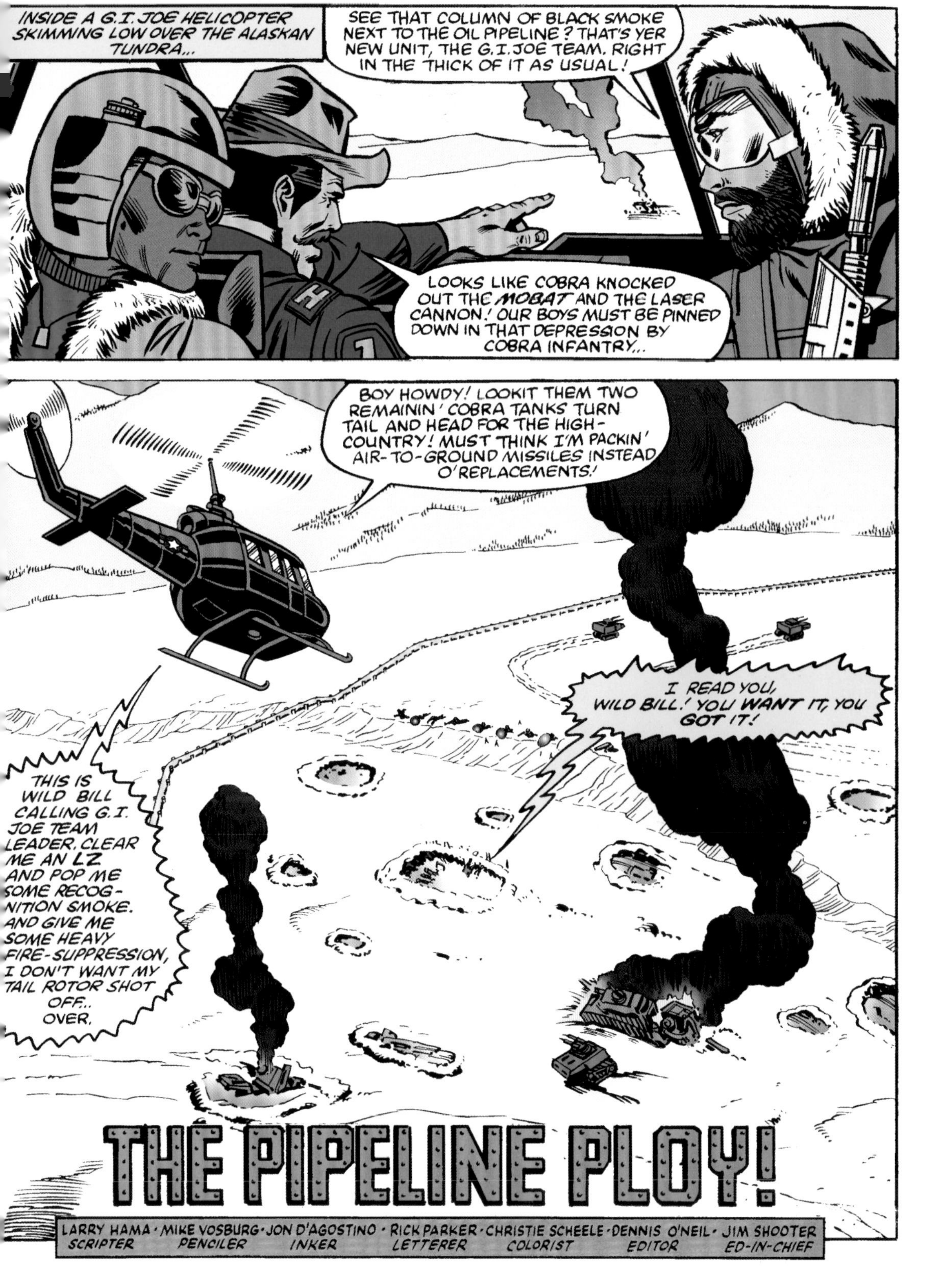
INSIDE A G.I. JOE HELICOPTER SKIMMING LOW OVER THE ALASKAN TUNDRA...
SEE THAT COLUMN OF BLACK SMOKE NEXT TO THE OIL PIPELINE? THAT'S YER NEW UNIT, THE G.I. JOE TEAM. RIGHT IN THE THICK OF IT AS USUAL!
LOOKS LIKE COBRA KNOCKED OUT THE MOBAT AND THE LASER CANNON! OUR BOYS MUST BE PINNED DOWN IN THAT DEPRESSION BY COBRA INFANTRY...
BOY HOWDY! LOOKIT THEM TWO REMAININ' COBRA TANKS TURN TAIL AND HEAD FOR THE HIGH-COUNTRY! MUST THINK I'M PACKIN' AIR-TO-GROUND MISSILES INSTEAD O'REPLACEMENTS!
THIS IS WILD BILL CALLING G.I. JOE TEAM LEADER. CLEAR ME AN LZ AND POP ME SOME RECOG-NITION SMOKE. AND GIVE ME SOME HEAVY FIRE-SUPPRESSION, I DON'T WANT MY TAIL ROTOR SHOT OFF... OVER.
I READ YOU, WILD BILL! YOU WANT IT, YOU GOT IT!
THE PIPELINE PLOY!
LARRY HAMA · MIKE VOSBURG · JON D'AGOSTINO · RICK PARKER · CHRISTIE SCHEELE · DENNIS O'NEIL · JIM SHOOTER
SCRIPTER PENCILER INKER LETTERER COLORIST EDITOR ED-IN-CHIEF

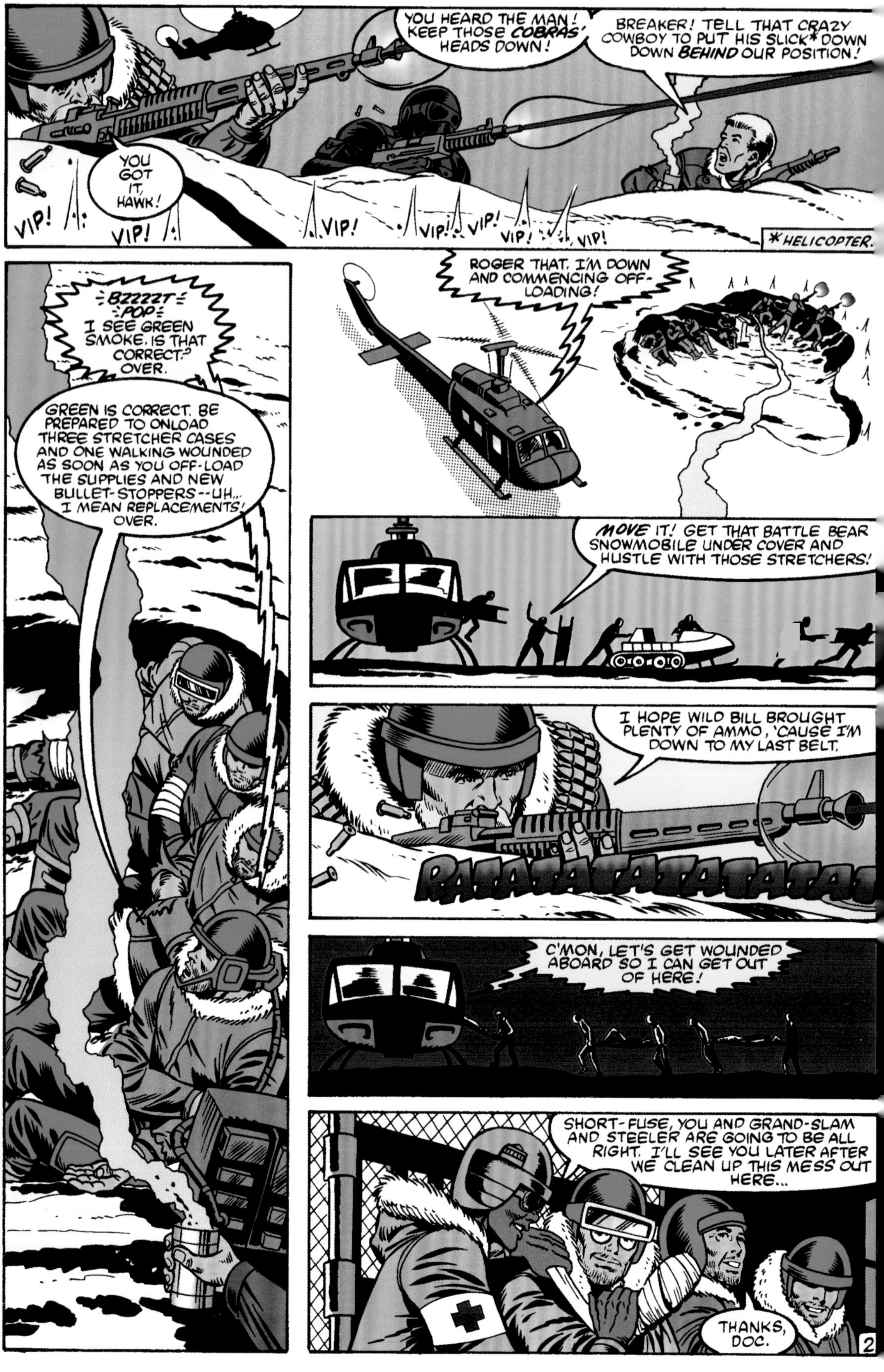
YOU HEARD THE MAN! KEEP THOSE COBRAS' HEADS DOWN!
YOU GOT IT, HAWK!
BREAKER! TELL THAT CRAZY COWBOY TO PUT HIS SLICK* DOWN DOWN BEHIND OUR POSITION!
VIP! VIP! VIP! VIP! VIP! VIP! VIP!
*HELICOPTER.
BZZZZT POP I SEE GREEN SMOKE. IS THAT CORRECT? OVER.
GREEN IS CORRECT. BE PREPARED TO ONLOAD THREE STRETCHER CASES AND ONE WALKING WOUNDED AS SOON AS YOU OFF-LOAD THE SUPPLIES AND NEW BULLET-STOPPERS--UH... I MEAN REPLACEMENTS! OVER.
ROGER THAT. I'M DOWN AND COMMENCING OFF-LOADING!
MOVE IT! GET THAT BATTLE BEAR SNOWMOBILE UNDER COVER AND HUSTLE WITH THOSE STRETCHERS!
I HOPE WILD BILL BROUGHT PLENTY OF AMMO, 'CAUSE I'M DOWN TO MY LAST BELT.
C'MON, LET'S GET WOUNDED ABOARD SO I CAN GET OUT OF HERE!
SHORT-FUSE, YOU AND GRAND-SLAM AND STEELER ARE GOING TO BE ALL RIGHT. I'LL SEE YOU LATER AFTER WE CLEAN UP THIS MESS OUT HERE...
THANKS, DOC.
2

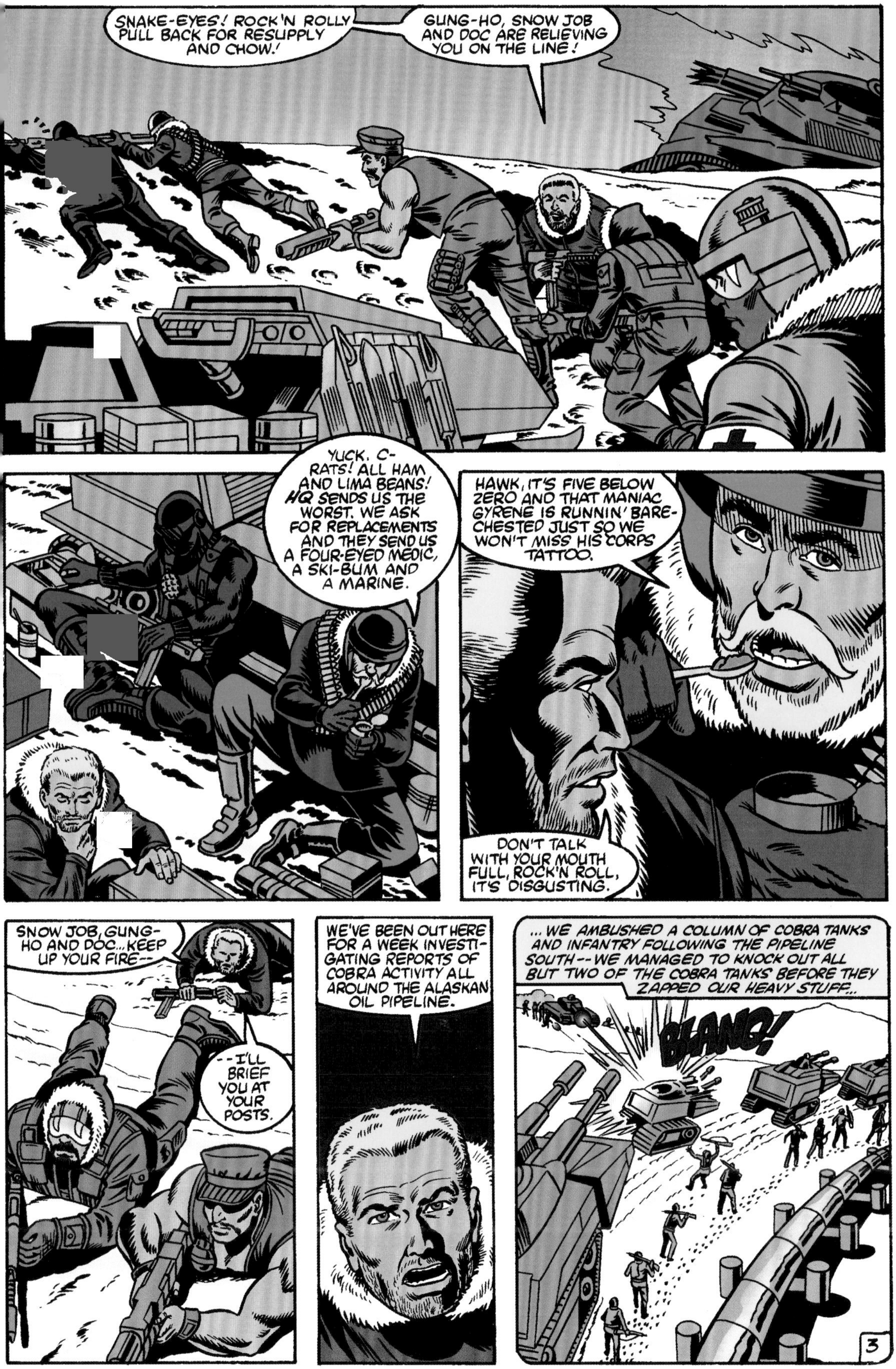
SNAKE-EYES! ROCK'N ROLLY PULL BACK FOR RESUPPLY AND CHOW.!
GUNG-HO, SNOW JOB AND DOC ARE RELIEVING YOU ON THE LINE!
YUCK. C-RATS! ALL HAM AND LIMA BEANS! HQ SENDS US THE WORST. WE ASK FOR REPLACEMENTS AND THEY SEND US A FOUR-EYED MEDIC, A SKI-BUM AND A MARINE.
HAWK, IT'S FIVE BELOW ZERO AND THAT MANIAC GYRENE IS RUNNIN' BARE-CHESTED JUST SO WE WON'T MISS HIS CORPS TATTOO.
DON'T TALK WITH YOUR MOUTH FULL, ROCK'N ROLL, IT'S DISGUSTING.
SNOW JOB, GUNG-HO AND DOC... KEEP UP YOUR FIRE--
--I'LL BRIEF YOU AT YOUR POSTS.
WE'VE BEEN OUT HERE FOR A WEEK INVESTIGATING REPORTS OF COBRA ACTIVITY ALL AROUND THE ALASKAN OIL PIPELINE.
...WE AMBUSHED A COLUMN OF COBRA TANKS AND INFANTRY FOLLOWING THE PIPELINE SOUTH--WE MANAGED TO KNOCK OUT ALL BUT TWO OF THE COBRA TANKS BEFORE THEY ZAPPED OUR HEAVY STUFF...
BLANG!
3

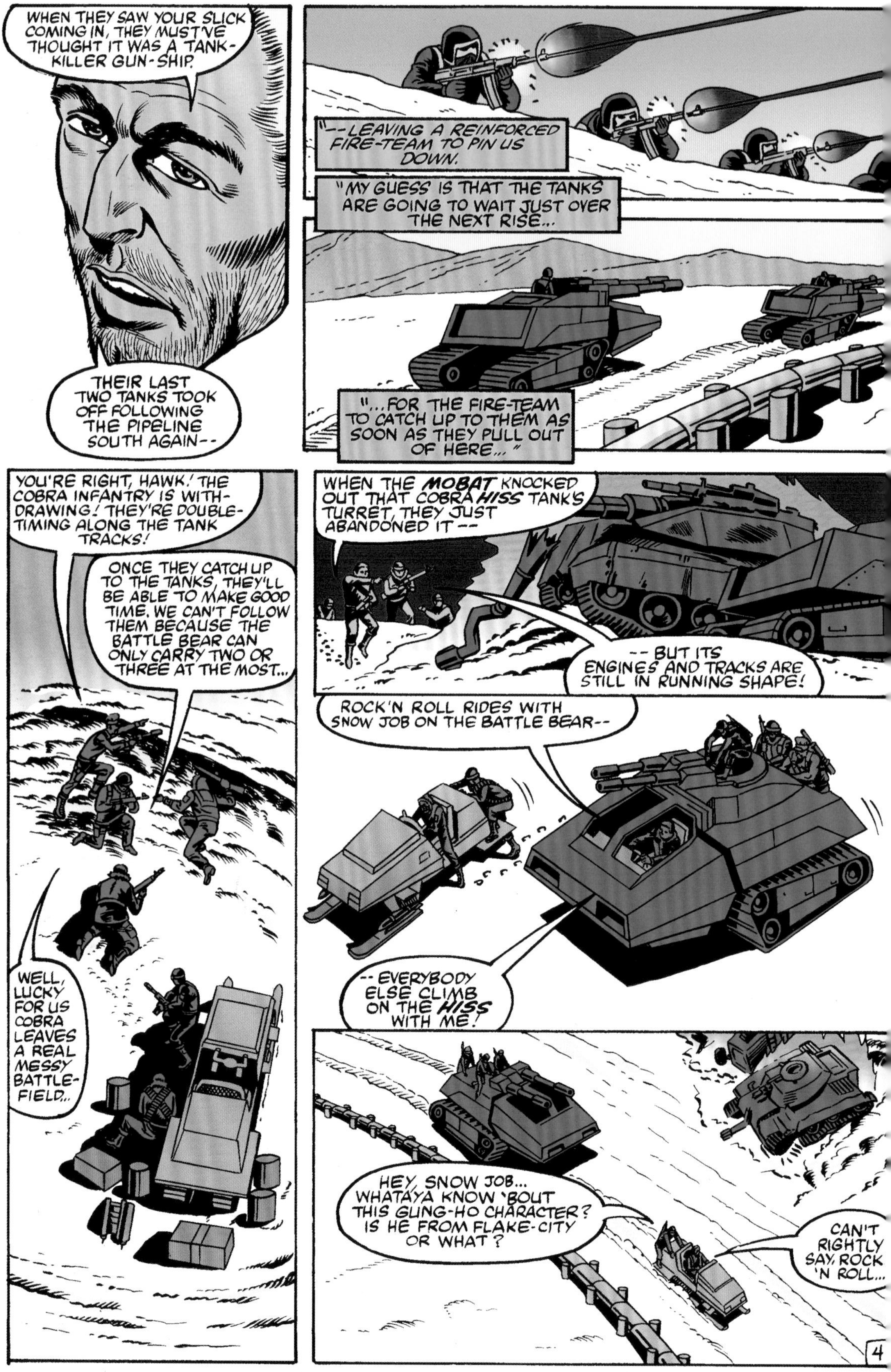
WHEN THEY SAW YOUR SLICK COMING IN, THEY MUST'VE THOUGHT IT WAS A TANK-KILLER GUN-SHIP.
THEIR LAST TWO TANKS TOOK OFF FOLLOWING THE PIPELINE SOUTH AGAIN--
"--LEAVING A REINFORCED FIRE-TEAM TO PIN US DOWN.
"MY GUESS IS THAT THE TANKS ARE GOING TO WAIT JUST OVER THE NEXT RISE...
"...FOR THE FIRE-TEAM TO CATCH UP TO THEM AS SOON AS THEY PULL OUT OF HERE..."
YOU'RE RIGHT, HAWK! THE COBRA INFANTRY IS WITH-DRAWING! THEY'RE DOUBLE-TIMING ALONG THE TANK TRACKS!
ONCE THEY CATCH UP TO THE TANKS, THEY'LL BE ABLE TO MAKE GOOD TIME. WE CAN'T FOLLOW THEM BECAUSE THE BATTLE BEAR CAN ONLY CARRY TWO OR THREE AT THE MOST...
WELL, LUCKY FOR US COBRA LEAVES A REAL MESSY BATTLE-FIELD...
WHEN THE MOBAT KNOCKED OUT THAT COBRA HISS TANK'S TURRET, THEY JUST ABANDONED IT --
-- BUT ITS ENGINES AND TRACKS ARE STILL IN RUNNING SHAPE!
ROCK'N ROLL RIDES WITH SNOW JOB ON THE BATTLE BEAR--
-- EVERYBODY ELSE CLIMB ON THE HISS WITH ME!
HEY, SNOW JOB... WHATAYA KNOW 'BOUT THIS GUNG-HO CHARACTER? IS HE FROM FLAKE-CITY OR WHAT?
CAN'T RIGHTLY SAY, ROCK 'N ROLL...
4

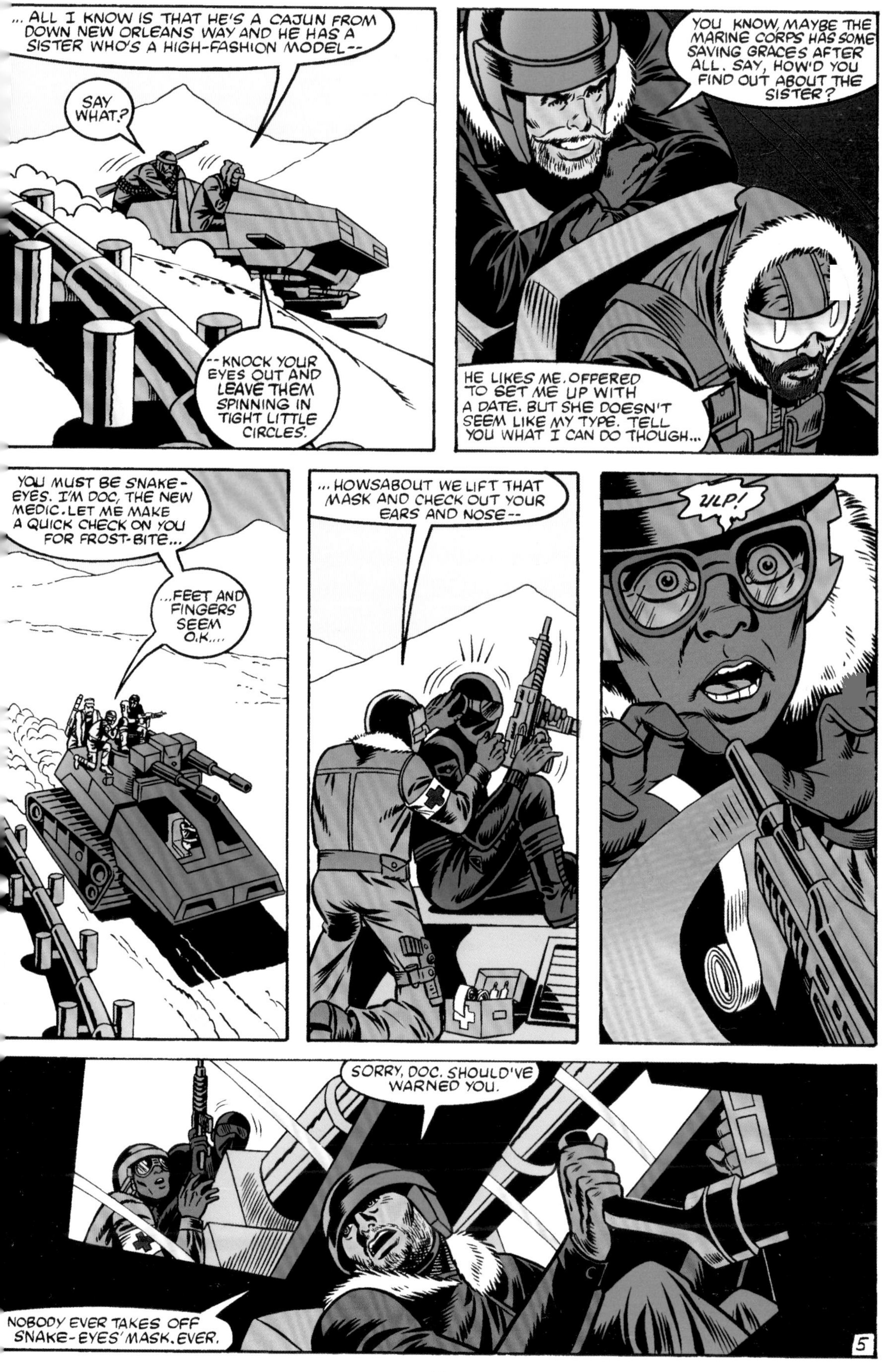
...ALL I KNOW IS THAT HE'S A CAJUN FROM DOWN NEW ORLEANS WAY AND HE HAS A SISTER WHO'S A HIGH-FASHION MODEL--
SAY WHAT?
--KNOCK YOUR EYES OUT AND LEAVE THEM SPINNING IN TIGHT LITTLE CIRCLES.
YOU KNOW, MAYBE THE MARINE CORPS HAS SOME SAVING GRACES AFTER ALL. SAY, HOW'D YOU FIND OUT ABOUT THE SISTER?
HE LIKES ME. OFFERED TO SET ME UP WITH A DATE. BUT SHE DOESN'T SEEM LIKE MY TYPE. TELL YOU WHAT I CAN DO THOUGH...
YOU MUST BE SNAKE-EYES. I'M DOC, THE NEW MEDIC. LET ME MAKE A QUICK CHECK ON YOU FOR FROST-BITE...
...FEET AND FINGERS SEEM O.K....
...HOWSABOUT WE LIFT THAT MASK AND CHECK OUT YOUR EARS AND NOSE--
ULP!
SORRY, DOC. SHOULD'VE WARNED YOU.
NOBODY EVER TAKES OFF SNAKE-EYES' MASK. EVER.
5

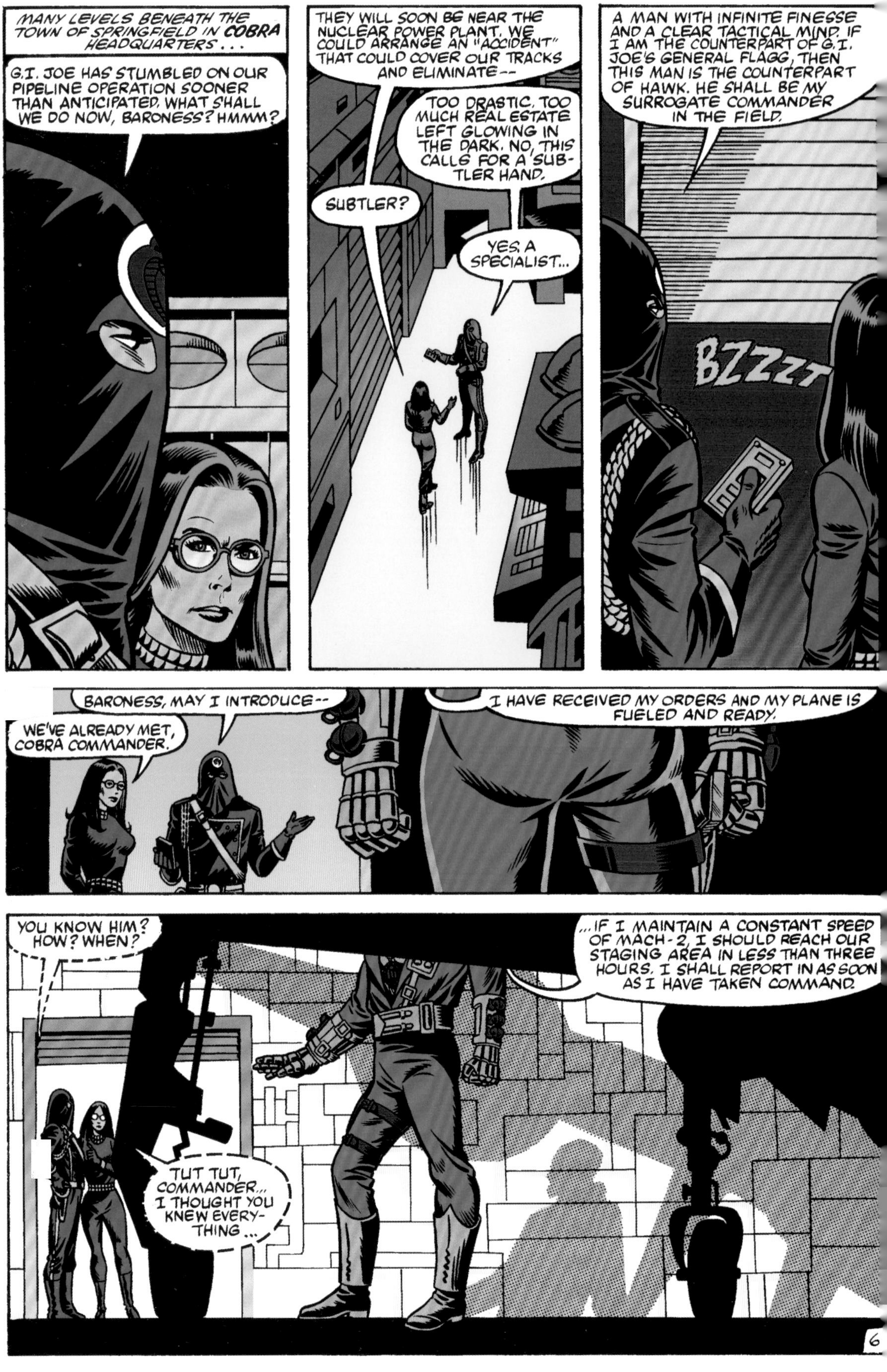
MANY LEVELS BENEATH THE TOWN OF SPRINGFIELD IN COBRA HEADQUARTERS . . .
G.I. JOE HAS STUMBLED ON OUR PIPELINE OPERATION SOONER THAN ANTICIPATED. WHAT SHALL WE DO NOW, BARONESS? HMMM?
THEY WILL SOON BE NEAR THE NUCLEAR POWER PLANT. WE COULD ARRANGE AN "ACCIDENT" THAT COULD COVER OUR TRACKS AND ELIMINATE--
TOO DRASTIC. TOO MUCH REAL ESTATE LEFT GLOWING IN THE DARK. NO, THIS CALLS FOR A SUB-TLER HAND.
SUBTLER?
YES, A SPECIALIST...
A MAN WITH INFINITE FINESSE AND A CLEAR TACTICAL MIND. IF I AM THE COUNTERPART OF G.I. JOE'S GENERAL FLAGG, THEN THIS MAN IS THE COUNTERPART OF HAWK. HE SHALL BE MY SURROGATE COMMANDER IN THE FIELD.
BZZZT
BARONESS, MAY I INTRODUCE--
WE'VE ALREADY MET, COBRA COMMANDER.
I HAVE RECEIVED MY ORDERS AND MY PLANE IS FUELED AND READY.
YOU KNOW HIM? HOW? WHEN?
...IF I MAINTAIN A CONSTANT SPEED OF MACH-2, I SHOULD REACH OUR STAGING AREA IN LESS THAN THREE HOURS. I SHALL REPORT IN AS SOON AS I HAVE TAKEN COMMAND.
TUT TUT, COMMANDER... I THOUGHT YOU KNEW EVERY-THING...
6

FOUR HOURS LATER, IN ALASKA...

WHAT IS IT, SNOW JOB?

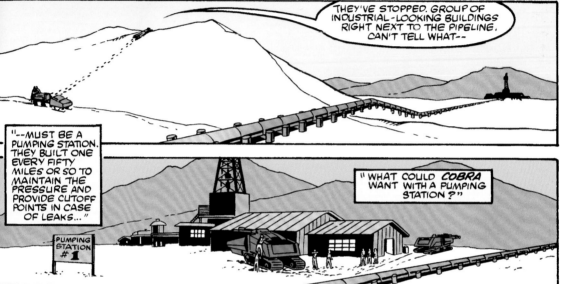

THEY'VE STOPPED. GROUP OF INDUSTRIAL-LOOKING BUILDINGS RIGHT NEXT TO THE PIPELINE. CAN'T TELL WHAT--

"--MUST BE A PUMPING STATION. THEY BUILT ONE EVERY FIFTY MILES OR SO TO MAINTAIN THE PRESSURE AND PROVIDE CUTOFF POINTS IN CASE OF LEAKS..."

"WHAT COULD *COBRA* WANT WITH A PUMPING STATION?"

PUMPING STATION #1

BETTER TELL HAWK TO GET UP HERE. SOMETHING'S GOING ON...

I HEAR YOU.

WELL, WELL, WELL... LOOKS LIKE THEY'RE UNLOADING CARGO FROM ONE OF THE TANKS...

MIGHTY STRANGE CARGO, TOO.

"...JUST WHAT IS IT YOU CARRY AROUND IN DOUBLE-WALLED STAINLESS STEEL CANISTERS?"

"LOOK! THE SECOND TANK'S MOVING OUT WITH MOST OF THE INFANTRY!"

1

7

WHAT DO YOU MAKE OF THIS, ROCK'N ROLL?

I THINK WE SHOULD SPLIT UP AND SEND THE STRONGER FORCE AFTER THE TANK AND INFANTRY...

... SINCE IT'S OBVIOUS THAT THEY'RE HEADED FOR THE MAIN OBJECTIVE AND THE SMALL PARTY IN THE PUMPING STATION IS JUST A REAR-GUARD.

SPLIT UP? NOT SO GOOD. I THINK BETTER TO TAKE OUT STATION FIRST, CAPTURE TANK AND THEN GO AFTER MAIN BODY. NO?

I THINK MAYBE THAT SNAKE-EYES HE AGREE WITH ME, HE NODDING LIKE HUNGRY 'GATOR...

SO DO I. BESIDES, I'M REAL CURIOUS ABOUT THOSE CANISTERS.

THAT GUNG-HO IS MAKING IT REAL DIFFICULT FOR ME TO LIKE HIM. YOU SURE ABOUT THAT SISTER OF HIS?

WOULD I LIE TO YOU?

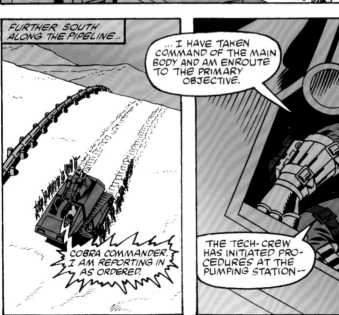

FURTHER SOUTH ALONG THE PIPELINE...

COBRA COMMANDER, I AM REPORTING IN AS ORDERED.

... I HAVE TAKEN COMMAND OF THE MAIN BODY AND AM ENROUTE TO THE PRIMARY OBJECTIVE.

THE TECH-CREW HAS INITIATED PROCEDURES AT THE PUMPING STATION--

THE G.I. JOE TEAM SHOULD HAVE THE STATION UNDER OBSERVATION BY NOW...

I HAVE TAKEN THAT INTO CONSIDERATION.

8

12

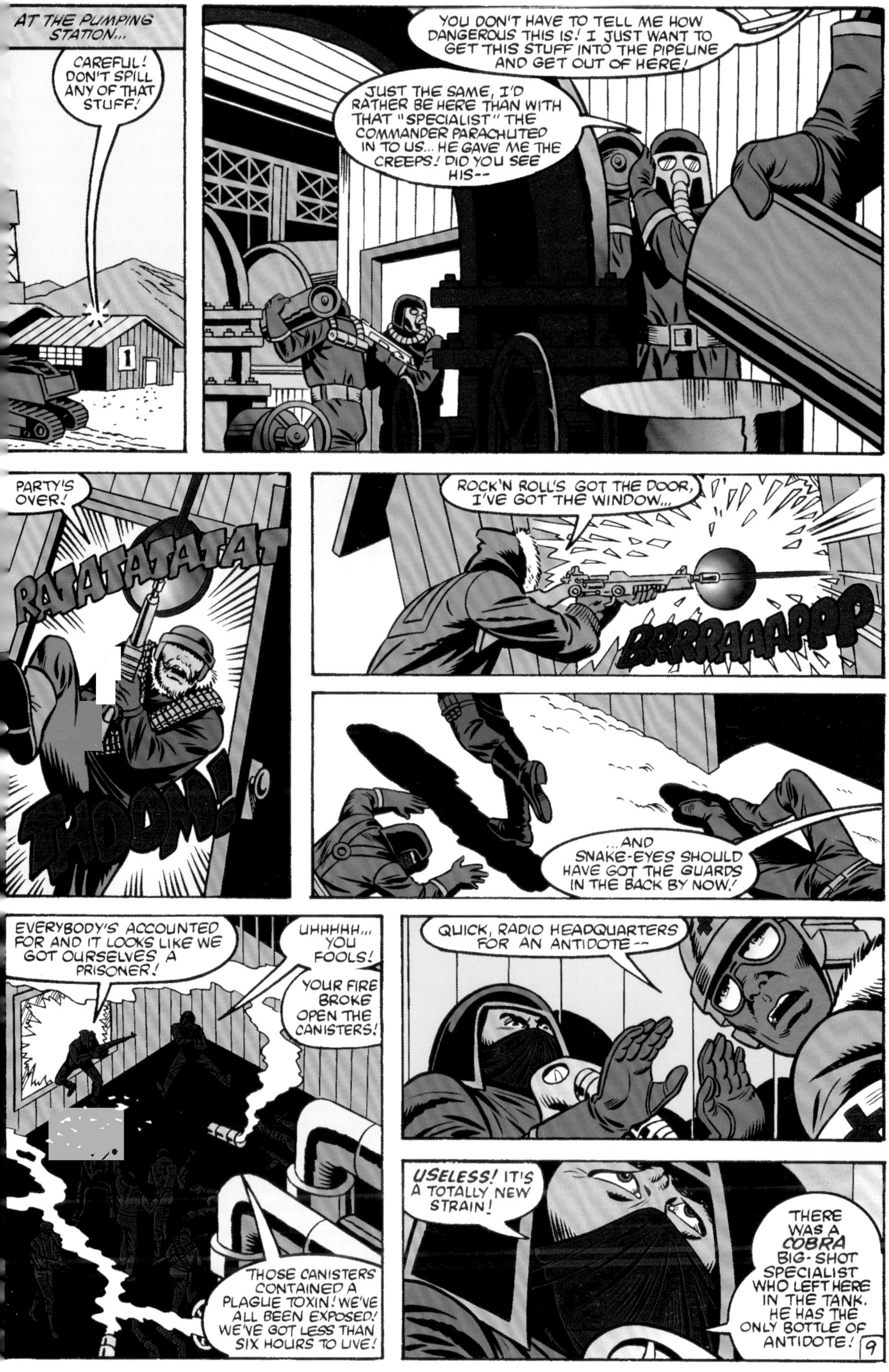
AT THE PUMPING STATION...
CAREFUL! DON'T SPILL ANY OF THAT STUFF!
YOU DON'T HAVE TO TELL ME HOW DANGEROUS THIS IS! I JUST WANT TO GET THIS STUFF INTO THE PIPELINE AND GET OUT OF HERE!
JUST THE SAME, I'D RATHER BE HERE THAN WITH THAT "SPECIALIST" THE COMMANDER PARACHUTED IN TO US... HE GAVE ME THE CREEPS! DID YOU SEE HIS--
1
PARTY'S OVER!
RATATATATAT
THOOM!
ROCK'N ROLL'S GOT THE DOOR, I'VE GOT THE WINDOW...
BRRRAAAPPP
...AND SNAKE-EYES SHOULD HAVE GOT THE GUARDS IN THE BACK BY NOW!
EVERYBODY'S ACCOUNTED FOR AND IT LOOKS LIKE WE GOT OURSELVES A PRISONER!
UHHHHH... YOU FOOLS!
YOUR FIRE BROKE OPEN THE CANISTERS!
THOSE CANISTERS CONTAINED A PLAGUE TOXIN! WE'VE ALL BEEN EXPOSED! WE'VE GOT LESS THAN SIX HOURS TO LIVE!
QUICK, RADIO HEADQUARTERS FOR AN ANTIDOTE--
USELESS! IT'S A TOTALLY NEW STRAIN!
THERE WAS A COBRA BIG-SHOT SPECIALIST WHO LEFT HERE IN THE TANK. HE HAS THE ONLY BOTTLE OF ANTIDOTE!
9

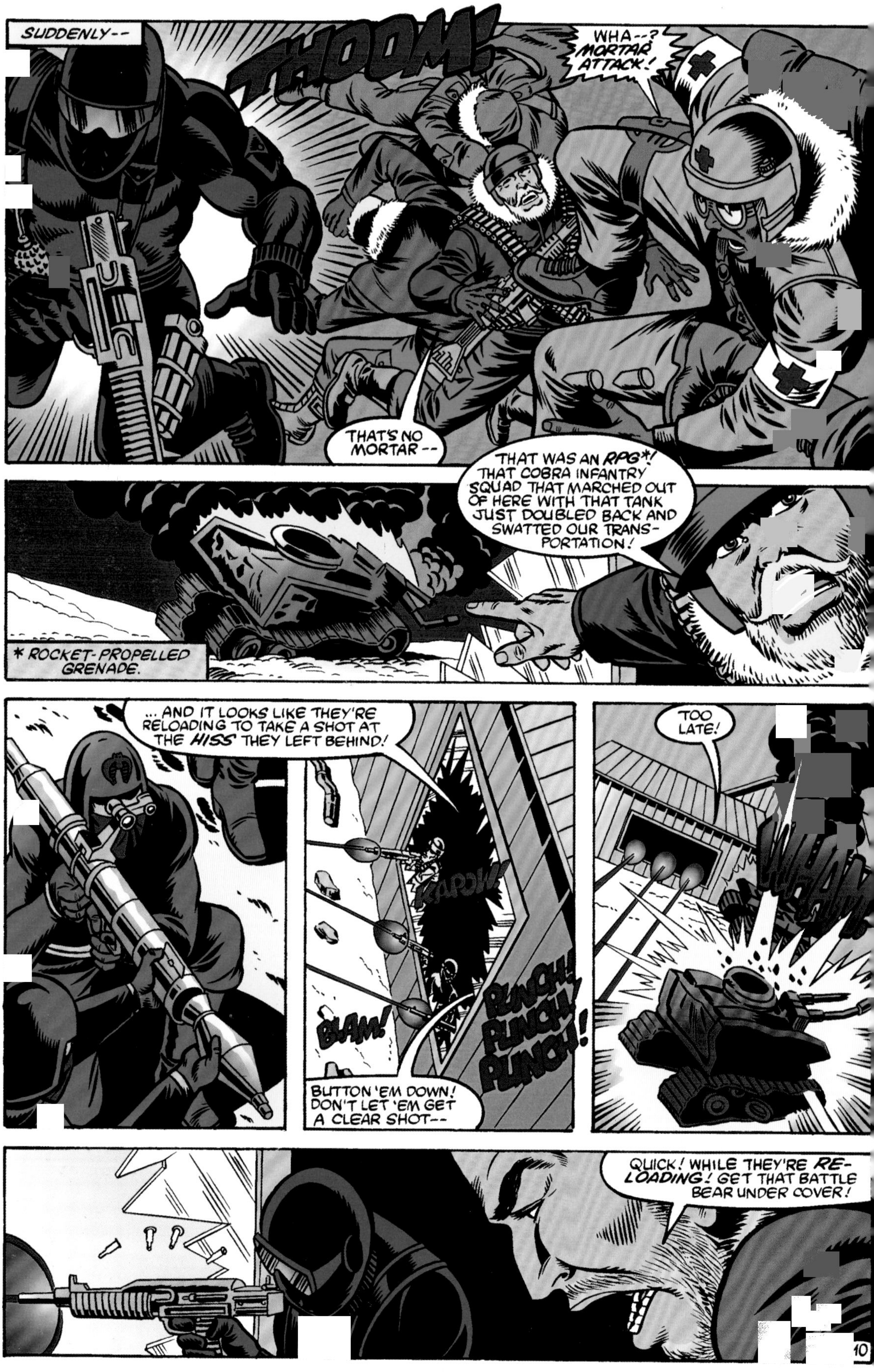
SUDDENLY--
THOOM!
WHA--? MORTAR ATTACK!
THAT'S NO MORTAR--
THAT WAS AN RPG*! THAT COBRA INFANTRY SQUAD THAT MARCHED OUT OF HERE WITH THAT TANK JUST DOUBLED BACK AND SWATTED OUR TRANSPORTATION!
* ROCKET-PROPELLED GRENADE.
...AND IT LOOKS LIKE THEY'RE RELOADING TO TAKE A SHOT AT THE HISS THEY LEFT BEHIND!
KAPOW!
BLAM!
PUNCH! PUNCH! PUNCH!
BUTTON 'EM DOWN! DON'T LET 'EM GET A CLEAR SHOT--
TOO LATE!
WHAM!
QUICK! WHILE THEY'RE RELOADING! GET THAT BATTLE BEAR UNDER COVER!
10

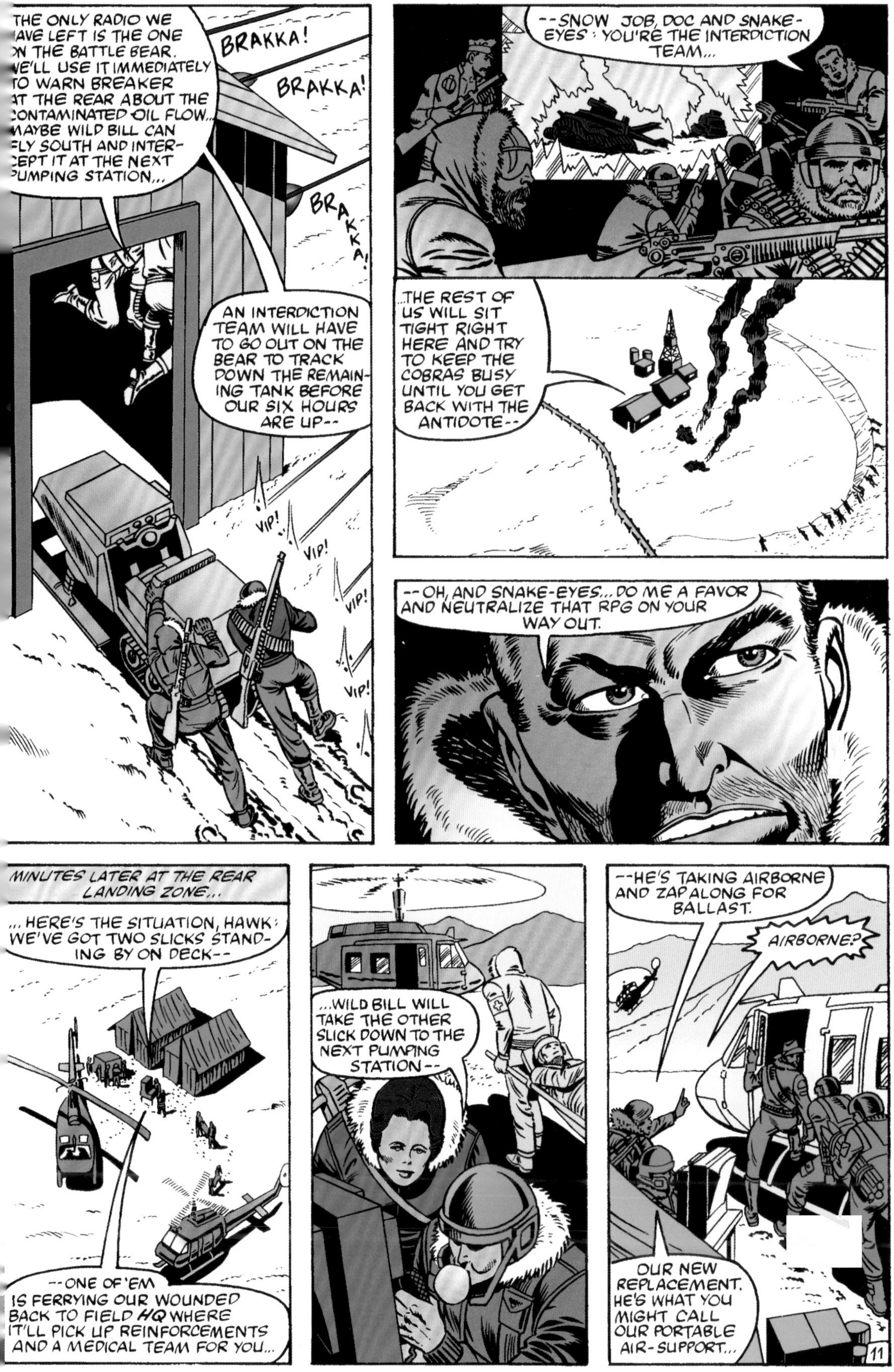
THE ONLY RADIO WE HAVE LEFT IS THE ONE ON THE BATTLE BEAR. WE'LL USE IT IMMEDIATELY TO WARN BREAKER AT THE REAR ABOUT THE CONTAMINATED OIL FLOW... MAYBE WILD BILL CAN FLY SOUTH AND INTERCEPT IT AT THE NEXT PUMPING STATION...
BRAKKA!
BRAKKA!
BRAKKA!
AN INTERDICTION TEAM WILL HAVE TO GO OUT ON THE BEAR TO TRACK DOWN THE REMAINING TANK BEFORE OUR SIX HOURS ARE UP--
VIP!
VIP!
VIP!
VIP!
--SNOW JOB, DOC AND SNAKE-EYES: YOU'RE THE INTERDICTION TEAM...
...THE REST OF US WILL SIT TIGHT RIGHT HERE AND TRY TO KEEP THE COBRAS BUSY UNTIL YOU GET BACK WITH THE ANTIDOTE--
--OH, AND SNAKE-EYES... DO ME A FAVOR AND NEUTRALIZE THAT RPG ON YOUR WAY OUT.
MINUTES LATER AT THE REAR LANDING ZONE...
...HERE'S THE SITUATION, HAWK: WE'VE GOT TWO SLICKS STANDING BY ON DECK--
--ONE OF 'EM IS FERRYING OUR WOUNDED BACK TO FIELD HQ WHERE IT'LL PICK UP REINFORCEMENTS AND A MEDICAL TEAM FOR YOU...
...WILD BILL WILL TAKE THE OTHER SLICK DOWN TO THE NEXT PUMPING STATION--
--HE'S TAKING AIRBORNE AND ZAP ALONG FOR BALLAST.
AIRBORNE?
OUR NEW REPLACEMENT. HE'S WHAT YOU MIGHT CALL OUR PORTABLE AIR-SUPPORT...
11

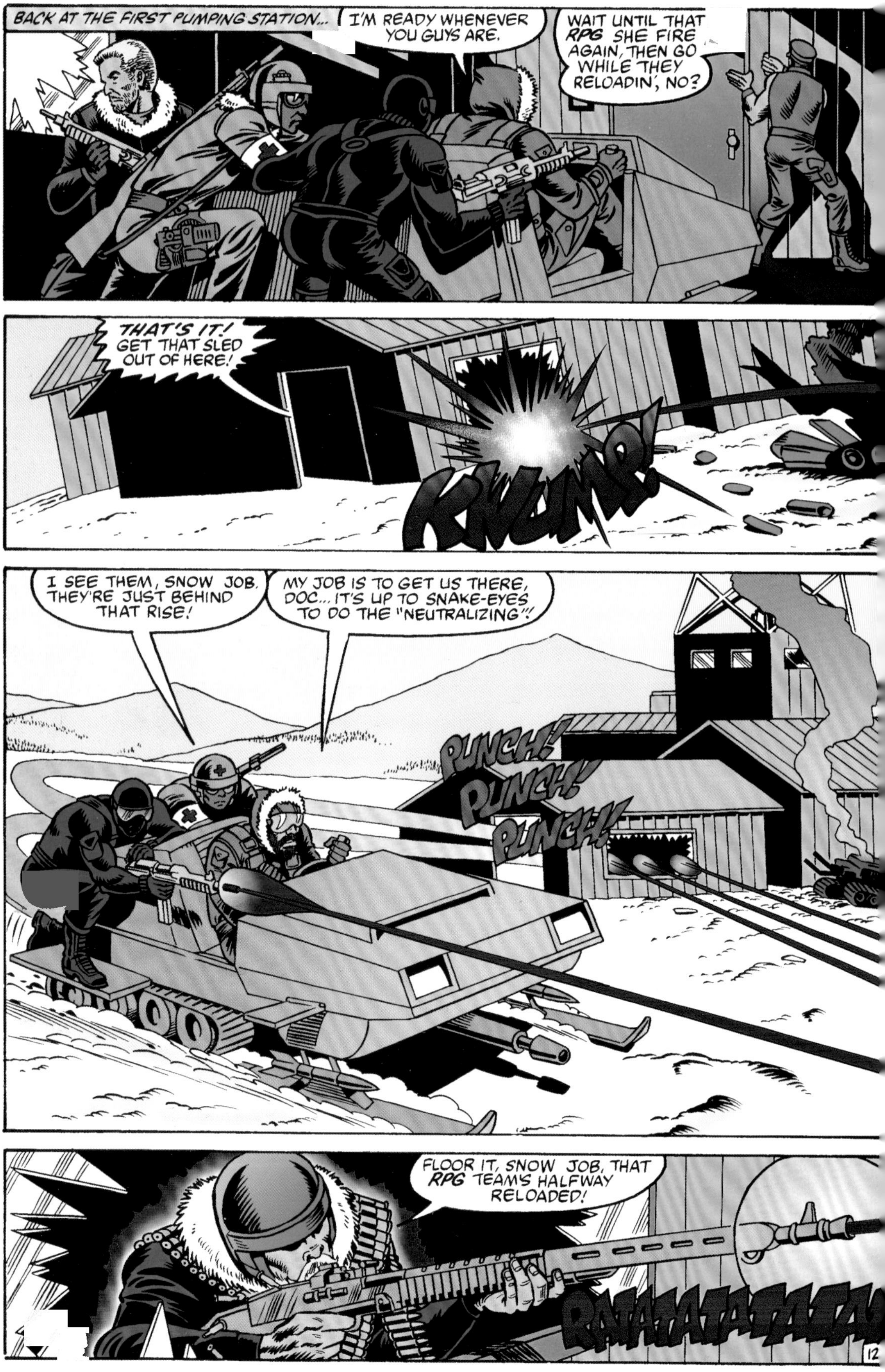
BACK AT THE FIRST PUMPING STATION...
I'M READY WHENEVER YOU GUYS ARE.
WAIT UNTIL THAT RPG SHE FIRE AGAIN, THEN GO WHILE THEY RELOADIN', NO?
THAT'S IT! GET THAT SLED OUT OF HERE!
KWUMP!
I SEE THEM, SNOW JOB. THEY'RE JUST BEHIND THAT RISE!
MY JOB IS TO GET US THERE, DOC... IT'S UP TO SNAKE-EYES TO DO THE "NEUTRALIZING"!
PUNCH! PUNCH! PUNCH!
FLOOR IT, SNOW JOB, THAT RPG TEAM'S HALFWAY RELOADED!
RATATATATATATA
12

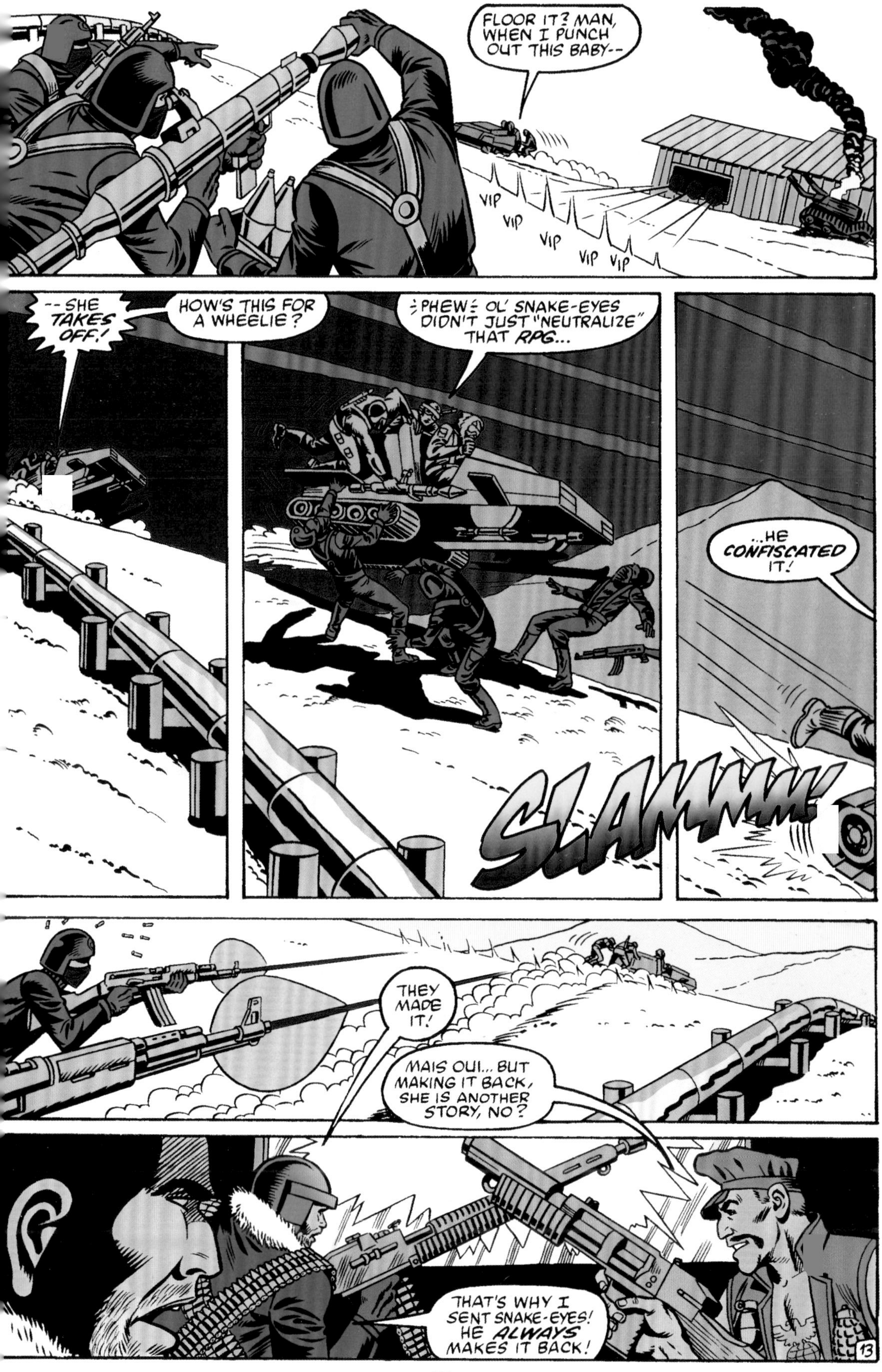

FLOOR IT? MAN, WHEN I PUNCH OUT THIS BABY--
VIP
VIP
VIP
VIP VIP
--SHE TAKES OFF!
HOW'S THIS FOR A WHEELIE?
PHEW! OL' SNAKE-EYES DIDN'T JUST "NEUTRALIZE" THAT RPG...
...HE CONFISCATED IT!
SLAMMM!
THEY MADE IT!
MAIS OUI... BUT MAKING IT BACK, SHE IS ANOTHER STORY, NO?
THAT'S WHY I SENT SNAKE-EYES! HE ALWAYS MAKES IT BACK!
13

...GENERAL FLAGG? THIS IS *BREAKER* AT FIELD HQ... WE ARE REQUESTING IMMEDIATE REINFORCEMENTS FOR HAWK'S TEAM AT THE FIRST PUMPING STATION AND ABSOLUTE QUARANTINE AND CONTAINMENT FOR THE NEXT TWO PUMPING STATIONS AND ALL THE PIPELINE BETWEEN THEM-- OVER.

FLAGG HERE. THAT'S A POSITIVE ON THE REINFORCEMENTS AND A QUALIFIED NEGATIVE ON THE QUARANTINE... WE HAVE BARELY ENOUGH PERSONNEL IN THE AREA TO COVER OTHER KEY STRATEGIC SITES, BUT I'LL SEE WHAT I CAN DO FOR YOU... OUT.

HA HA HA HA! *EAVESDROPPING* HAS BECOME CHILD'S PLAY SINCE WE STOLE THE PROGRAM FOR THE G.I. JOE CRYPTO-SCRAMBLER! SOON ALL THE SECURITY FORCES IN THE REGION WILL BE SPREAD OUT OVER 50 MILES OF PIPELINE!

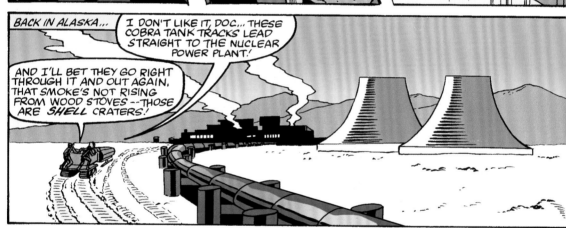

BACK IN ALASKA...

I DON'T LIKE IT, DOC... THESE COBRA TANK TRACKS LEAD STRAIGHT TO THE NUCLEAR POWER PLANT!

AND I'LL BET THEY GO RIGHT THROUGH IT AND OUT AGAIN. THAT SMOKE'S NOT RISING FROM WOOD STOVES --THOSE ARE *SHELL* CRATERS!

SHORTLY...

--THEY JUST PLOWED THROUGH SO FAST... WE DIDN'T HAVE A CHANCE! --THE *PLUTONIUM!* THEY HAULED AWAY ENOUGH PLUTONIUM TO START WW III!

TAKE IT EASY, FELLA. WE'LL FIX YOU UP.

HE CAN FIX HIMSELF UP! WE'VE GOT TO CATCH UP TO THAT TANK!

YOU'RE RIGHT. I'LL MANAGE! THE TANK CUT BACK THROUGH THAT OPEN GROUND, HEADING SOUTH. I THINK THEY WERE HEADING FOR THE PIPELINE...

THANKS, PAL. WE'LL SEND HELP IF WE MAKE IT...

14

MINUTES LATER...

RATATATAT BRRAP

PING!

TUP TUP TUP TUP TUP TUP TUP TUP

SNOW JOB, THIS IS WILD BILL... LOOKS LIKE YOU BOYS GOT YOUR-SELVES A PROBLEM: COBRA HANG-GLIDER STYLE!

OH, IT'S NOTHING A COUPLE O' BURSTS FROM YOUR DOORGUNNER COULDN'T SOLVE...

TRUE, BUT I CAN'T STOP. GOT PRIORITY BUSINESS DOWN AT PUMPING STATION #2!

BEST I CAN DO IS EVEN UP THE ODDS A BIT!

15

HEH-HEH-HEH! COBRA AIR SUPERIORITY WILL CRUSH THESE INSUF-FERABLE G.I. JOES LIKE--

ROKKA ROKKA ROKKA ROK

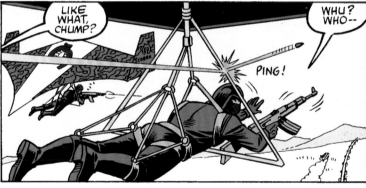

LIKE WHAT, CHUMP?

WHU? WHO--

PING!

THE NAME'S AIRBORNE, AND I'M THE NEW JOE IN TOWN!

PUNCH PUNCH PUNC

AIRBORNE

19

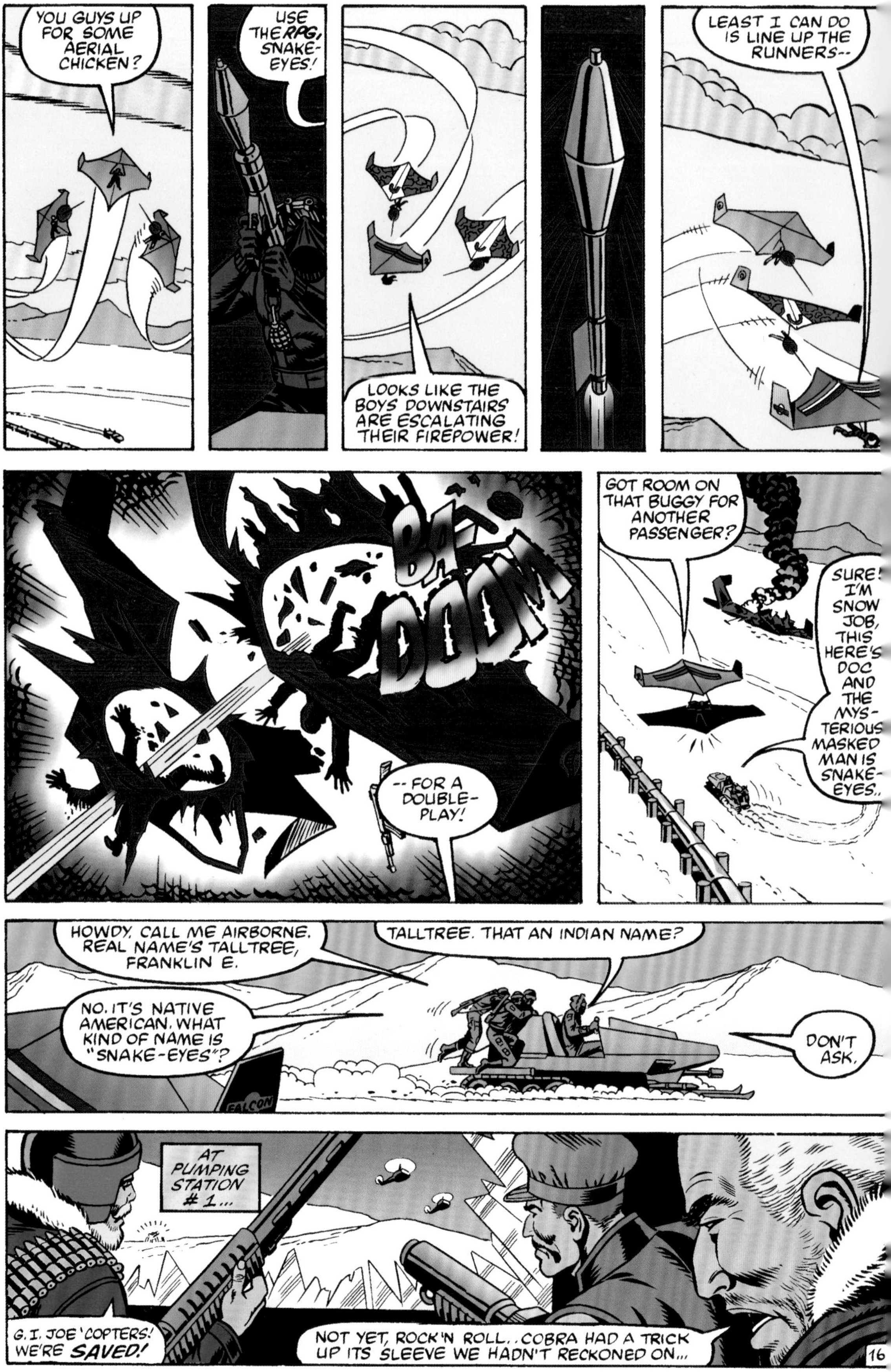

YOU GUYS UP FOR SOME AERIAL CHICKEN?
USE THE RPG, SNAKE-EYES!
LOOKS LIKE THE BOYS DOWNSTAIRS ARE ESCALATING THEIR FIREPOWER!
LEAST I CAN DO IS LINE UP THE RUNNERS--
BA-DOOM
--FOR A DOUBLE-PLAY!
GOT ROOM ON THAT BUGGY FOR ANOTHER PASSENGER?
SURE! I'M SNOW JOB, THIS HERE'S DOC AND THE MYSTERIOUS MASKED MAN IS SNAKE-EYES..
HOWDY. CALL ME AIRBORNE. REAL NAME'S TALLTREE, FRANKLIN E.
TALLTREE. THAT AN INDIAN NAME?
NO. IT'S NATIVE AMERICAN. WHAT KIND OF NAME IS "SNAKE-EYES"?
DON'T ASK.
FALCON
AT PUMPING STATION #1...
G.I. JOE 'COPTERS! WE'RE SAVED!
NOT YET, ROCK'N ROLL.. COBRA HAD A TRICK UP ITS SLEEVE WE HADN'T RECKONED ON...
16

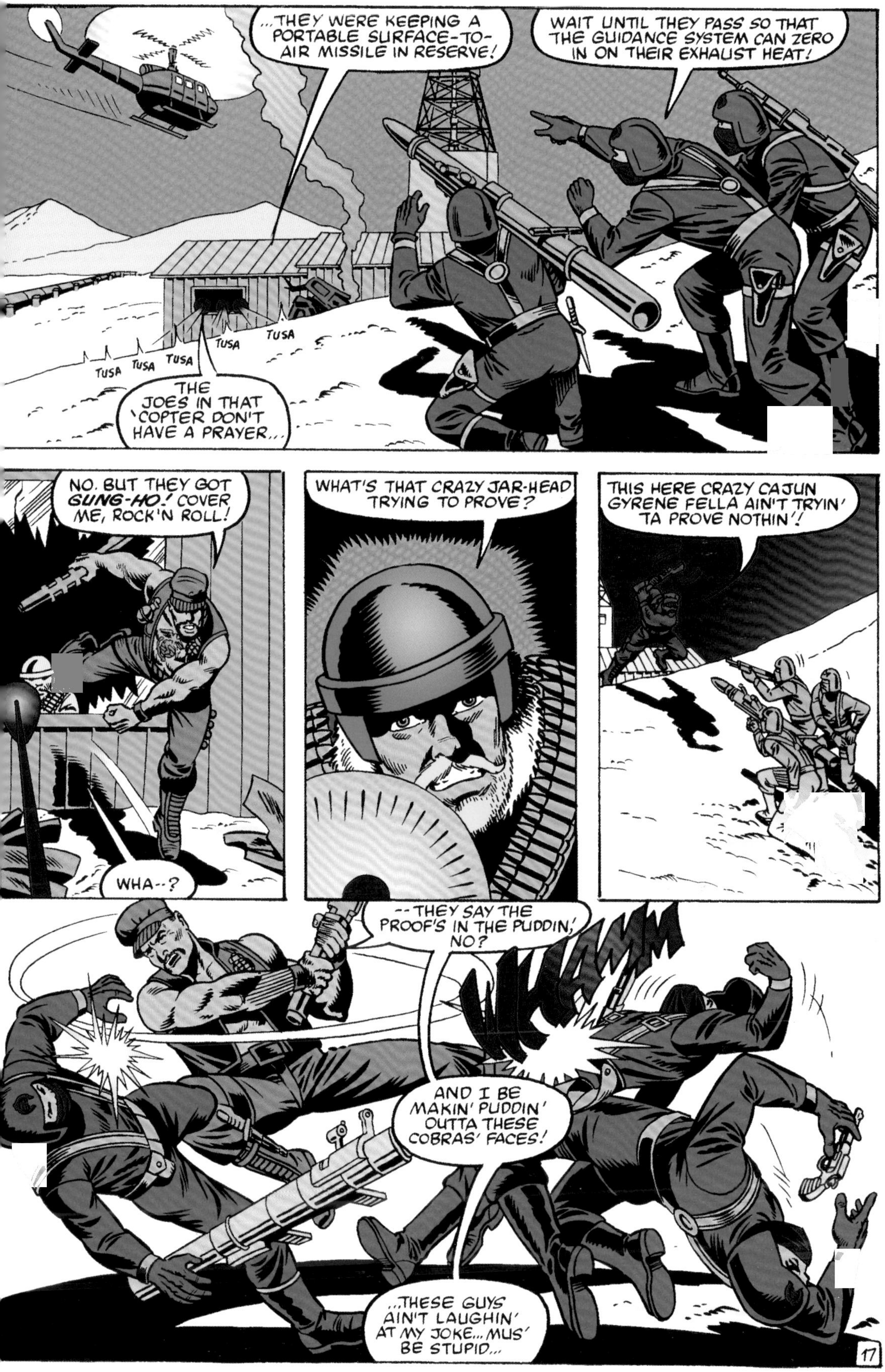
...THEY WERE KEEPING A PORTABLE SURFACE-TO-AIR MISSILE IN RESERVE!
WAIT UNTIL THEY PASS SO THAT THE GUIDANCE SYSTEM CAN ZERO IN ON THEIR EXHAUST HEAT!
TUSA TUSA TUSA TUSA TUSA
THE JOES IN THAT 'COPTER DON'T HAVE A PRAYER...
NO. BUT THEY GOT GUNG-HO! COVER ME, ROCK'N ROLL!
WHA--?
WHAT'S THAT CRAZY JAR-HEAD TRYING TO PROVE?
THIS HERE CRAZY CAJUN GYRENE FELLA AIN'T TRYIN' TA PROVE NOTHIN'!
--THEY SAY THE PROOF'S IN THE PUDDIN', NO?
WHAMM
AND I BE MAKIN' PUDDIN' OUTTA THESE COBRAS' FACES!
...THESE GUYS AIN'T LAUGHIN' AT MY JOKE... MUS' BE STUPID...
17

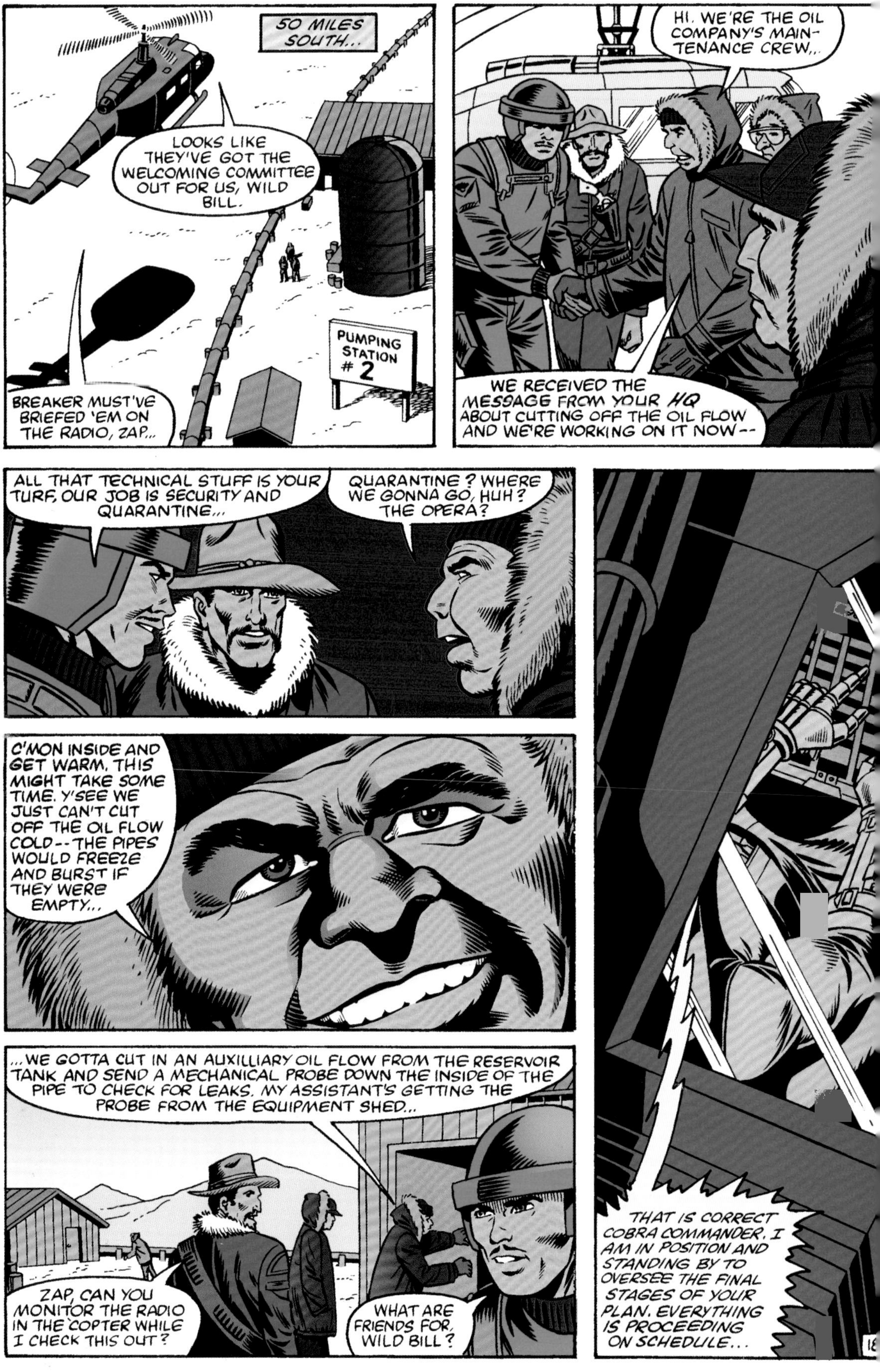
50 MILES SOUTH...
LOOKS LIKE THEY'VE GOT THE WELCOMING COMMITTEE OUT FOR US, WILD BILL.
BREAKER MUST'VE BRIEFED 'EM ON THE RADIO, ZAP...
PUMPING STATION # 2
HI. WE'RE THE OIL COMPANY'S MAINTENANCE CREW...
WE RECEIVED THE MESSAGE FROM YOUR HQ ABOUT CUTTING OFF THE OIL FLOW AND WE'RE WORKING ON IT NOW--
ALL THAT TECHNICAL STUFF IS YOUR TURF, OUR JOB IS SECURITY AND QUARANTINE...
QUARANTINE? WHERE WE GONNA GO, HUH? THE OPERA?
C'MON INSIDE AND GET WARM. THIS MIGHT TAKE SOME TIME. Y'SEE WE JUST CAN'T CUT OFF THE OIL FLOW COLD--THE PIPES WOULD FREEZE AND BURST IF THEY WERE EMPTY...
...WE GOTTA CUT IN AN AUXILIARY OIL FLOW FROM THE RESERVOIR TANK AND SEND A MECHANICAL PROBE DOWN THE INSIDE OF THE PIPE TO CHECK FOR LEAKS. MY ASSISTANT'S GETTING THE PROBE FROM THE EQUIPMENT SHED...
ZAP, CAN YOU MONITOR THE RADIO IN THE 'COPTER WHILE I CHECK THIS OUT?
WHAT ARE FRIENDS FOR, WILD BILL?
THAT IS CORRECT COBRA COMMANDER. I AM IN POSITION AND STANDING BY TO OVERSEE THE FINAL STAGES OF YOUR PLAN. EVERYTHING IS PROCEEDING ON SCHEDULE...

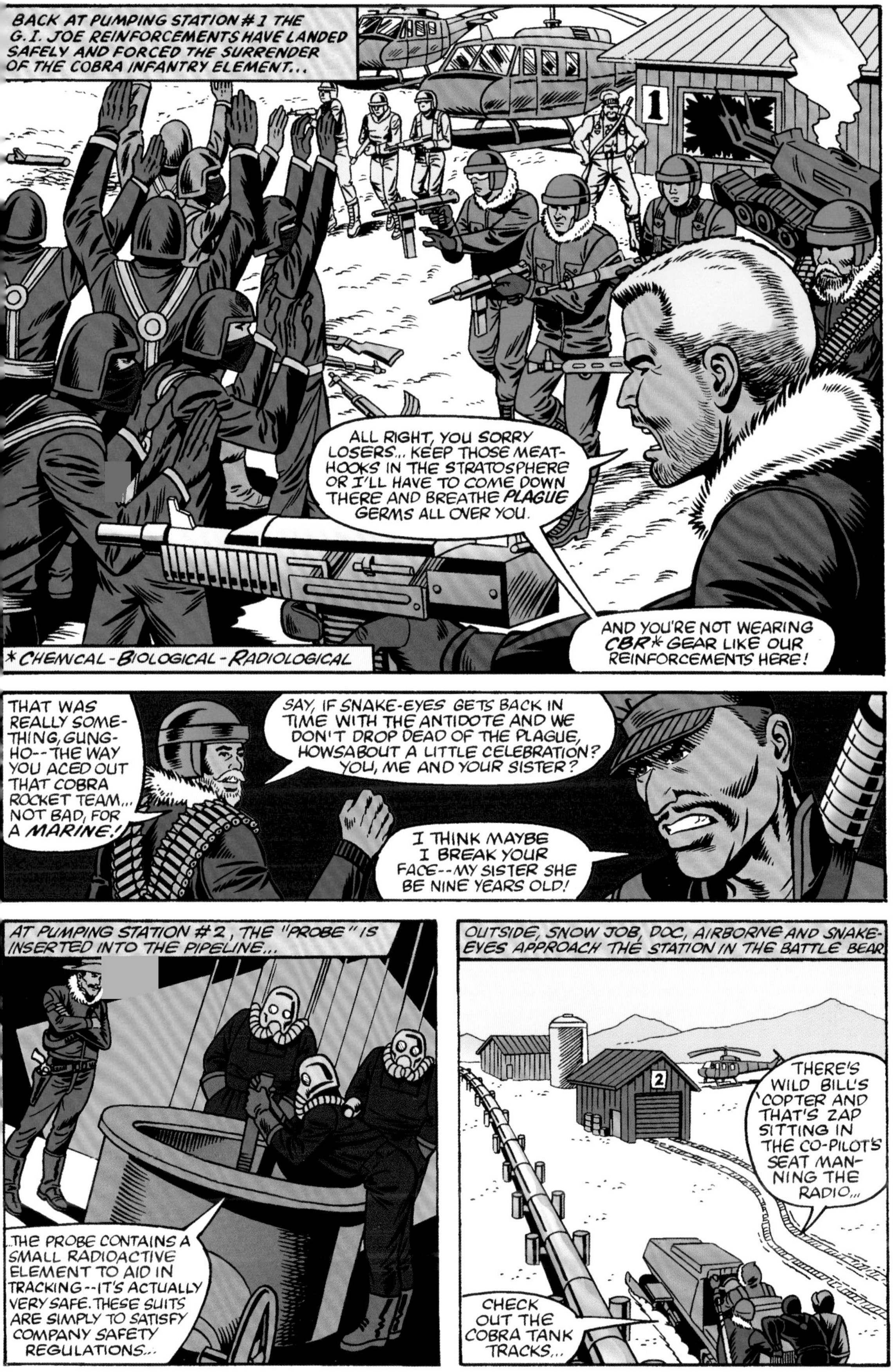

BACK AT PUMPING STATION #1 THE G.I. JOE REINFORCEMENTS HAVE LANDED SAFELY AND FORCED THE SURRENDER OF THE COBRA INFANTRY ELEMENT...
1
ALL RIGHT, YOU SORRY LOSERS... KEEP THOSE MEAT-HOOKS IN THE STRATOSPHERE OR I'LL HAVE TO COME DOWN THERE AND BREATHE THE PLAGUE GERMS ALL OVER YOU.
AND YOU'RE NOT WEARING CBR* GEAR LIKE OUR REINFORCEMENTS HERE!
*CHEMICAL-BIOLOGICAL-RADIOLOGICAL
THAT WAS REALLY SOME-THING, GUNG-HO--THE WAY YOU ACED OUT THAT COBRA ROCKET TEAM... NOT BAD, FOR A MARINE!
SAY, IF SNAKE-EYES GETS BACK IN TIME WITH THE ANTIDOTE AND WE DON'T DROP DEAD OF THE PLAGUE, HOWSABOUT A LITTLE CELEBRATION? YOU, ME AND YOUR SISTER?
I THINK MAYBE I BREAK YOUR FACE--MY SISTER SHE BE NINE YEARS OLD!
AT PUMPING STATION #2, THE "PROBE" IS INSERTED INTO THE PIPELINE...
...THE PROBE CONTAINS A SMALL RADIOACTIVE ELEMENT TO AID IN TRACKING--IT'S ACTUALLY VERY SAFE. THESE SUITS ARE SIMPLY TO SATISFY COMPANY SAFETY REGULATIONS...
OUTSIDE, SNOW JOB, DOC, AIRBORNE AND SNAKE-EYES APPROACH THE STATION IN THE BATTLE BEAR.
2
THERE'S WILD BILL'S 'COPTER AND THAT'S ZAP SITTING IN THE CO-PILOT'S SEAT MAN-NING THE RADIO...
CHECK OUT THE COBRA TANK TRACKS...

...THOSE TRACKS LEAD INTO THAT UTILITY SHED AND THEY DON'T COME OUT! THE COBRA TANK MUST HAVE ENTERED THE SHED BEFORE WILD BILL LANDED. OTHERWIZE ZAP WOULD'VE SEEN IT!

SO WHOEVER THE HECK WILD BILL IS HOB-NOBBING WITH INSIDE THE STATION AREN'T WHAT THEY APPEAR TO BE!

COBRA! THEY'VE BEEN ONE JUMP AHEAD OF US FROM THE START!

ZAP, THIS IS SNOW JOB. WE'RE NEXT TO THE PIPELINE APPROACHING THE UTILITY SHED. THERE'S A COBRA TANK IN THE SHED--

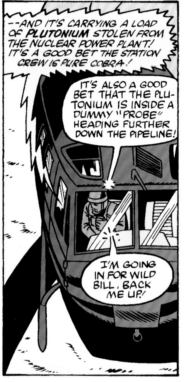

--AND IT'S CARRYING A LOAD OF PLUTONIUM STOLEN FROM THE NUCLEAR POWER PLANT! IT'S A GOOD BET THE STATION CREW IS PURE COBRA!

IT'S ALSO A GOOD BET THAT THE PLUTONIUM IS INSIDE A DUMMY "PROBE" HEADING FURTHER DOWN THE PIPELINE!

I'M GOING IN FOR WILD BILL, BACK ME UP!

SNAKE-EYES IS GOING AFTER THE COBRA TANK BY HIMSELF?

IT'S ONLY ONE TANK, RIGHT?

ZAP, WHAT THE--

TAKE 'EM OUT WILD BILL! THEY'RE COBRA!

SLAM!

HA! YOU'RE BOTH DEAD MEN--

--WE'VE ALREADY BEATEN YOU TO THE DRAW!

KA POW

THAT'LL BE THE DAY!

BLAM!

BLAM!

BLAM!

20

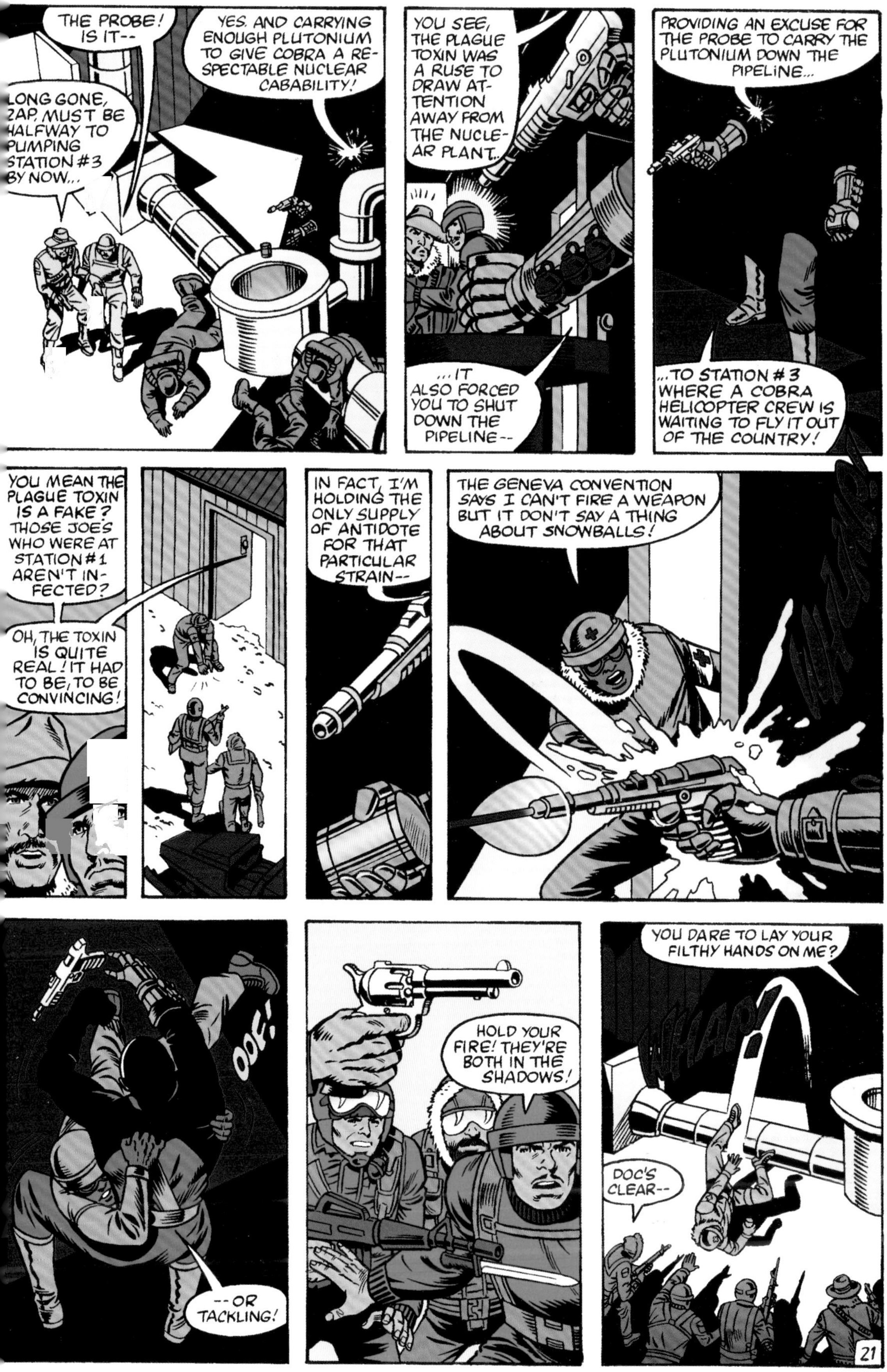
THE PROBE! IS IT--
YES. AND CARRYING ENOUGH PLUTONIUM TO GIVE COBRA A RESPECTABLE NUCLEAR CABABILITY!
LONG GONE, ZAP. MUST BE HALFWAY TO PUMPING STATION #3 BY NOW...
YOU SEE, THE PLAGUE TOXIN WAS A RUSE TO DRAW ATTENTION AWAY FROM THE NUCLEAR PLANT...
...IT ALSO FORCED YOU TO SHUT DOWN THE PIPELINE--
PROVIDING AN EXCUSE FOR THE PROBE TO CARRY THE PLUTONIUM DOWN THE PIPELINE...
...TO STATION #3 WHERE A COBRA HELICOPTER CREW IS WAITING TO FLY IT OUT OF THE COUNTRY!
YOU MEAN THE PLAGUE TOXIN IS A FAKE? THOSE JOES WHO WERE AT STATION #1 AREN'T INFECTED?
OH, THE TOXIN IS QUITE REAL! IT HAD TO BE, TO BE CONVINCING!
IN FACT, I'M HOLDING THE ONLY SUPPLY OF ANTIDOTE FOR THAT PARTICULAR STRAIN--
THE GENEVA CONVENTION SAYS I CAN'T FIRE A WEAPON BUT IT DON'T SAY A THING ABOUT SNOWBALLS!
OOF!
--OR TACKLING!
HOLD YOUR FIRE! THEY'RE BOTH IN THE SHADOWS!
YOU DARE TO LAY YOUR FILTHY HANDS ON ME?
DOC'S CLEAR--
21

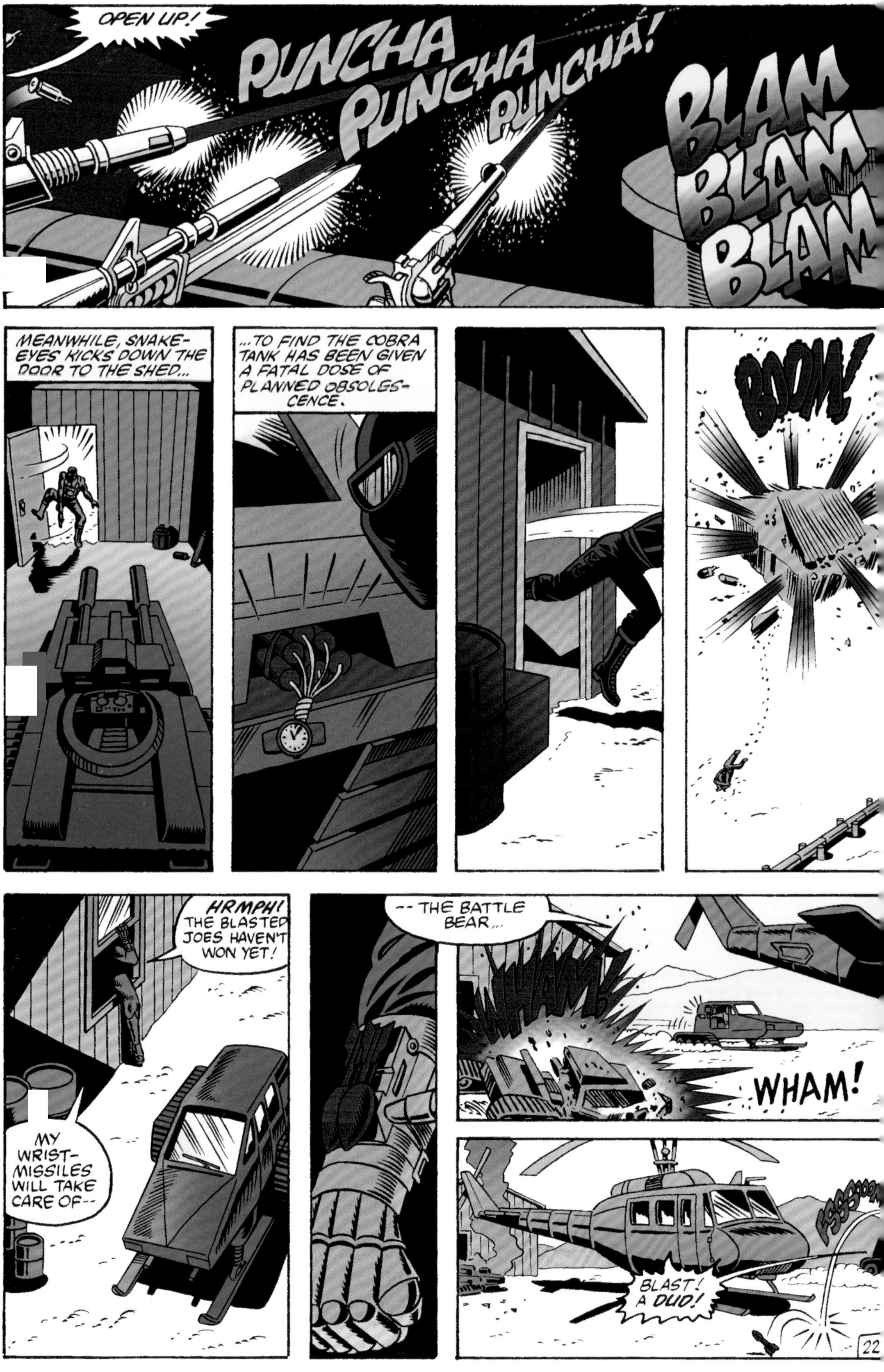
OPEN UP!
PUNCHA PUNCHA PUNCHA!
BLAM BLAM BLAM
MEANWHILE, SNAKE-EYES KICKS DOWN THE DOOR TO THE SHED...
...TO FIND THE COBRA TANK HAS BEEN GIVEN A FATAL DOSE OF PLANNED OBSOLESCENCE.
BOOM!
HRMPH! THE BLASTED JOES HAVEN'T WON YET!
MY WRIST-MISSILES WILL TAKE CARE OF--
-- THE BATTLE BEAR...
WHAM!
BLAST! A DUD!
22

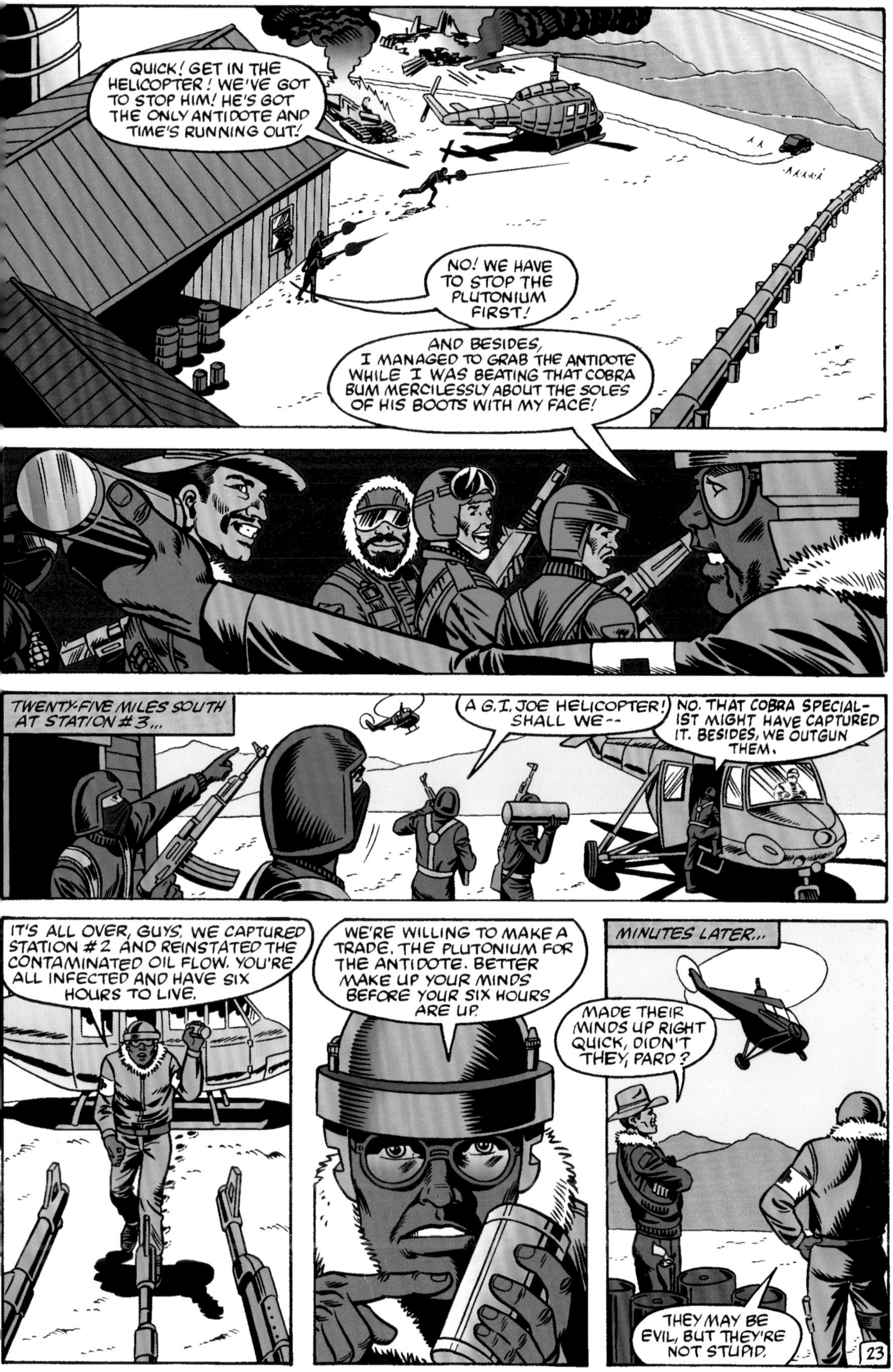
QUICK! GET IN THE HELICOPTER! WE'VE GOT TO STOP HIM! HE'S GOT THE ONLY ANTIDOTE AND TIME'S RUNNING OUT!
NO! WE HAVE TO STOP THE PLUTONIUM FIRST!
AND BESIDES, I MANAGED TO GRAB THE ANTIDOTE WHILE I WAS BEATING THAT COBRA BUM MERCILESSLY ABOUT THE SOLES OF HIS BOOTS WITH MY FACE!
TWENTY-FIVE MILES SOUTH AT STATION #3...
A G.I. JOE HELICOPTER! SHALL WE--
NO. THAT COBRA SPECIALIST MIGHT HAVE CAPTURED IT. BESIDES, WE OUTGUN THEM.
IT'S ALL OVER, GUYS. WE CAPTURED STATION #2 AND REINSTATED THE CONTAMINATED OIL FLOW. YOU'RE ALL INFECTED AND HAVE SIX HOURS TO LIVE.
WE'RE WILLING TO MAKE A TRADE. THE PLUTONIUM FOR THE ANTIDOTE. BETTER MAKE UP YOUR MINDS BEFORE YOUR SIX HOURS ARE UP.
MINUTES LATER...
MADE THEIR MINDS UP RIGHT QUICK, DIDN'T THEY, PARD?
THEY MAY BE EVIL, BUT THEY'RE NOT STUPID.
23

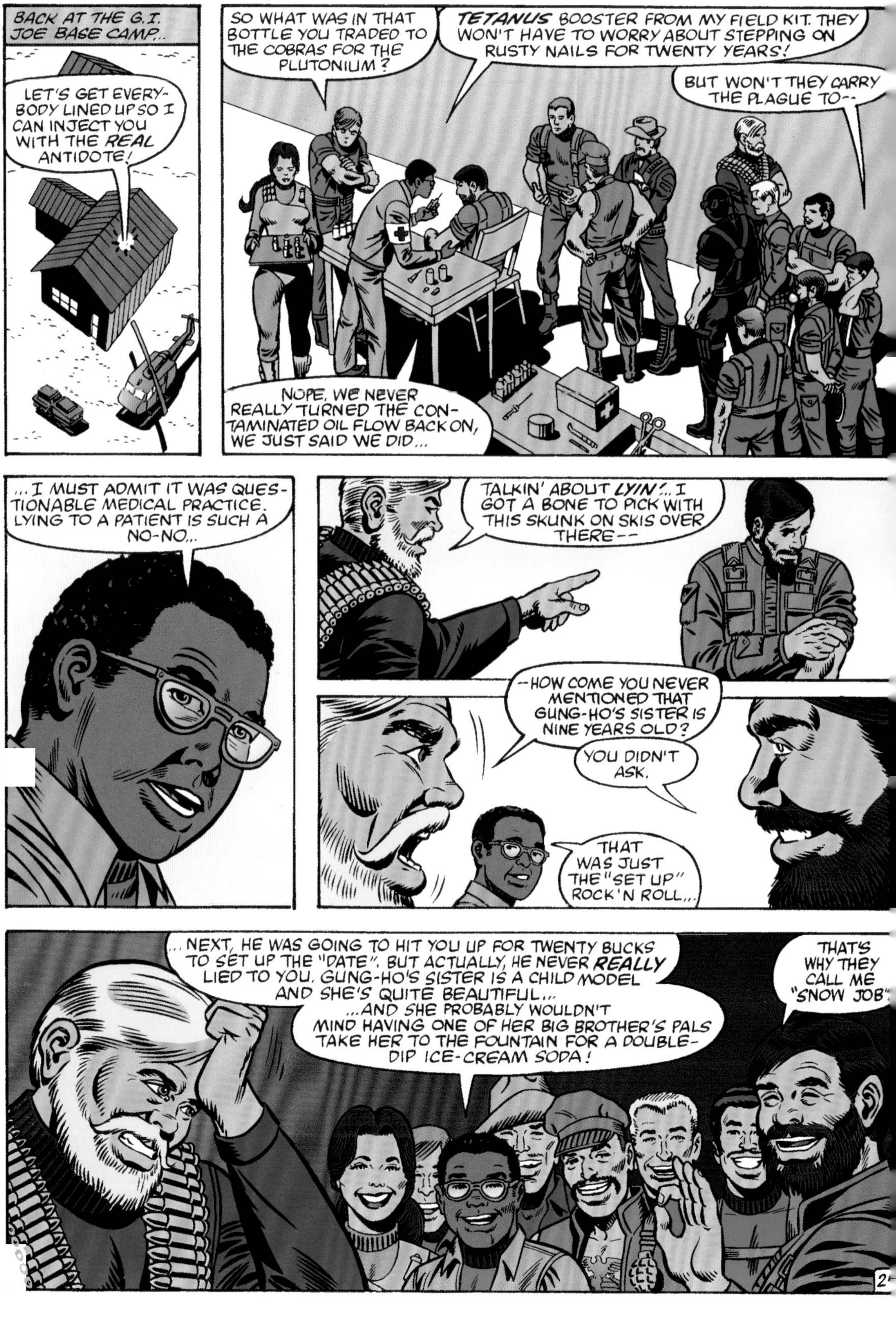
BACK AT THE G.I. JOE BASE CAMP...
LET'S GET EVERY-BODY LINED UP SO I CAN INJECT YOU WITH THE REAL ANTIDOTE!
SO WHAT WAS IN THAT BOTTLE YOU TRADED TO THE COBRAS FOR THE PLUTONIUM?
TETANUS BOOSTER FROM MY FIELD KIT. THEY WON'T HAVE TO WORRY ABOUT STEPPING ON RUSTY NAILS FOR TWENTY YEARS!
BUT WON'T THEY CARRY THE PLAGUE TO--
NOPE, WE NEVER REALLY TURNED THE CON-TAMINATED OIL FLOW BACK ON, WE JUST SAID WE DID...
...I MUST ADMIT IT WAS QUES-TIONABLE MEDICAL PRACTICE. LYING TO A PATIENT IS SUCH A NO-NO...
TALKIN' ABOUT LYIN'!.. I GOT A BONE TO PICK WITH THIS SKUNK ON SKIS OVER THERE--
--HOW COME YOU NEVER MENTIONED THAT GUNG-HO'S SISTER IS NINE YEARS OLD?
YOU DIDN'T ASK.
THAT WAS JUST THE "SET UP" ROCK 'N ROLL...
...NEXT, HE WAS GOING TO HIT YOU UP FOR TWENTY BUCKS TO SET UP THE "DATE". BUT ACTUALLY, HE NEVER REALLY LIED TO YOU. GUNG-HO'S SISTER IS A CHILD MODEL AND SHE'S QUITE BEAUTIFUL...
...AND SHE PROBABLY WOULDN'T MIND HAVING ONE OF HER BIG BROTHER'S PALS TAKE HER TO THE FOUNTAIN FOR A DOUBLE-DIP ICE-CREAM SODA!
THAT'S WHY THEY CALL ME "SNOW JOB"
2

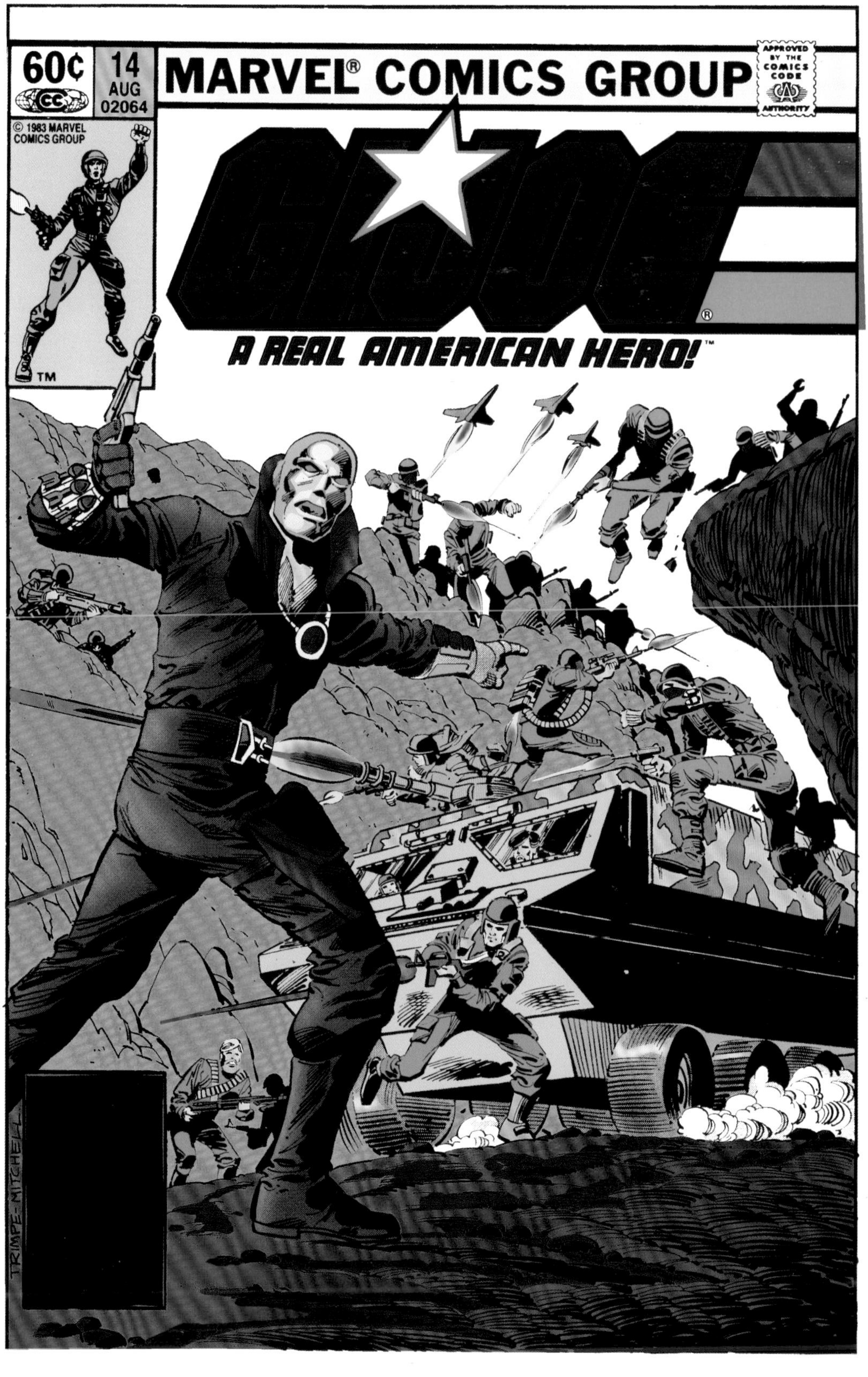

60¢
14
AUG
02064
MARVEL® COMICS GROUP
APPROVED BY THE COMICS CODE AUTHORITY
© 1983 MARVEL COMICS GROUP
TM
G.I. JOE®
A REAL AMERICAN HERO!™
TRIMPE-MITCHELL

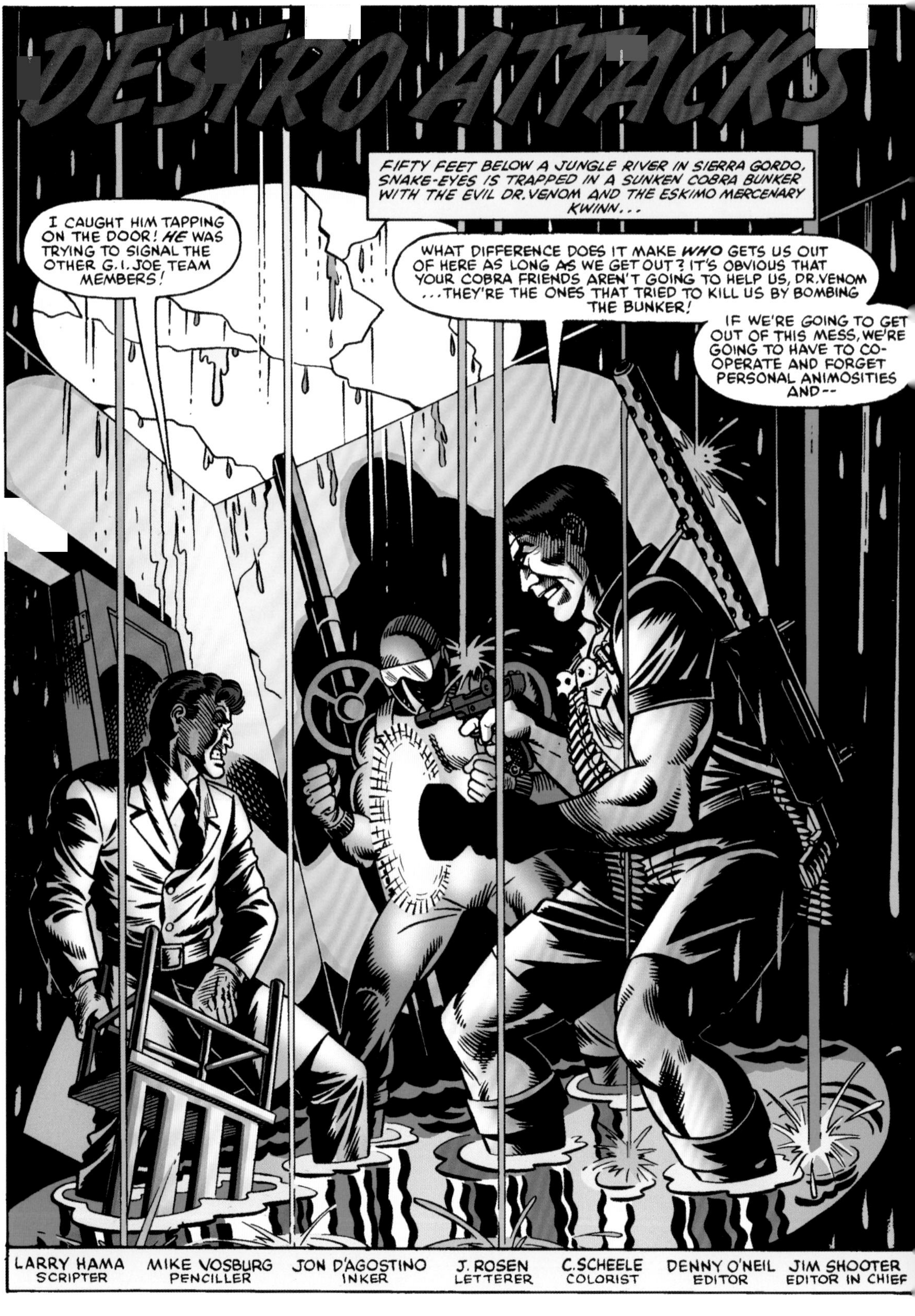
DESTRO ATTACKS
FIFTY FEET BELOW A JUNGLE RIVER IN SIERRA GORDO, SNAKE-EYES IS TRAPPED IN A SUNKEN COBRA BUNKER WITH THE EVIL DR. VENOM AND THE ESKIMO MERCENARY KWINN...
I CAUGHT HIM TAPPING ON THE DOOR! *HE* WAS TRYING TO SIGNAL THE OTHER G.I. JOE TEAM MEMBERS!
WHAT DIFFERENCE DOES IT MAKE *WHO* GETS US OUT OF HERE AS LONG AS WE GET OUT? IT'S OBVIOUS THAT YOUR COBRA FRIENDS AREN'T GOING TO HELP US, DR. VENOM ...THEY'RE THE ONES THAT TRIED TO KILL US BY BOMBING THE BUNKER!
IF WE'RE GOING TO GET OUT OF THIS MESS, WE'RE GOING TO HAVE TO CO-OPERATE AND FORGET PERSONAL ANIMOSITIES AND--

LARRY HAMA SCRIPTER | MIKE VOSBURG PENCILLER | JON D'AGOSTINO INKER | J. ROSEN LETTERER | C. SCHEELE COLORIST | DENNY O'NEIL EDITOR | JIM SHOOTER EDITOR IN CHIEF

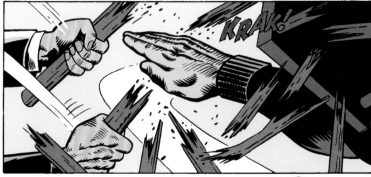

FORGET?! NEVER!!! I SHALL KILL THIS SNAKE-EYES WITH MY BARE--

NNNNNGGG!!

STOP IT! DON'T YOU UNDERSTAND? WE EITHER HELP EACH OTHER OR ELSE WE ALL DIE!

DO YOU FEAR DEATH, KWINN?

FEAR? NO. I'D CALL IT A HEALTHY RESPECT...

THERE ARE DEATHS THAT ONE *SHOULD* FEAR, KWINN...

...PROLONGED, AGONIZED, WRETCHED EXPIRATIONS--

--SUCH AS ARE CONTAINED IN THIS VIAL, THE PLAGUE TOXIN THE BARONESS MISTAKENLY ASSUMES TO BE IN SCAR-FACE'S BRIEFCASE!

IN G.I. JOE HEADQUARTERS DEEP BELOW FORT WADSWORTH IN STATEN ISLAND...

THIS MICRO-DOT MAP FRAGMENT THAT STALKER FOUND IN THE COBRA RESEARCH STATION IN SIERRA GORDO IS LABELED IN CODE...

...WE'VE BEEN RUNNING A MATCHING PROGRAM WITH EVERY KNOWN MAP IN THE WORLD WORKING FROM GEOGRAPHICAL FEATURES ALONE...

HAWK, BREAKER'S GOT A PRINT-OUT...

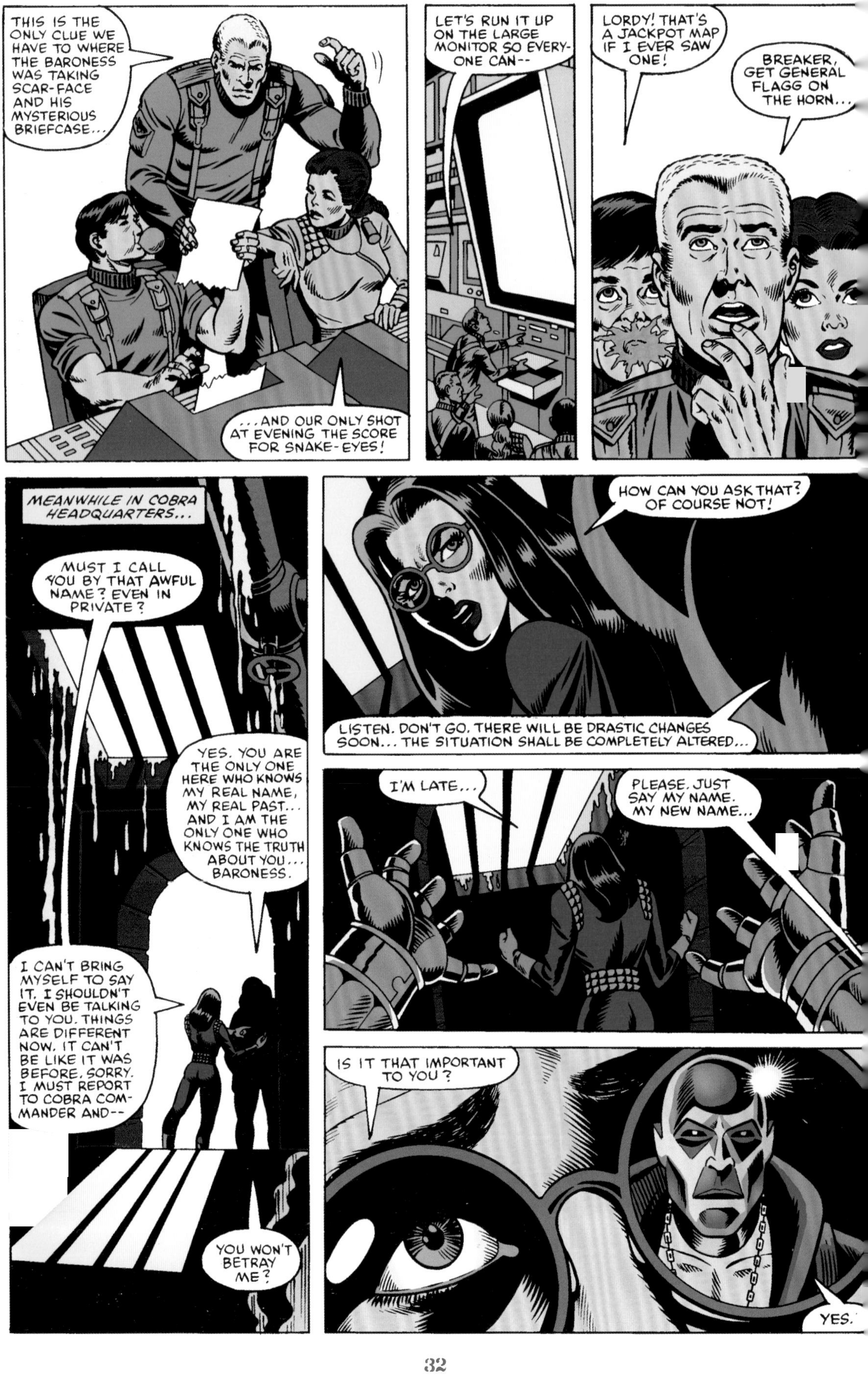
THIS IS THE ONLY CLUE WE HAVE TO WHERE THE BARONESS WAS TAKING SCAR-FACE AND HIS MYSTERIOUS BRIEFCASE...
...AND OUR ONLY SHOT AT EVENING THE SCORE FOR SNAKE-EYES!
LET'S RUN IT UP ON THE LARGE MONITOR SO EVERY-ONE CAN--
LORDY! THAT'S A JACKPOT MAP IF I EVER SAW ONE!
BREAKER, GET GENERAL FLAGG ON THE HORN...
MEANWHILE IN COBRA HEADQUARTERS...
MUST I CALL YOU BY THAT AWFUL NAME? EVEN IN PRIVATE?
YES. YOU ARE THE ONLY ONE HERE WHO KNOWS MY REAL NAME, MY REAL PAST... AND I AM THE ONLY ONE WHO KNOWS THE TRUTH ABOUT YOU... BARONESS.
I CAN'T BRING MYSELF TO SAY IT. I SHOULDN'T EVEN BE TALKING TO YOU. THINGS ARE DIFFERENT NOW. IT CAN'T BE LIKE IT WAS BEFORE. SORRY. I MUST REPORT TO COBRA COM-MANDER AND--
YOU WON'T BETRAY ME?
HOW CAN YOU ASK THAT? OF COURSE NOT!
LISTEN. DON'T GO. THERE WILL BE DRASTIC CHANGES SOON... THE SITUATION SHALL BE COMPLETELY ALTERED...
I'M LATE...
PLEASE. JUST SAY MY NAME. MY NEW NAME...
IS IT THAT IMPORTANT TO YOU?
YES.

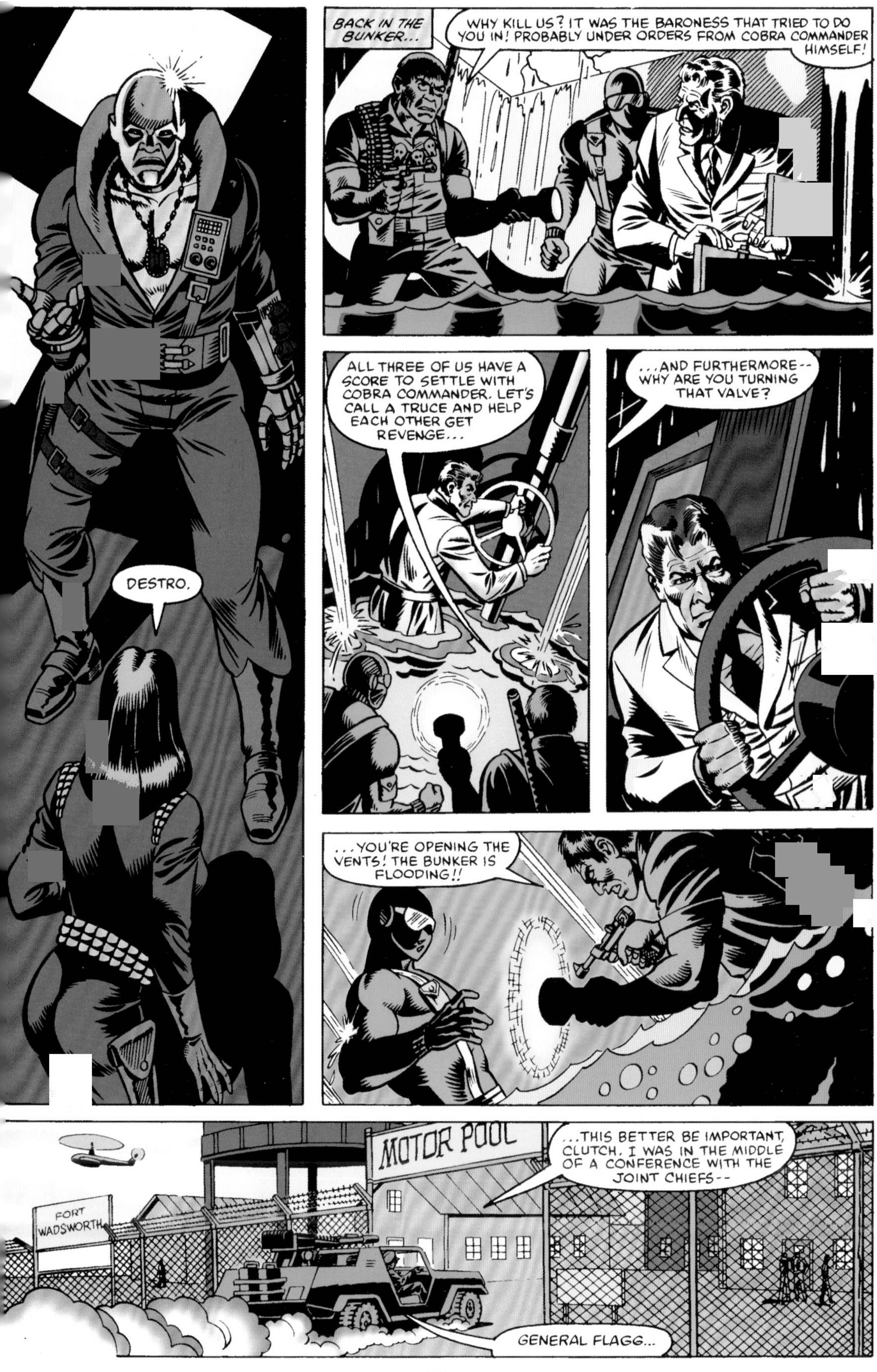
DESTRO.
BACK IN THE BUNKER...
WHY KILL US? IT WAS THE BARONESS THAT TRIED TO DO YOU IN! PROBABLY UNDER ORDERS FROM COBRA COMMANDER HIMSELF!
ALL THREE OF US HAVE A SCORE TO SETTLE WITH COBRA COMMANDER. LET'S CALL A TRUCE AND HELP EACH OTHER GET REVENGE...
...AND FURTHERMORE-- WHY ARE YOU TURNING THAT VALVE?
...YOU'RE OPENING THE VENTS! THE BUNKER IS FLOODING!!
FORT WADSWORTH
MOTOR POOL
...THIS BETTER BE IMPORTANT, CLUTCH. I WAS IN THE MIDDLE OF A CONFERENCE WITH THE JOINT CHIEFS--
GENERAL FLAGG...

...IF WHAT WE HAVE DOWN-STAIRS PANS OUT--

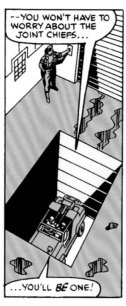

--YOU WON'T HAVE TO WORRY ABOUT THE JOINT CHIEFS...

...YOU'LL *BE* ONE!

MOMENTS LATER...

...WE HAVE AN EXACT COMPUTER MATCH-UP. THE COBRA MICRO-DOT MAP FRAGMENT SHOWS A FIVE MILE SQUARE SECTION OF VERMONT...

COULD MEAN ANY-THING, HAWK. MAYBE COBRA COMMANDER LIKES TO SKI...

NO SIR. HIS ONLY HOBBY IS TARGET SHOOTING WITH MACHINE-GUNS...

SPRINGFIELD.

...IF YOU'LL SEE FOR YOURSELF, SIR, THE NAME OF THE TOWN DEAD CENTER IN THIS MAP FRAGMENT, YOU UNDERSTAND OUR CONCERN

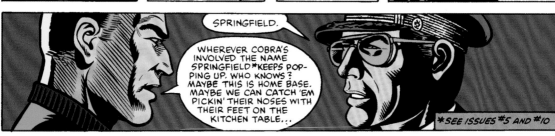

SPRINGFIELD.

WHEREVER COBRA'S INVOLVED THE NAME SPRINGFIELD*KEEPS POP-PING UP. WHO KNOWS? MAYBE THIS IS HOME BASE. MAYBE WE CAN CATCH 'EM PICKIN' THEIR NOSES WITH THEIR FEET ON THE KITCHEN TABLE...

*SEE ISSUES #5 AND #10

COBRA HEADQUARTERS...

SO, MY DEAR BARONESS... DID THE JOES SNAP UP THE MICRO-DOT WE PLANTED AT THE RESEARCH STATION IN SIERRA GORDO?

YES, COBRA COMMANDER. OUR REMOTE SENSORS RECORDED THE PICKUP. THE MAP FRAGMENT INDICATED THE LOCATION OF COBRA HEAD-QUARTERS AS BEING UNDER THE CHAPLAIN'S ASSISTANT SCHOOL IN FORT WADSWORTH...

....THE JOES WILL WASTE THEIR TIME POKING AROUND THAT INNOCENT LITTLE ARMY POST-- AND STAY FAR AWAY FROM SPRINGFIELD, VERMONT, OUR PLAGUE TOXIN TEST SITE...

DOES SCAR-FACE KNOW WHAT HE CARRIED IN THE BRIEFCASE?

NO.

AND YOU'RE SURE DR. VENOM IS DEAD?

CERTAIN. ALONG WITH SNAKE-EYES AND KWINN.

DID YOU PLANT THE MICRO-DOT YOURSELF?

OF COURSE. WHY SHOULDN'T?

34

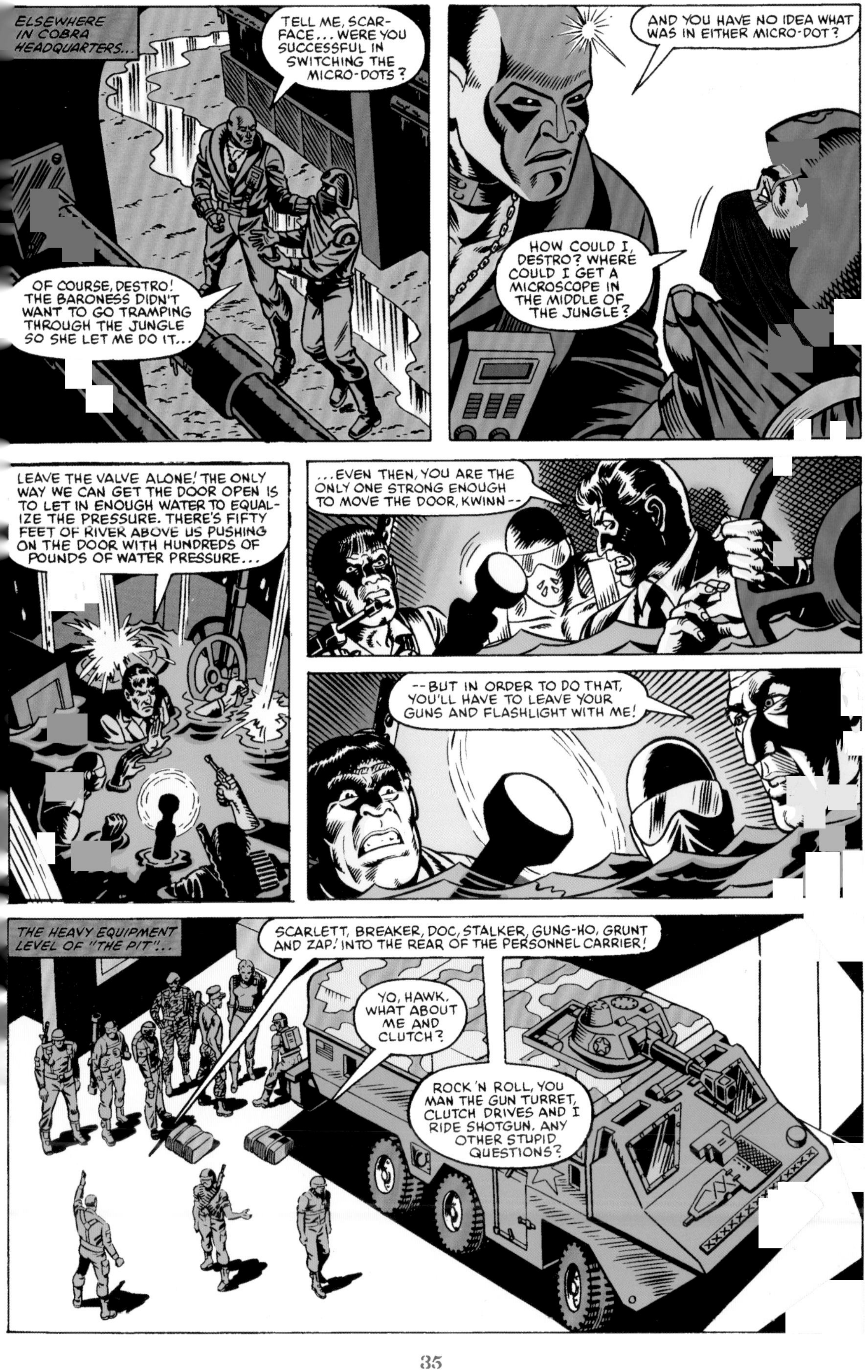
ELSEWHERE IN COBRA HEADQUARTERS...
TELL ME, SCAR-FACE... WERE YOU SUCCESSFUL IN SWITCHING THE MICRO-DOTS?
OF COURSE, DESTRO! THE BARONESS DIDN'T WANT TO GO TRAMPING THROUGH THE JUNGLE SO SHE LET ME DO IT...
AND YOU HAVE NO IDEA WHAT WAS IN EITHER MICRO-DOT?
HOW COULD I, DESTRO? WHERE COULD I GET A MICROSCOPE IN THE MIDDLE OF THE JUNGLE?
LEAVE THE VALVE ALONE! THE ONLY WAY WE CAN GET THE DOOR OPEN IS TO LET IN ENOUGH WATER TO EQUALIZE THE PRESSURE. THERE'S FIFTY FEET OF RIVER ABOVE US PUSHING ON THE DOOR WITH HUNDREDS OF POUNDS OF WATER PRESSURE...
...EVEN THEN, YOU ARE THE ONLY ONE STRONG ENOUGH TO MOVE THE DOOR, KWINN--
--BUT IN ORDER TO DO THAT, YOU'LL HAVE TO LEAVE YOUR GUNS AND FLASHLIGHT WITH ME!
THE HEAVY EQUIPMENT LEVEL OF "THE PIT"...
SCARLETT, BREAKER, DOC, STALKER, GUNG-HO, GRUNT AND ZAP! INTO THE REAR OF THE PERSONNEL CARRIER!
YO, HAWK, WHAT ABOUT ME AND CLUTCH?
ROCK 'N ROLL, YOU MAN THE GUN TURRET, CLUTCH DRIVES AND I RIDE SHOTGUN. ANY OTHER STUPID QUESTIONS?

LET'S GO! MOVE US ON TO THE HEAVY EQUIPMENT LIFT, CLUTCH.

WE GONNA DRIVE ALL THE WAY TO VERMONT? WE'D BETTER STOP AT A GAS STATION AND GET A MAP...

WE'RE ONLY DRIVING AS FAR AS THE FORT WADSWORTH BASEBALL FIELD, CLUTCH...

...PUT IT ON THE PITCHER'S MOUND AND SHUT OFF THE ENGINE.

HEY! WHAT'S THE IDEA?

WE GOT A MAJOR PLAY-OFF GOING ON HERE BETWEEN THE CHAPLAIN'S ASSISTANTS AND THE PERMANENT LATRINE ORDER- LIES!

SORRY, BUT ORDERS IS ORDERS...

HUH? PRIORITY TRANSPORTA- TION ORDERS SIGNED BY GENERAL FLAGG?

HOW DO YOU TRANSPORT A PC FROM THE MIDDLE OF A BALL DIAMOND?

ULP. HERE COMES THE ANSWER!

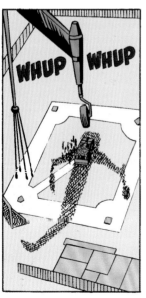

WHUP WHUP

WHUP WHUP

CLAMPS SECURED?

VEHICLE CLAMPS SECURED, WILD BILL ...TAKE US UP!

HANG ON TIGHT, PARDS...NEXT STOP IS SPRINGFIELD!

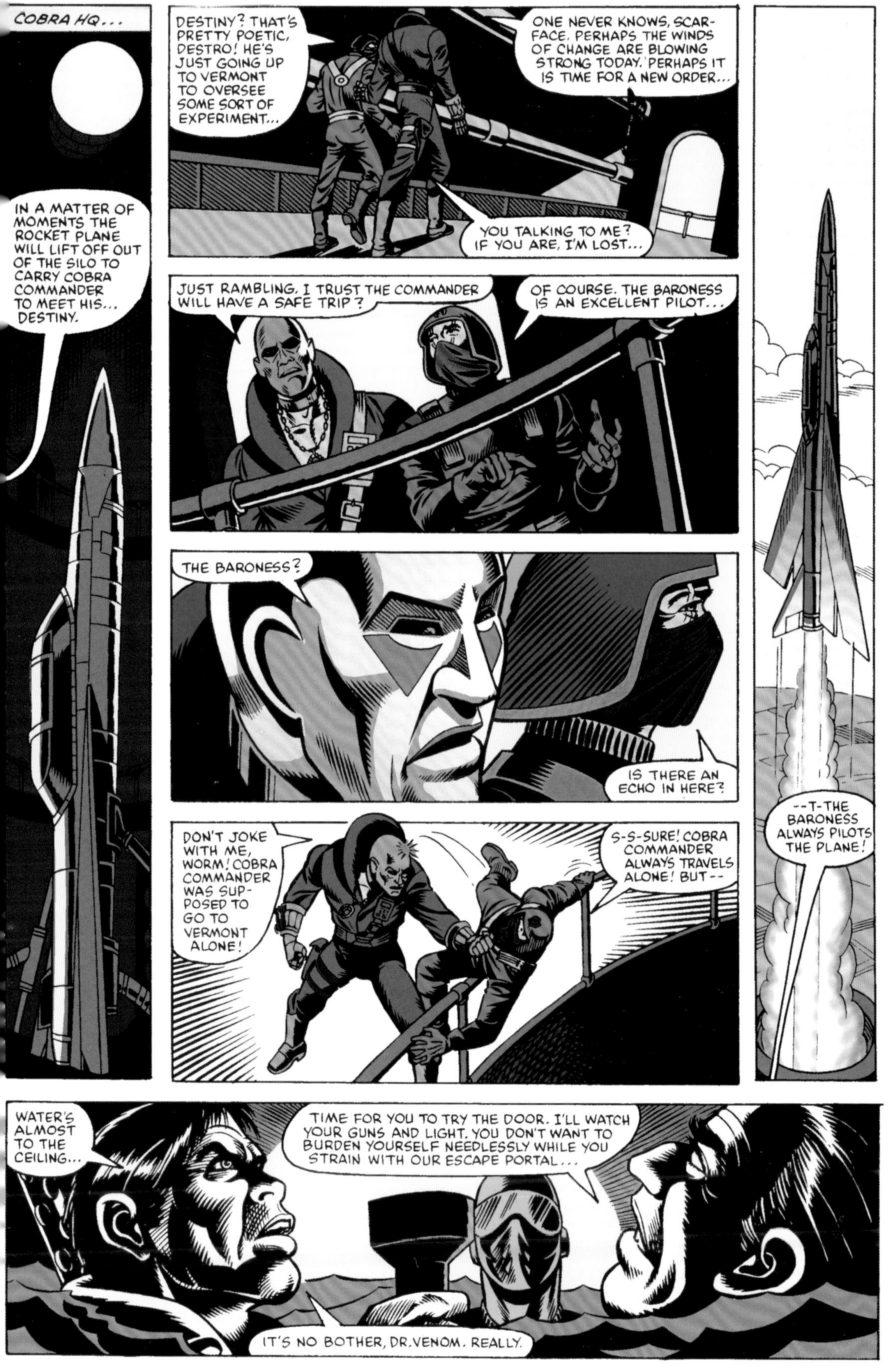

COBRA HQ...
DESTINY? THAT'S PRETTY POETIC, DESTRO! HE'S JUST GOING UP TO VERMONT TO OVERSEE SOME SORT OF EXPERIMENT...
ONE NEVER KNOWS, SCAR-FACE. PERHAPS THE WINDS OF CHANGE ARE BLOWING STRONG TODAY. PERHAPS IT IS TIME FOR A NEW ORDER...
YOU TALKING TO ME? IF YOU ARE, I'M LOST...
IN A MATTER OF MOMENTS THE ROCKET PLANE WILL LIFT OFF OUT OF THE SILO TO CARRY COBRA COMMANDER TO MEET HIS... DESTINY.
JUST RAMBLING. I TRUST THE COMMANDER WILL HAVE A SAFE TRIP?
OF COURSE. THE BARONESS IS AN EXCELLENT PILOT...
THE BARONESS?
IS THERE AN ECHO IN HERE?
DON'T JOKE WITH ME, WORM! COBRA COMMANDER WAS SUP-POSED TO GO TO VERMONT ALONE!
S-S-SURE! COBRA COMMANDER ALWAYS TRAVELS ALONE! BUT--
--T-THE BARONESS ALWAYS PILOTS THE PLANE!
WATER'S ALMOST TO THE CEILING...
TIME FOR YOU TO TRY THE DOOR. I'LL WATCH YOUR GUNS AND LIGHT. YOU DON'T WANT TO BURDEN YOURSELF NEEDLESSLY WHILE YOU STRAIN WITH OUR ESCAPE PORTAL...
IT'S NO BOTHER, DR. VENOM. REALLY.

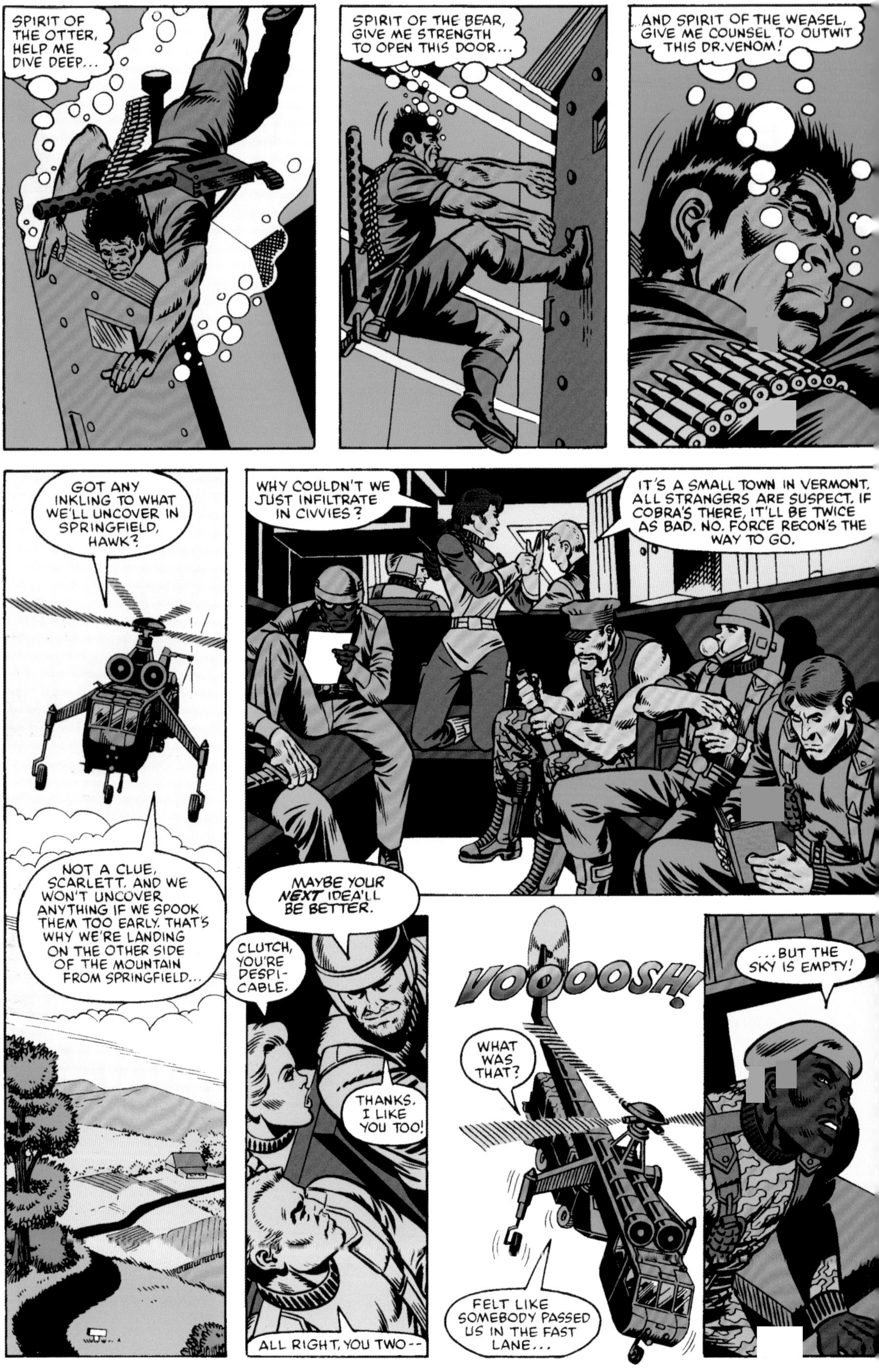
SPIRIT OF THE OTTER, HELP ME DIVE DEEP...
SPIRIT OF THE BEAR, GIVE ME STRENGTH TO OPEN THIS DOOR...
...AND SPIRIT OF THE WEASEL, GIVE ME COUNSEL TO OUTWIT THIS DR.VENOM!
GOT ANY INKLING TO WHAT WE'LL UNCOVER IN SPRINGFIELD, HAWK?
NOT A CLUE, SCARLETT. AND WE WON'T UNCOVER ANYTHING IF WE SPOOK THEM TOO EARLY. THAT'S WHY WE'RE LANDING ON THE OTHER SIDE OF THE MOUNTAIN FROM SPRINGFIELD...
WHY COULDN'T WE JUST INFILTRATE IN CIVVIES?
IT'S A SMALL TOWN IN VERMONT. ALL STRANGERS ARE SUSPECT. IF COBRA'S THERE, IT'LL BE TWICE AS BAD. NO. FORCE RECON'S THE WAY TO GO.
MAYBE YOUR NEXT IDEA'LL BE BETTER.
CLUTCH, YOU'RE DESPI-CABLE.
THANKS. I LIKE YOU TOO!
ALL RIGHT, YOU TWO--
VOOOOOSH!
WHAT WAS THAT?
FELT LIKE SOMEBODY PASSED US IN THE FAST LANE...
...BUT THE SKY IS EMPTY!

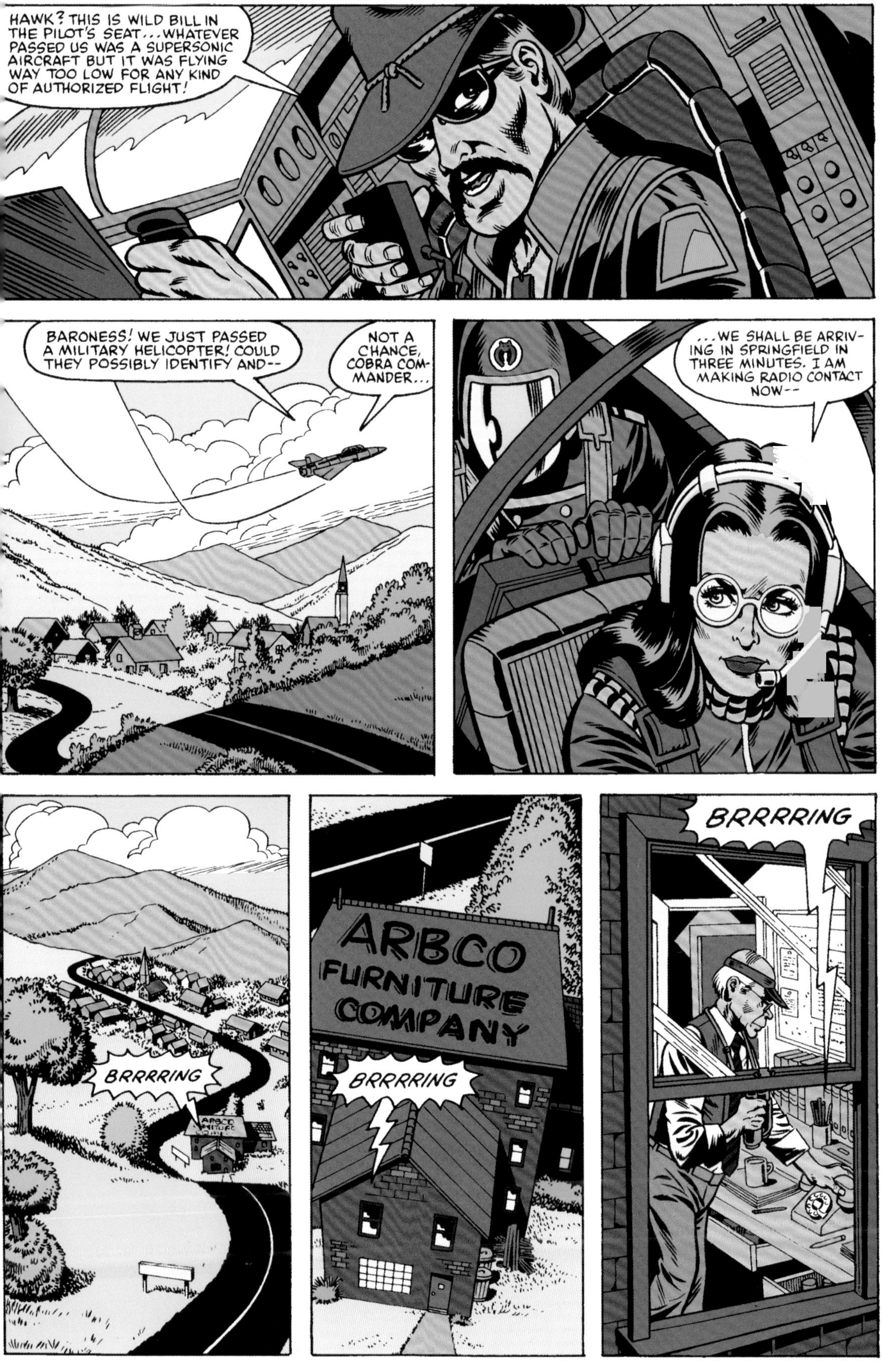

HAWK? THIS IS WILD BILL IN THE PILOT'S SEAT... WHATEVER PASSED US WAS A SUPERSONIC AIRCRAFT BUT IT WAS FLYING WAY TOO LOW FOR ANY KIND OF AUTHORIZED FLIGHT!
BARONESS! WE JUST PASSED A MILITARY HELICOPTER! COULD THEY POSSIBLY IDENTIFY AND--
NOT A CHANCE, COBRA COMMANDER...
...WE SHALL BE ARRIVING IN SPRINGFIELD IN THREE MINUTES. I AM MAKING RADIO CONTACT NOW--
BRRRRING
ARBCO FURNITURE COMPANY
BRRRRING
BRRRRING

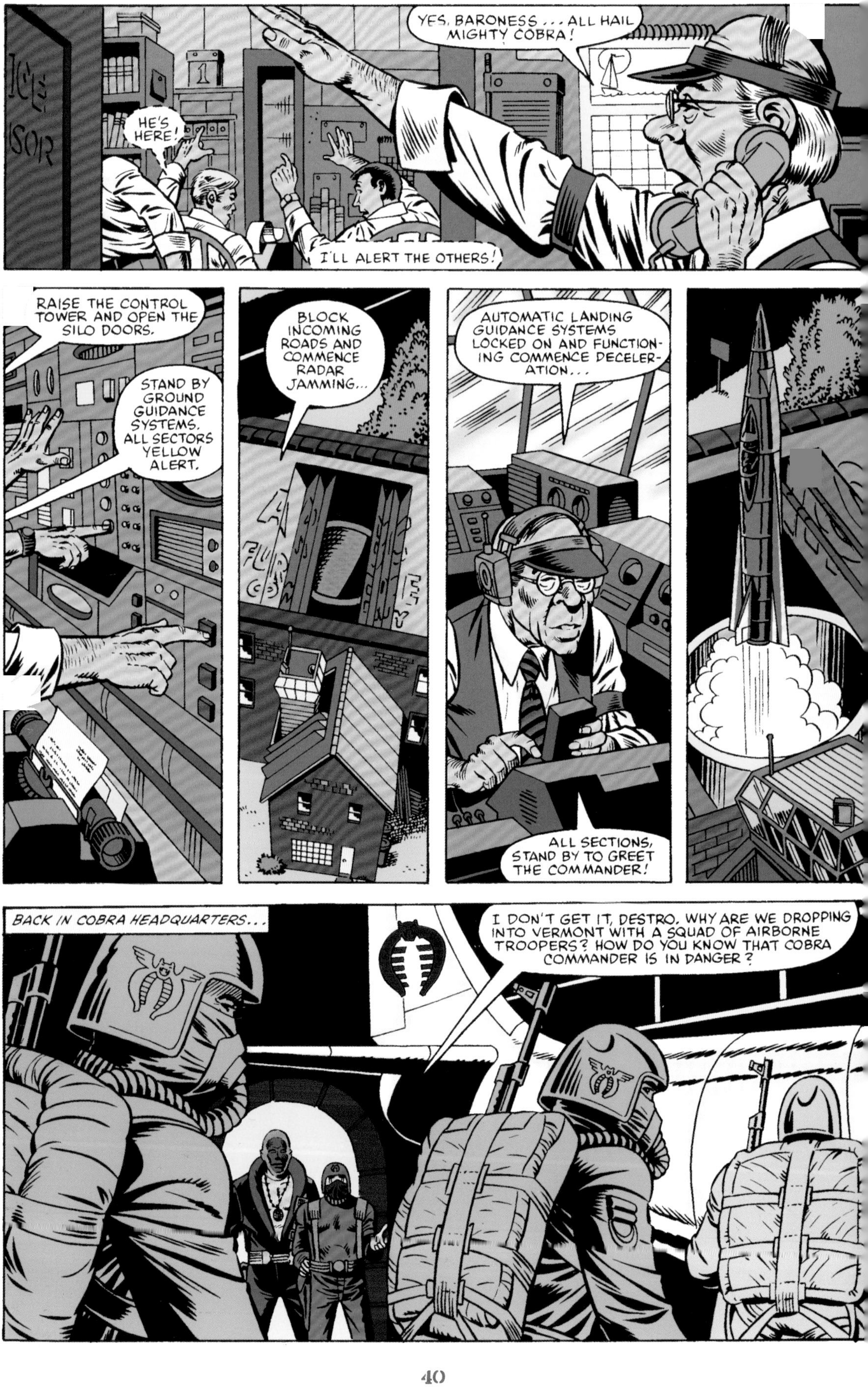
YES, BARONESS... ALL HAIL MIGHTY COBRA!
HE'S HERE!
I'LL ALERT THE OTHERS!
RAISE THE CONTROL TOWER AND OPEN THE SILO DOORS.
STAND BY GROUND GUIDANCE SYSTEMS. ALL SECTORS YELLOW ALERT.
BLOCK INCOMING ROADS AND COMMENCE RADAR JAMMING...
AUTOMATIC LANDING GUIDANCE SYSTEMS LOCKED ON AND FUNCTIONING COMMENCE DECELERATION...
ALL SECTIONS, STAND BY TO GREET THE COMMANDER!
BACK IN COBRA HEADQUARTERS...
I DON'T GET IT, DESTRO. WHY ARE WE DROPPING INTO VERMONT WITH A SQUAD OF AIRBORNE TROOPERS? HOW DO YOU KNOW THAT COBRA COMMANDER IS IN DANGER?

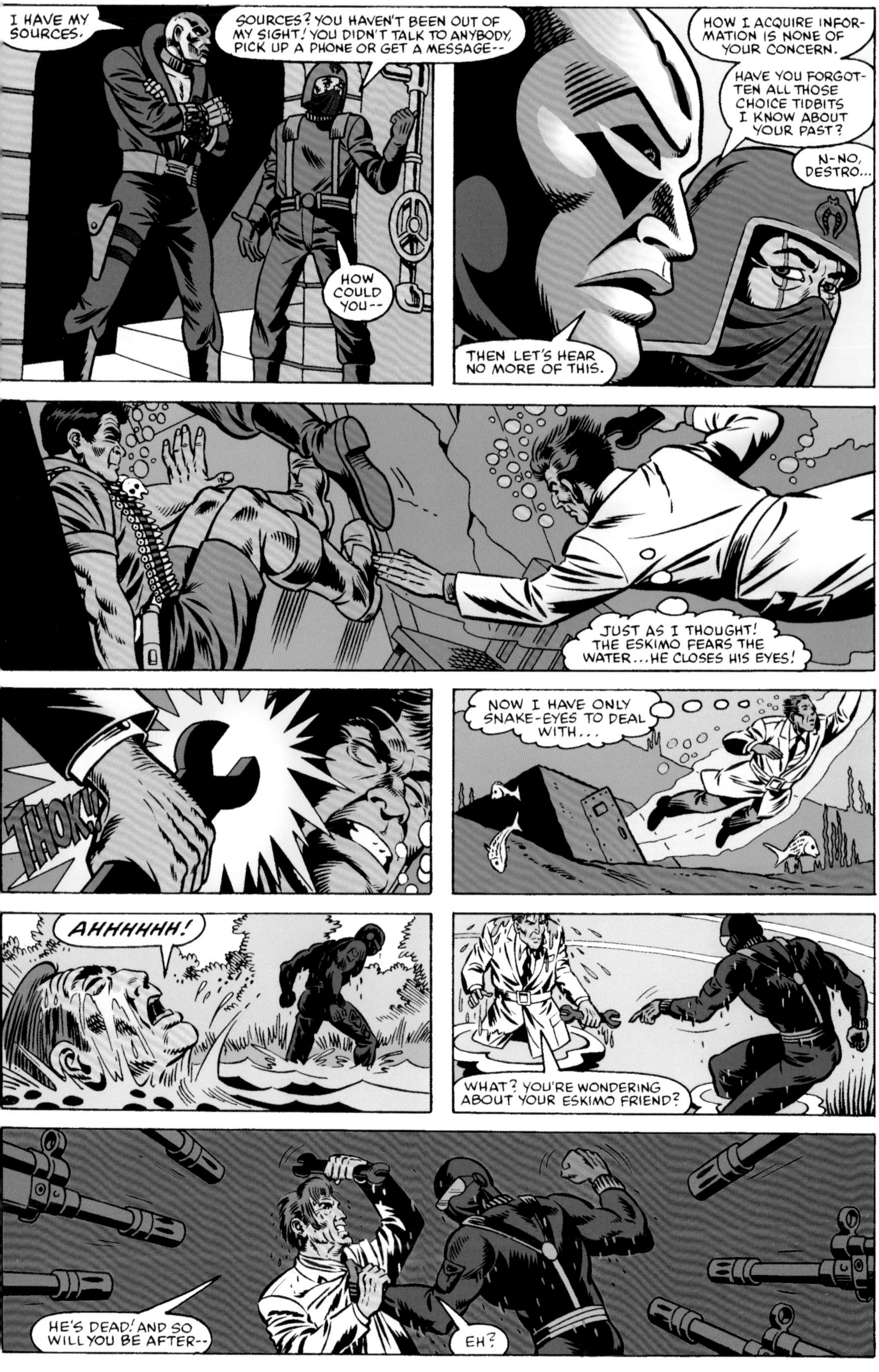
I HAVE MY SOURCES.
SOURCES? YOU HAVEN'T BEEN OUT OF MY SIGHT! YOU DIDN'T TALK TO ANYBODY, PICK UP A PHONE OR GET A MESSAGE--
HOW COULD YOU--
HOW I ACQUIRE INFORMATION IS NONE OF YOUR CONCERN.
HAVE YOU FORGOTTEN ALL THOSE CHOICE TIDBITS I KNOW ABOUT YOUR PAST?
N-NO, DESTRO...
THEN LET'S HEAR NO MORE OF THIS.
JUST AS I THOUGHT! THE ESKIMO FEARS THE WATER... HE CLOSES HIS EYES!
THOK!!
NOW I HAVE ONLY SNAKE-EYES TO DEAL WITH...
AHHHHHH!
WHAT? YOU'RE WONDERING ABOUT YOUR ESKIMO FRIEND?
HE'S DEAD! AND SO WILL YOU BE AFTER--
EH?

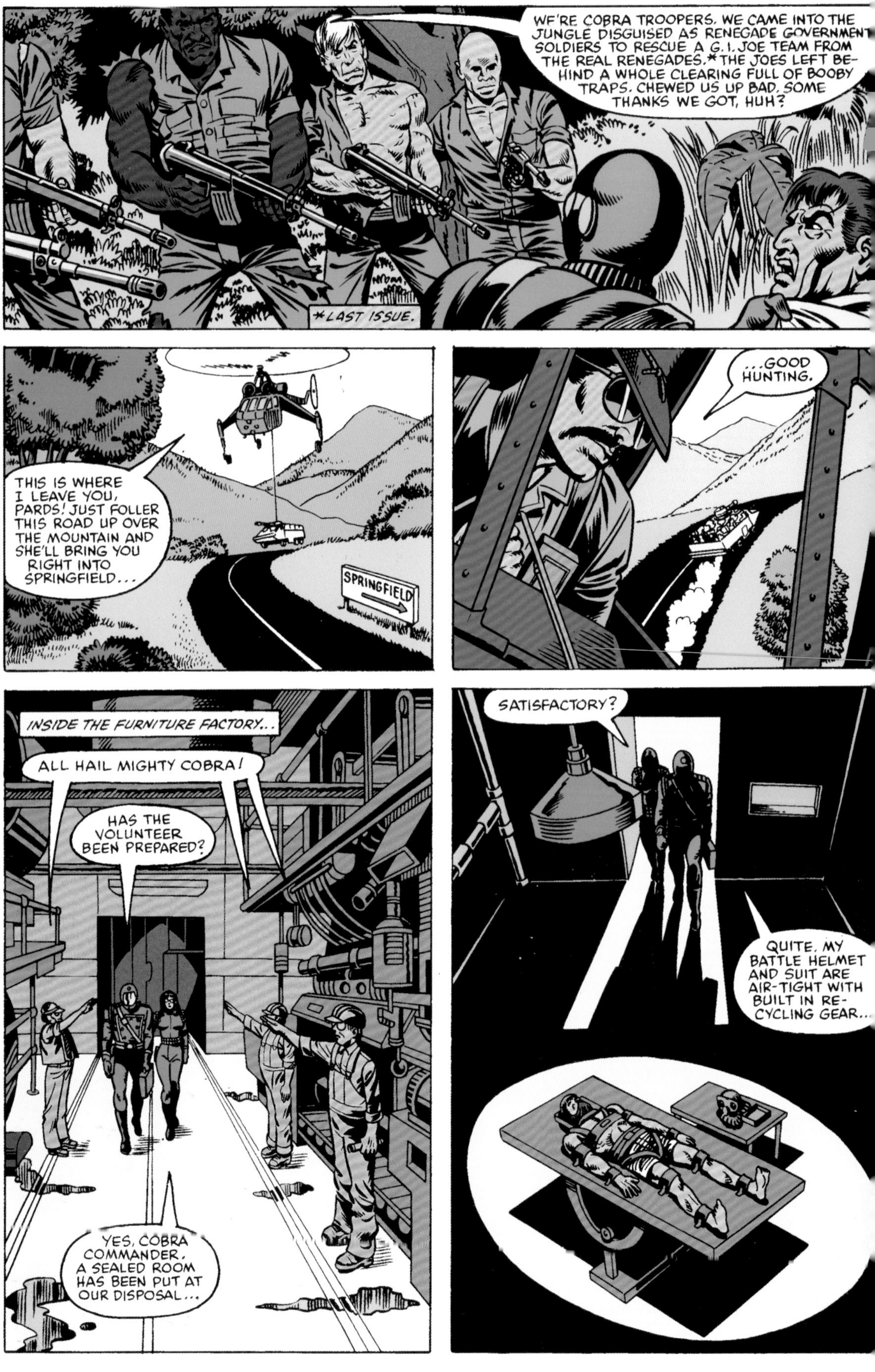
WE'RE COBRA TROOPERS. WE CAME INTO THE JUNGLE DISGUISED AS RENEGADE GOVERNMENT SOLDIERS TO RESCUE A G.I. JOE TEAM FROM THE REAL RENEGADES.* THE JOES LEFT BEHIND A WHOLE CLEARING FULL OF BOOBY TRAPS. CHEWED US UP BAD. SOME THANKS WE GOT, HUH?
*LAST ISSUE.
THIS IS WHERE I LEAVE YOU, PARDS! JUST FOLLER THIS ROAD UP OVER THE MOUNTAIN AND SHE'LL BRING YOU RIGHT INTO SPRINGFIELD...
SPRINGFIELD
...GOOD HUNTING.
INSIDE THE FURNITURE FACTORY...
ALL HAIL MIGHTY COBRA!
HAS THE VOLUNTEER BEEN PREPARED?
YES, COBRA COMMANDER. A SEALED ROOM HAS BEEN PUT AT OUR DISPOSAL...
SATISFACTORY?
QUITE. MY BATTLE HELMET AND SUIT ARE AIR-TIGHT WITH BUILT IN RECYCLING GEAR...

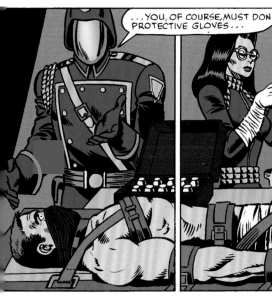

...YOU, OF COURSE, MUST DON PROTECTIVE GLOVES...

AND MASK...

BEFORE WE BREAK THE SEALS OF THE VIALS!

FIVE MILES FROM SPRINGFIELD...

HERE COME STALKER AND GUNG-HO BACK FROM THEIR SCOUTING MISSION...

ANYTHING TO REPORT?

SPRINGFIELD ITSELF LOOKS CLEAN...

...BUT THIS FURNITURE FACTORY ON THE OUTSKIRTS IS A TAD FISHY.

ANY PARTICULAR REASON OR JUST GUT FEELING?

ARBCO IS AN ANAGRAM FOR COBRA.

BINGO.

YOU'VE NO GRUDGE AGAINST ME! IT'S THE JOES WHO DID YOU DIRT! I'M ONE OF YOU--

CAN IT, VENOM! COBRA COMMANDER WANTED YOU DEAD!

THE WAY I SEE IT, I CAN MAKE MYSELF SOME BROWNIE POINTS BY FINISHING THE JOB THE BARONESS BOTCHED UP!

PLEASE! I H-HAVE M-M-MONEY! SWISS ACCOUNTS! PLEASE--

43

IN VERMONT...

SCAR-FACE, YOU'RE OUR LAND NAVIGATOR. PLOT A COURSE THAT WILL TAKE US TO SPRINGFIELD BEFORE THE G.I. JOE TEAM!

SPRINGFIELD IS DUE EAST OF HERE, FIVE MILES AS THE CROW FLIES...

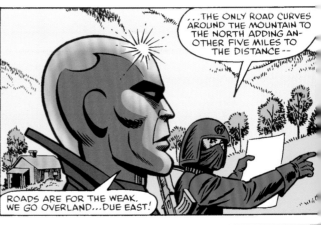

...THE ONLY ROAD CURVES AROUND THE MOUNTAIN TO THE NORTH ADDING ANOTHER FIVE MILES TO THE DISTANCE--

ROADS ARE FOR THE WEAK. WE GO OVERLAND...DUE EAST!

SKY-DIVING JOGGERS WITH COSTUMES! WHAT WILL THEY THINK OF NEXT, SETH?

MUST BE FROM NEW YORK, EVERYBODY'S CRAZY DOWN THERE.

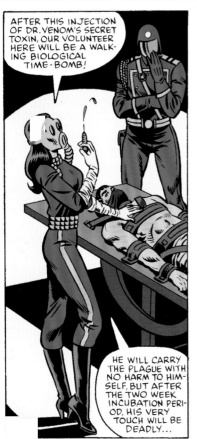

AFTER THIS INJECTION OF DR. VENOM'S SECRET TOXIN, OUR VOLUNTEER HERE WILL BE A WALKING BIOLOGICAL TIME-BOMB!

HE WILL CARRY THE PLAGUE WITH NO HARM TO HIMSELF, BUT AFTER THE TWO WEEK INCUBATION PERIOD, HIS VERY TOUCH WILL BE DEADLY...

...AND BY THAT TIME HE SHOULD BE DEEP WITHIN G.I. JOE HEADQUARTERS!

EVERYBODY BACK ON THE APC! WE'RE GOING TO CHECK OUT THIS FURNITURE FACTORY! HOW FAR IS IT, CLUTCH?

WE'LL HAVE TO TAKE THE ROAD THAT SWINGS NORTH FIVE MILES WORTH, BUT IT'S ONLY TWO MILES AWAY AS THE CROW FLIES...DUE WEST!

SPRINGFIELD

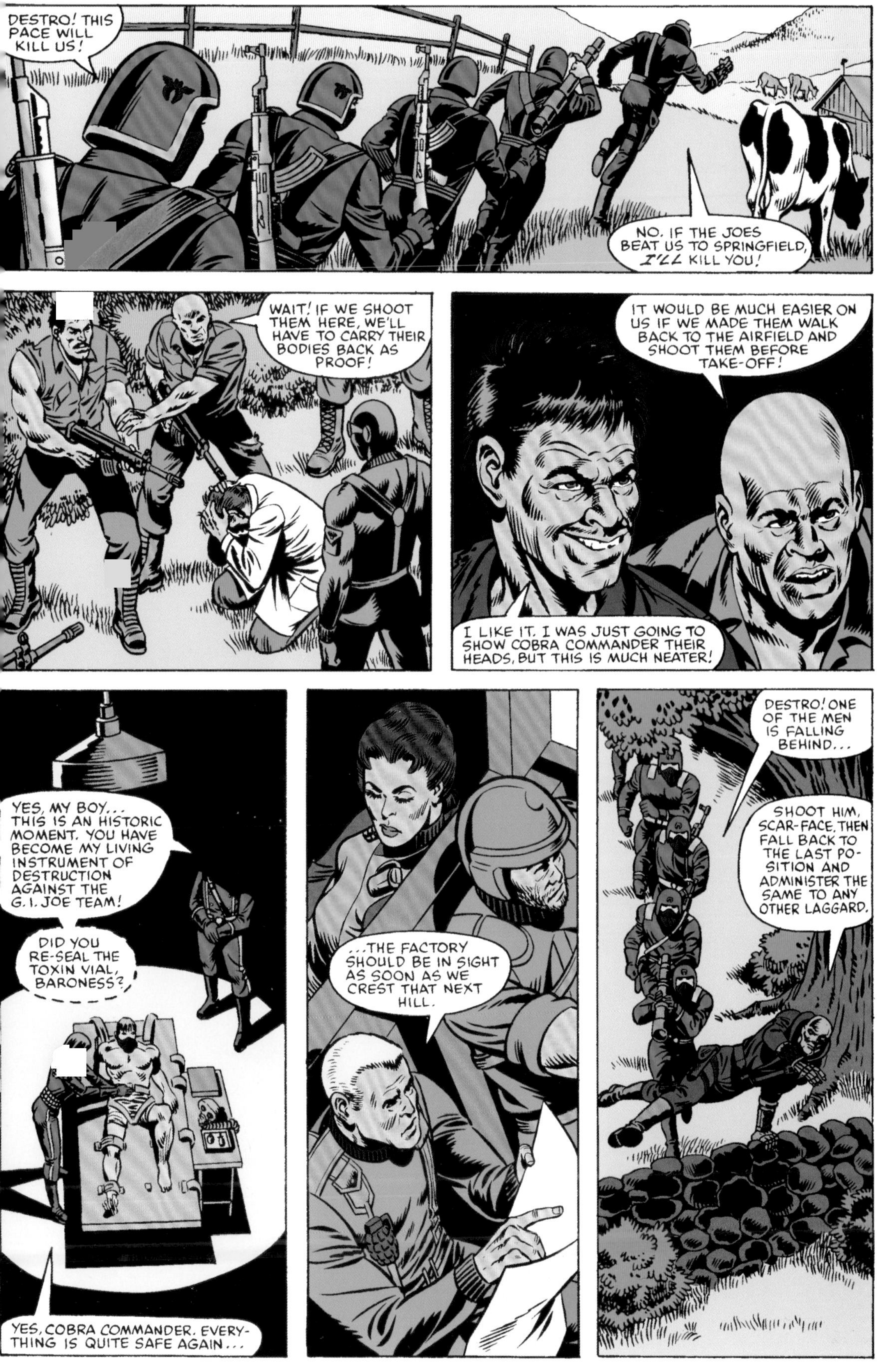
DESTRO! THIS PACE WILL KILL US!
NO. IF THE JOES BEAT US TO SPRINGFIELD, I'LL KILL YOU!
WAIT! IF WE SHOOT THEM HERE, WE'LL HAVE TO CARRY THEIR BODIES BACK AS PROOF!
IT WOULD BE MUCH EASIER ON US IF WE MADE THEM WALK BACK TO THE AIRFIELD AND SHOOT THEM BEFORE TAKE-OFF!
I LIKE IT. I WAS JUST GOING TO SHOW COBRA COMMANDER THEIR HEADS, BUT THIS IS MUCH NEATER!
YES, MY BOY... THIS IS AN HISTORIC MOMENT. YOU HAVE BECOME MY LIVING INSTRUMENT OF DESTRUCTION AGAINST THE G. I. JOE TEAM!
DID YOU RE-SEAL THE TOXIN VIAL, BARONESS?
YES, COBRA COMMANDER. EVERY-THING IS QUITE SAFE AGAIN...
...THE FACTORY SHOULD BE IN SIGHT AS SOON AS WE CREST THAT NEXT HILL.
DESTRO! ONE OF THE MEN IS FALLING BEHIND...
SHOOT HIM, SCAR-FACE, THEN FALL BACK TO THE LAST PO-SITION AND ADMINISTER THE SAME TO ANY OTHER LAGGARD.

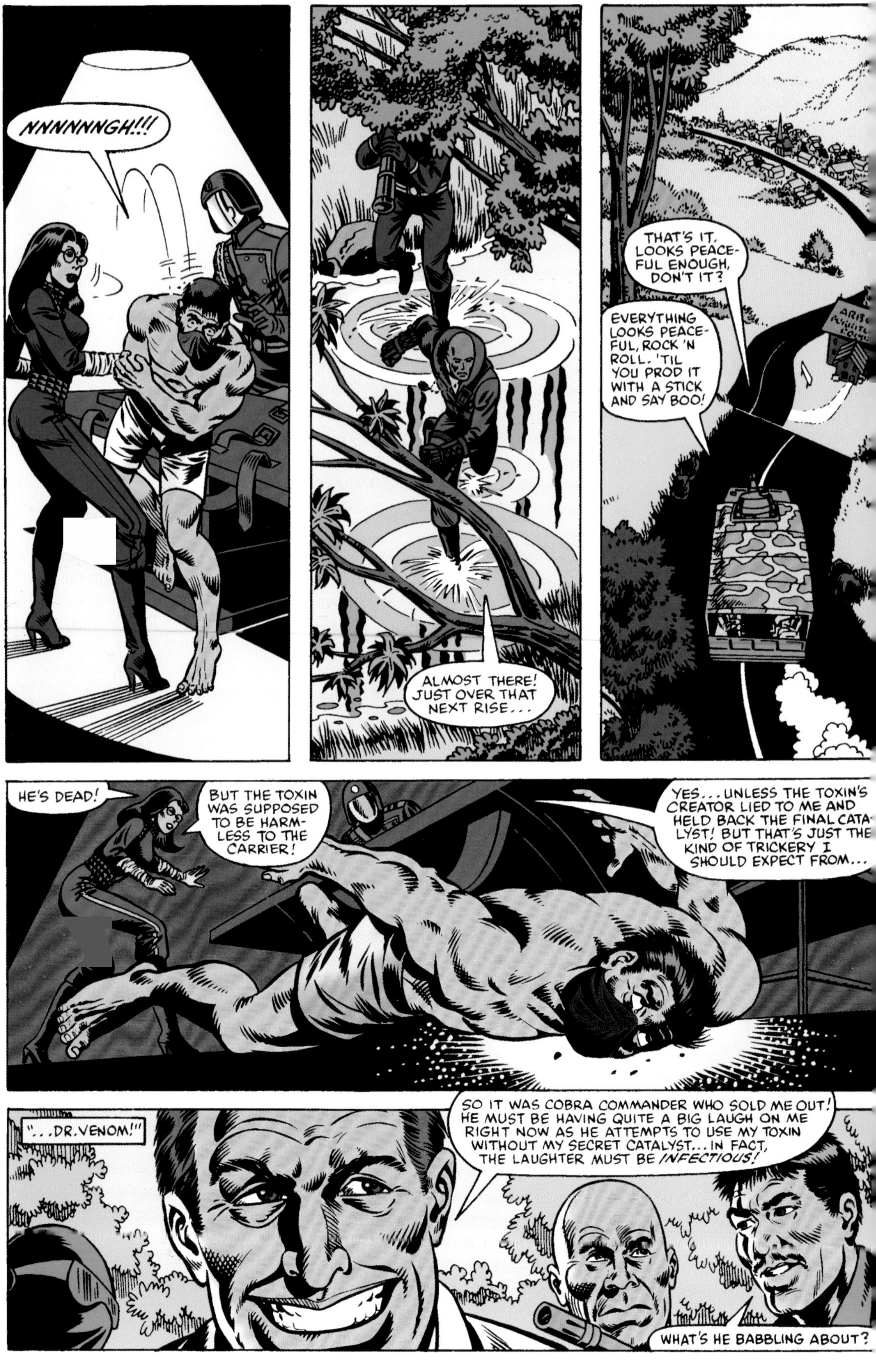

NNNNNNGH!!!
ALMOST THERE! JUST OVER THAT NEXT RISE...
THAT'S IT, LOOKS PEACEFUL ENOUGH, DON'T IT?
EVERYTHING LOOKS PEACEFUL, ROCK 'N ROLL. 'TIL YOU PROD IT WITH A STICK AND SAY BOO!
HE'S DEAD!
BUT THE TOXIN WAS SUPPOSED TO BE HARMLESS TO THE CARRIER!
YES... UNLESS THE TOXIN'S CREATOR LIED TO ME AND HELD BACK THE FINAL CATALYST! BUT THAT'S JUST THE KIND OF TRICKERY I SHOULD EXPECT FROM...
"...DR. VENOM!"
SO IT WAS COBRA COMMANDER WHO SOLD ME OUT! HE MUST BE HAVING QUITE A BIG LAUGH ON ME RIGHT NOW AS HE ATTEMPTS TO USE MY TOXIN WITHOUT MY SECRET CATALYST... IN FACT, THE LAUGHTER MUST BE *INFECTIOUS!*
WHAT'S HE BABBLING ABOUT?

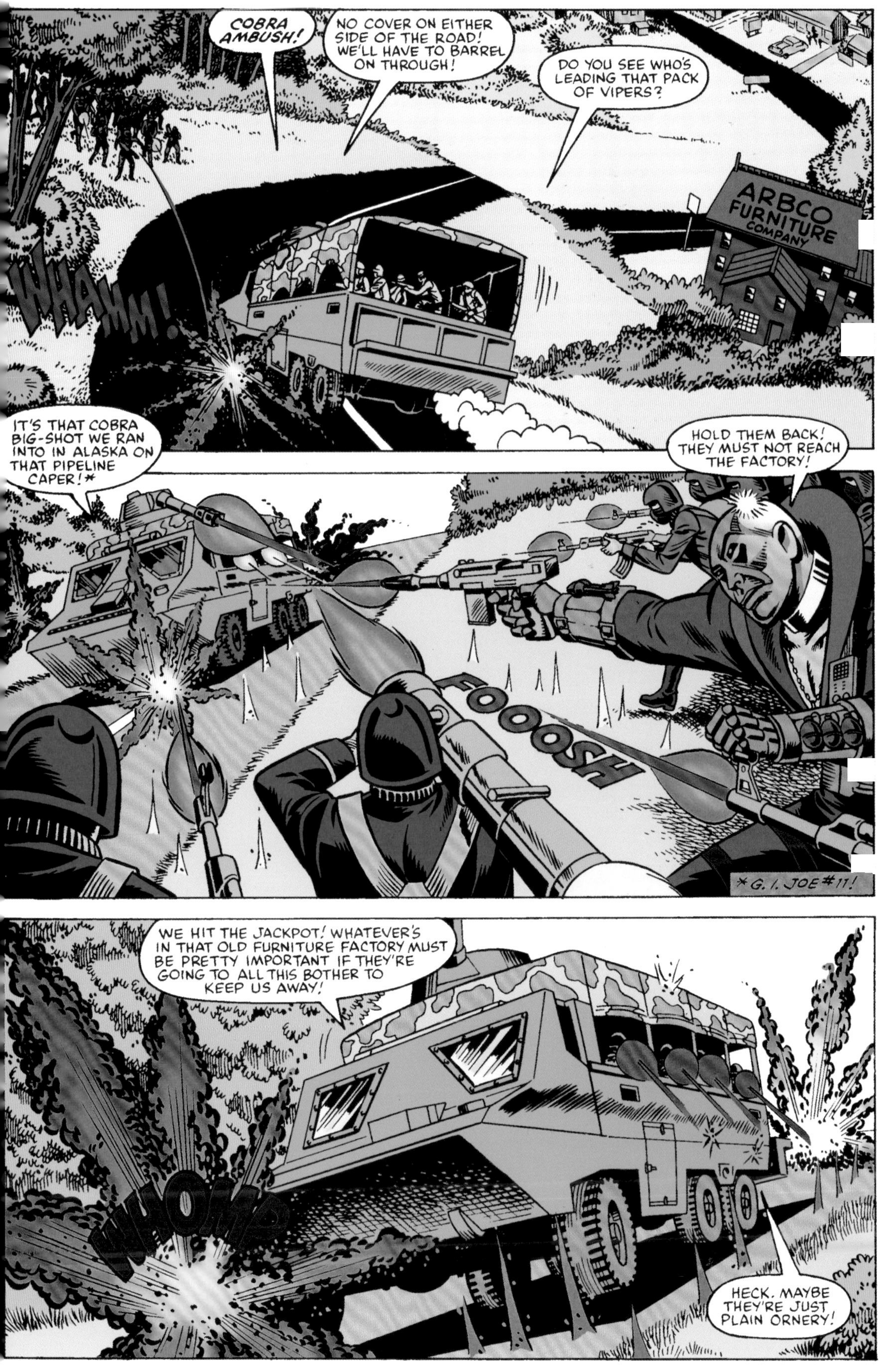
COBRA AMBUSH!
NO COVER ON EITHER SIDE OF THE ROAD! WE'LL HAVE TO BARREL ON THROUGH!
DO YOU SEE WHO'S LEADING THAT PACK OF VIPERS?
ARBCO FURNITURE COMPANY
WHAMM!
IT'S THAT COBRA BIG-SHOT WE RAN INTO IN ALASKA ON THAT PIPELINE CAPER!*
HOLD THEM BACK! THEY MUST NOT REACH THE FACTORY!
FOOOSH
*G. I. JOE #11!
WE HIT THE JACKPOT! WHATEVER'S IN THAT OLD FURNITURE FACTORY MUST BE PRETTY IMPORTANT IF THEY'RE GOING TO ALL THIS BOTHER TO KEEP US AWAY!
WHOMP
HECK, MAYBE THEY'RE JUST PLAIN ORNERY!

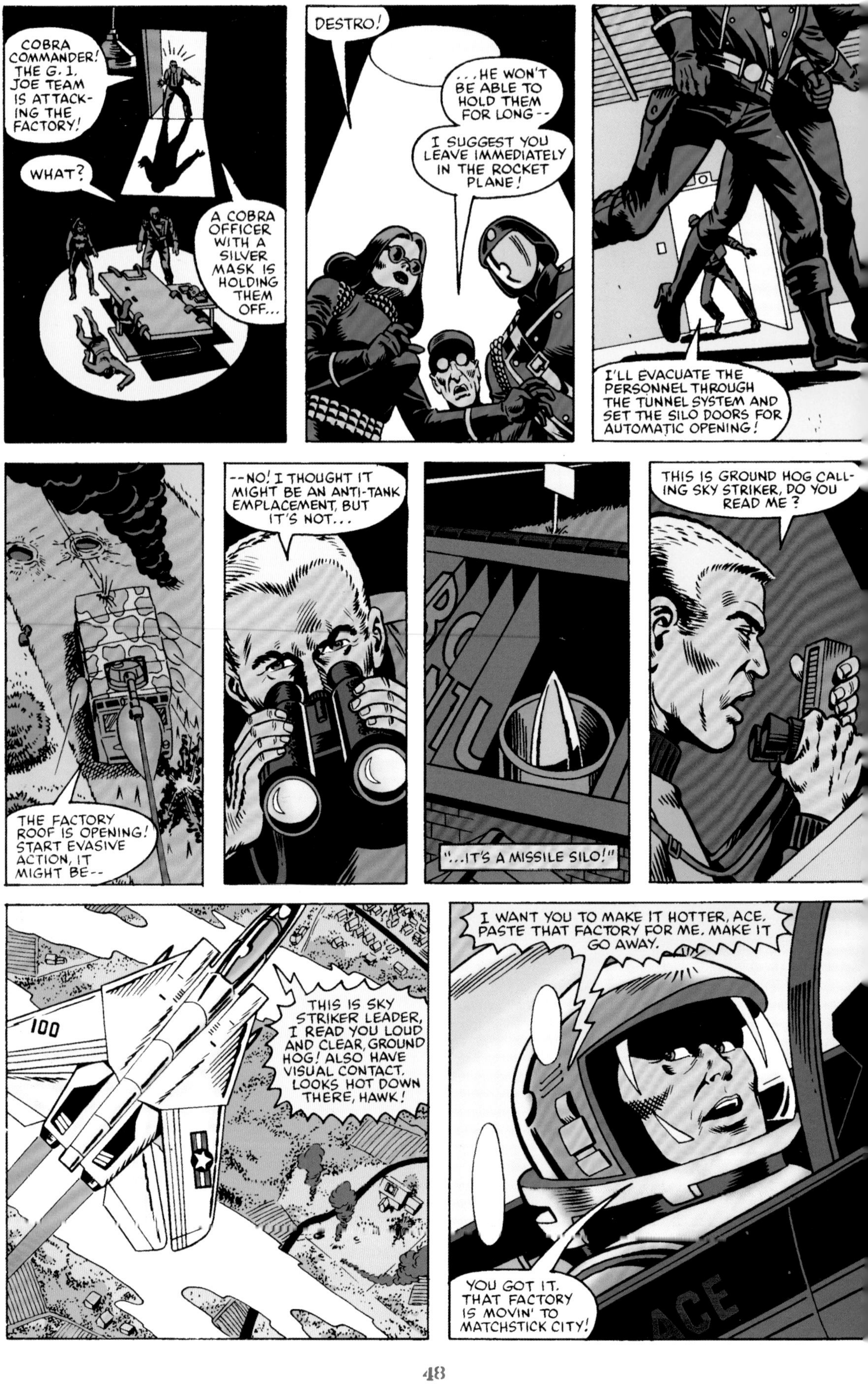
COBRA COMMANDER! THE G.I. JOE TEAM IS ATTACKING THE FACTORY!
WHAT?
A COBRA OFFICER WITH A SILVER MASK IS HOLDING THEM OFF...
DESTRO!
...HE WON'T BE ABLE TO HOLD THEM FOR LONG--
I SUGGEST YOU LEAVE IMMEDIATELY IN THE ROCKET PLANE!
I'LL EVACUATE THE PERSONNEL THROUGH THE TUNNEL SYSTEM AND SET THE SILO DOORS FOR AUTOMATIC OPENING!
THE FACTORY ROOF IS OPENING! START EVASIVE ACTION, IT MIGHT BE--
--NO! I THOUGHT IT MIGHT BE AN ANTI-TANK EMPLACEMENT, BUT IT'S NOT...
"...IT'S A MISSILE SILO!"
THIS IS GROUND HOG CALLING SKY STRIKER, DO YOU READ ME?
100
THIS IS SKY STRIKER LEADER, I READ YOU LOUD AND CLEAR, GROUND HOG! ALSO HAVE VISUAL CONTACT. LOOKS HOT DOWN THERE, HAWK!
I WANT YOU TO MAKE IT HOTTER, ACE. PASTE THAT FACTORY FOR ME. MAKE IT GO AWAY.
YOU GOT IT. THAT FACTORY IS MOVIN' TO MATCHSTICK CITY!
ACE

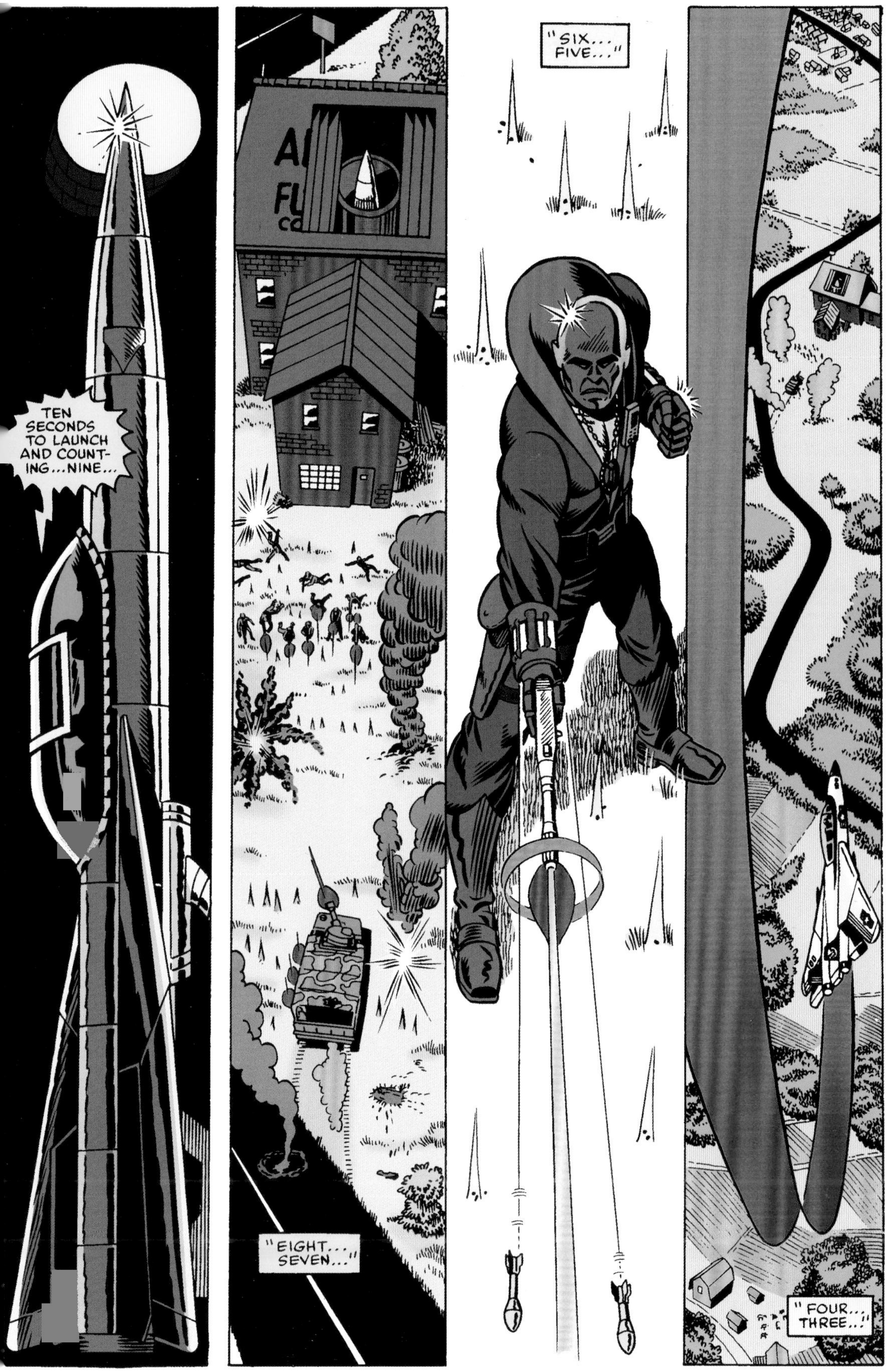
TEN SECONDS TO LAUNCH AND COUNTING...NINE...
"EIGHT... SEVEN..."
"SIX... FIVE..."
"FOUR... THREE..."

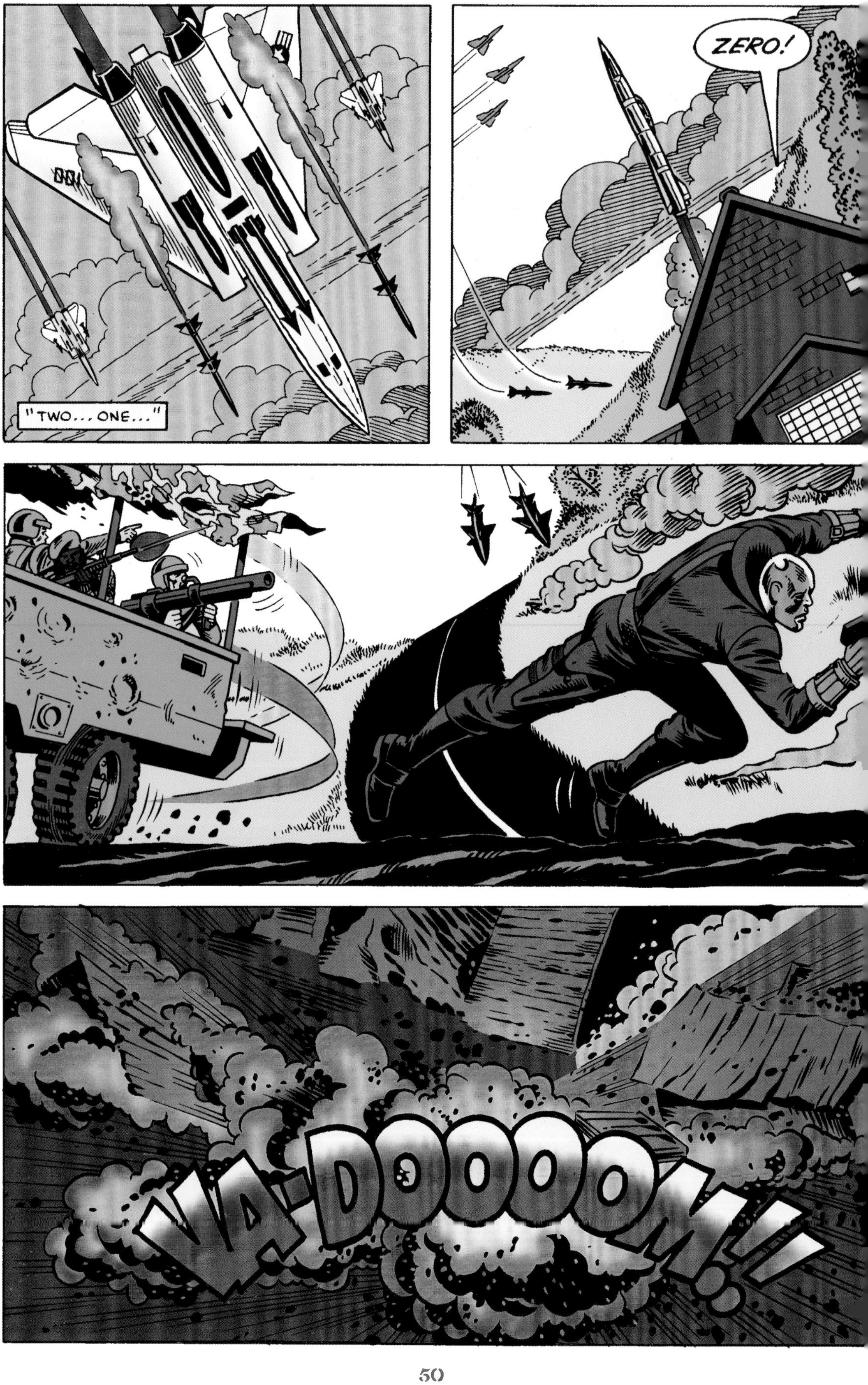
"TWO... ONE..."
ZERO!
VA-DOOOOOM!!

TH-THE ROCKET PLANE GOT AWAY... THE BARONESS IS SAFE...

YOU DID IT, DESTRO, YOU SAVED COBRA COMMANDER!

YES... THAT TOO...

WELL, IT WASN'T AN ICBM IN THAT SILO AFTER ALL...

SOME SORT OF ROCKET PLANE. IT'LL OUT-RUN OUR JETS IN SECONDS...

THIS OL' APC DONE GOOD. TOOK A LICKIN' AND KEPT ON TICKIN'!

LOOKS LIKE WE'RE BACK TO SQUARE ONE, HAWK. WE DIDN'T PASS "GO" AND WE DIDN'T COLLECT $200...

BACK IN SIERRA GORDO...

WAIT, WEREN'T THERE THREE OF YOU IN THAT BUNKER? WHAT HAPPENED TO THE ESKIMO, KWINN?

I CAVED IN THE BACK OF HIS HEAD WITH A WRENCH...

...HE'S DEAD.

YOU HAVEN'T TOLD US THE TRUTH SO FAR, WHY SHOULD WE BELIEVE--

KWINN'S DEAD...

...IF HE HASN'T COME UP BY NOW, HE'S DROWNED FOR SURE!

TO THE AIRFIELD, THEN!

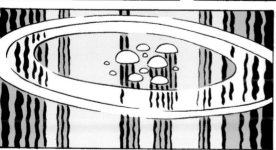

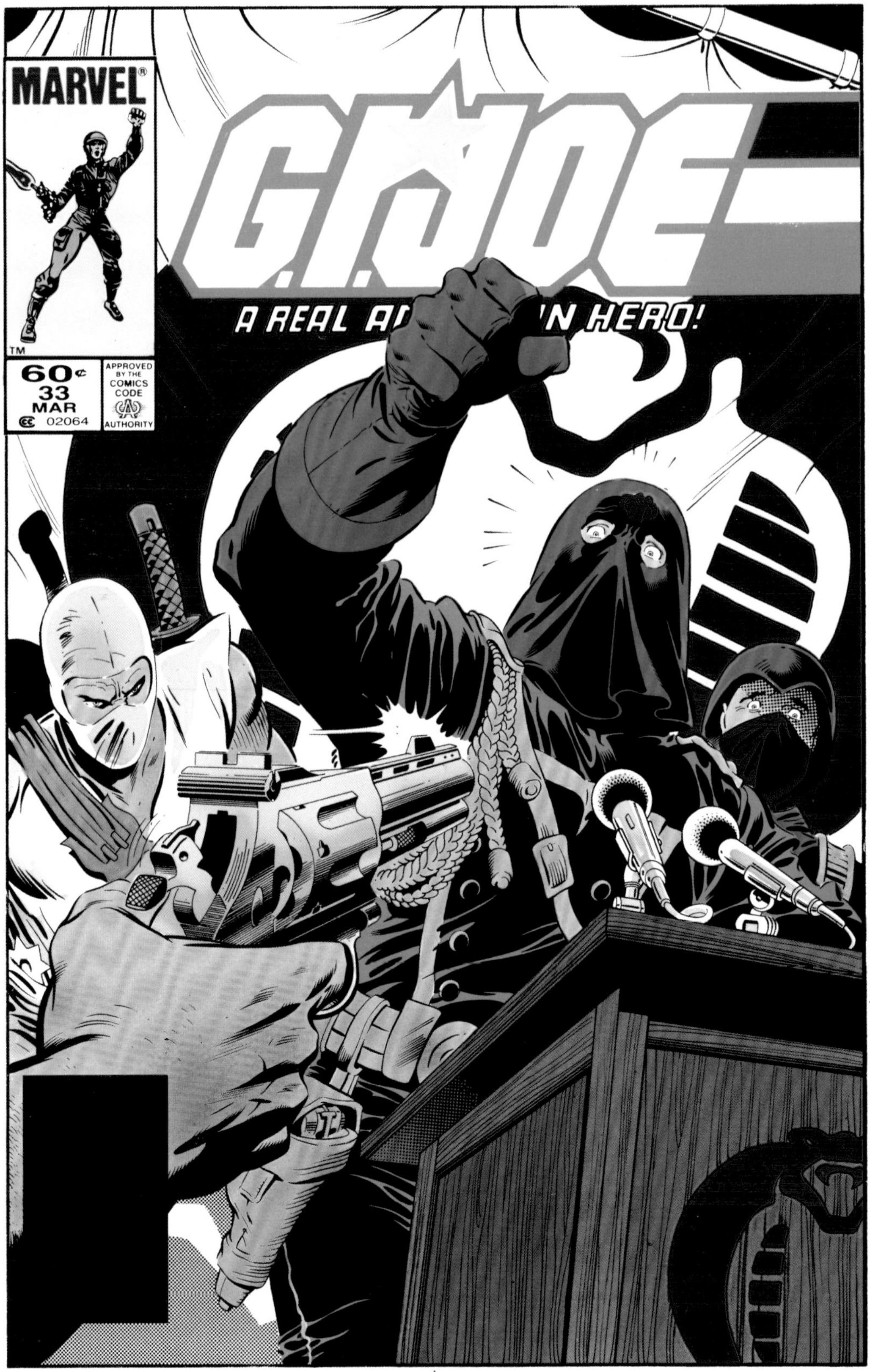
MARVEL®
G.I. JOE
A REAL A
N HERO!
TM
60¢
33
MAR
02064
APPROVED BY THE COMICS CODE AUTHORITY

Stan Lee PRESENTS: THE G.I. JOE TEAM IN:

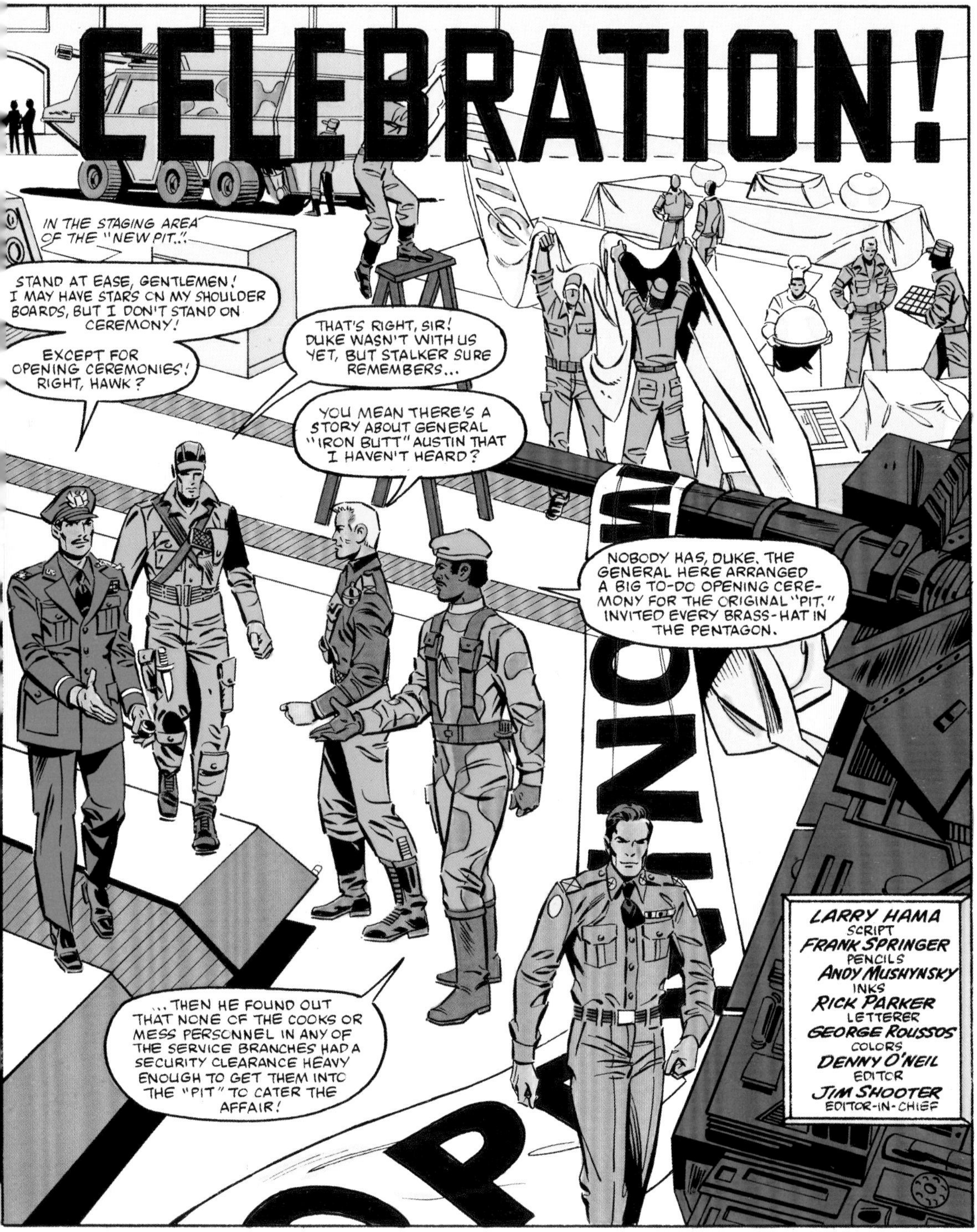
CELEBRATION!
IN THE STAGING AREA OF THE "NEW PIT."
STAND AT EASE, GENTLEMEN! I MAY HAVE STARS ON MY SHOULDER BOARDS, BUT I DON'T STAND ON CEREMONY!
EXCEPT FOR OPENING CEREMONIES! RIGHT, HAWK?
THAT'S RIGHT, SIR! DUKE WASN'T WITH US YET, BUT STALKER SURE REMEMBERS...
YOU MEAN THERE'S A STORY ABOUT GENERAL "IRON BUTT" AUSTIN THAT I HAVEN'T HEARD?
NOBODY HAS, DUKE. THE GENERAL HERE ARRANGED A BIG TO-DO OPENING CEREMONY FOR THE ORIGINAL "PIT." INVITED EVERY BRASS-HAT IN THE PENTAGON.
...THEN HE FOUND OUT THAT NONE OF THE COOKS OR MESS PERSONNEL IN ANY OF THE SERVICE BRANCHES HAD A SECURITY CLEARANCE HEAVY ENOUGH TO GET THEM INTO THE "PIT" TO CATER THE AFFAIR!
LARRY HAMA SCRIPT
FRANK SPRINGER PENCILS
ANDY MUSHYNSKY INKS
RICK PARKER LETTERER
GEORGE ROUSSOS COLORS
DENNY O'NEIL EDITOR
JIM SHOOTER EDITOR-IN-CHIEF

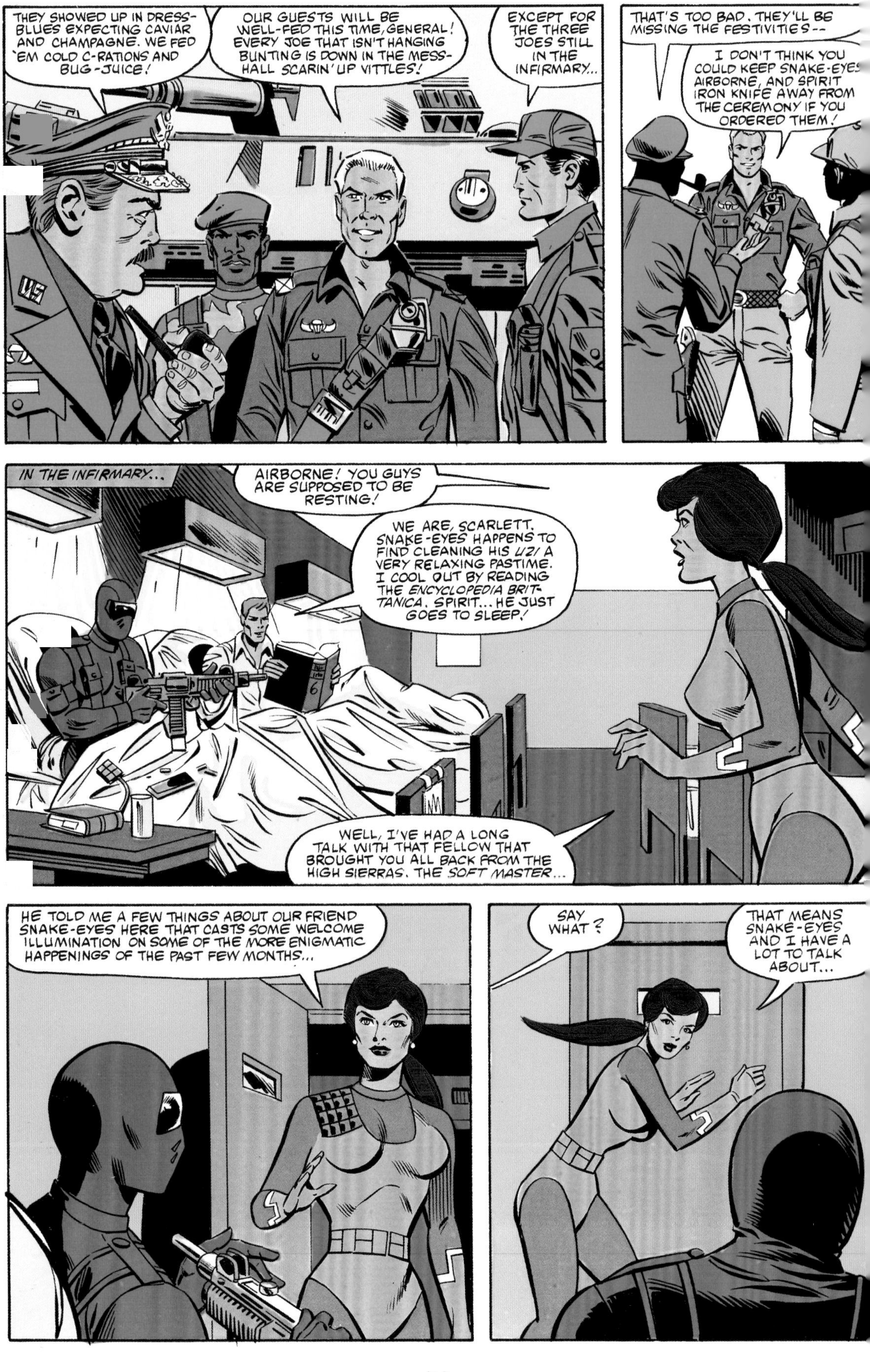
THEY SHOWED UP IN DRESS-BLUES EXPECTING CAVIAR AND CHAMPAGNE. WE FED 'EM COLD C-RATIONS AND BUG-JUICE!
OUR GUESTS WILL BE WELL-FED THIS TIME, GENERAL! EVERY JOE THAT ISN'T HANGING BUNTING IS DOWN IN THE MESS-HALL SCARIN' UP VITTLES!
EXCEPT FOR THE THREE JOES STILL IN THE INFIRMARY...
THAT'S TOO BAD. THEY'LL BE MISSING THE FESTIVITIES--
I DON'T THINK YOU COULD KEEP SNAKE-EYES AIRBORNE, AND SPIRIT IRON KNIFE AWAY FROM THE CEREMONY IF YOU ORDERED THEM!
IN THE INFIRMARY...
AIRBORNE! YOU GUYS ARE SUPPOSED TO BE RESTING!
WE ARE, SCARLETT. SNAKE-EYES HAPPENS TO FIND CLEANING HIS UZI A VERY RELAXING PASTIME. I COOL OUT BY READING THE ENCYCLOPEDIA BRITTANICA. SPIRIT... HE JUST GOES TO SLEEP!
WELL, I'VE HAD A LONG TALK WITH THAT FELLOW THAT BROUGHT YOU ALL BACK FROM THE HIGH SIERRAS. THE SOFT MASTER...
HE TOLD ME A FEW THINGS ABOUT OUR FRIEND SNAKE-EYES HERE THAT CASTS SOME WELCOME ILLUMINATION ON SOME OF THE MORE ENIGMATIC HAPPENINGS OF THE PAST FEW MONTHS...
SAY WHAT?
THAT MEANS SNAKE-EYES AND I HAVE A LOT TO TALK ABOUT...

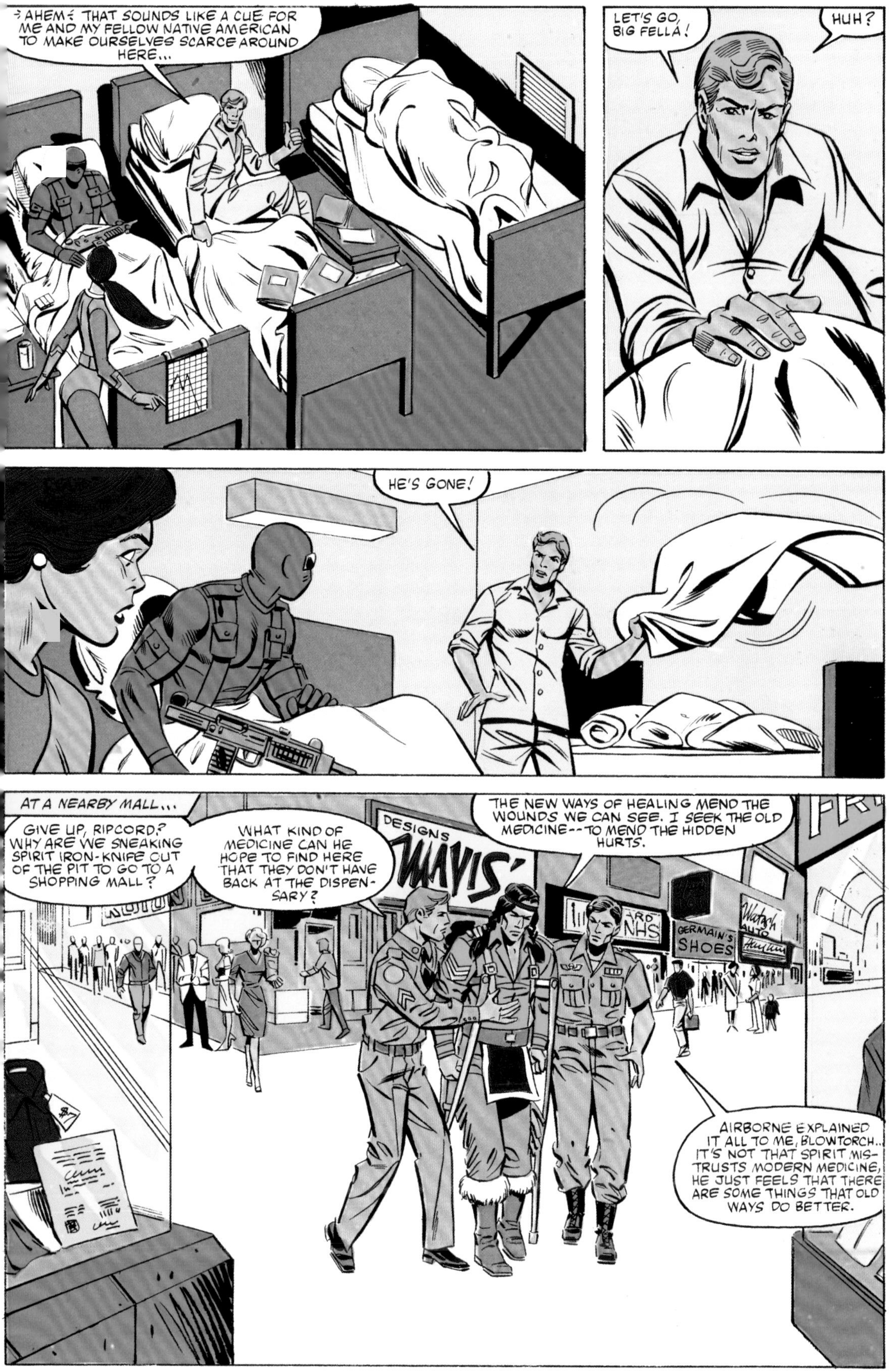

AHEM THAT SOUNDS LIKE A CUE FOR ME AND MY FELLOW NATIVE AMERICAN TO MAKE OURSELVES SCARCE AROUND HERE...
LET'S GO, BIG FELLA!
HUH?
HE'S GONE!
AT A NEARBY MALL...
GIVE UP, RIPCORD? WHY ARE WE SNEAKING SPIRIT IRON-KNIFE OUT OF THE PIT TO GO TO A SHOPPING MALL?
WHAT KIND OF MEDICINE CAN HE HOPE TO FIND HERE THAT THEY DON'T HAVE BACK AT THE DISPENSARY?
THE NEW WAYS OF HEALING MEND THE WOUNDS WE CAN SEE. I SEEK THE OLD MEDICINE--TO MEND THE HIDDEN HURTS.
AIRBORNE EXPLAINED IT ALL TO ME, BLOWTORCH... IT'S NOT THAT SPIRIT MISTRUSTS MODERN MEDICINE, HE JUST FEELS THAT THERE ARE SOME THINGS THAT OLD WAYS DO BETTER.
DESIGNS
MAVIS'
GERMAIN'S SHOES

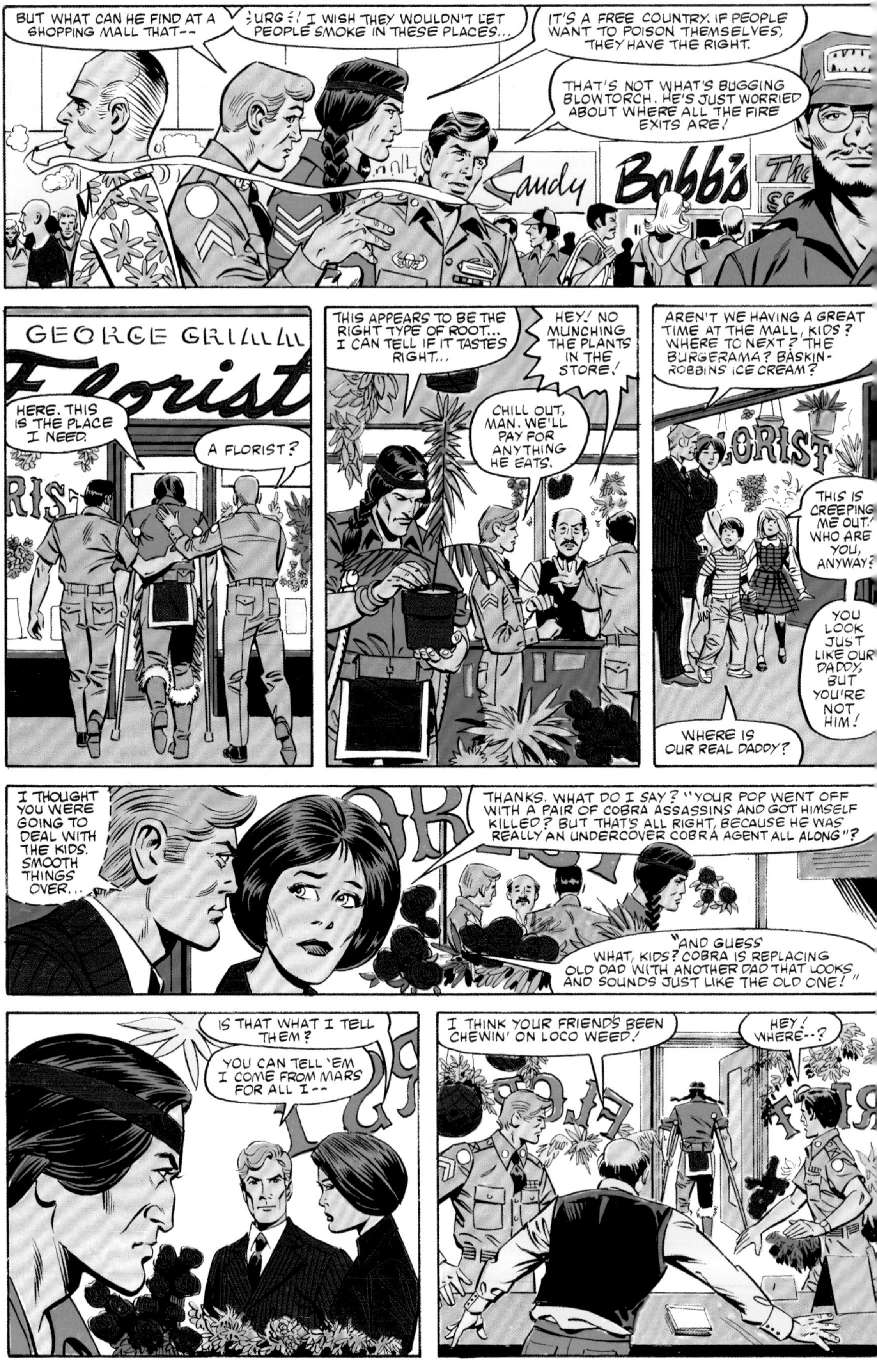
BUT WHAT CAN HE FIND AT A SHOPPING MALL THAT--
URG! I WISH THEY WOULDN'T LET PEOPLE SMOKE IN THESE PLACES...
IT'S A FREE COUNTRY. IF PEOPLE WANT TO POISON THEMSELVES, THEY HAVE THE RIGHT.
THAT'S NOT WHAT'S BUGGING BLOWTORCH. HE'S JUST WORRIED ABOUT WHERE ALL THE FIRE EXITS ARE!
Candy
Bobb's
GEORGE GRIMM
Florist
HERE. THIS IS THE PLACE I NEED.
A FLORIST?
THIS APPEARS TO BE THE RIGHT TYPE OF ROOT... I CAN TELL IF IT TASTES RIGHT...
HEY! NO MUNCHING THE PLANTS IN THE STORE!
CHILL OUT, MAN. WE'LL PAY FOR ANYTHING HE EATS.
AREN'T WE HAVING A GREAT TIME AT THE MALL, KIDS? WHERE TO NEXT? THE BURGERAMA? BASKIN-ROBBINS ICE CREAM?
FLORIST
THIS IS CREEPING ME OUT! WHO ARE YOU, ANYWAY?
YOU LOOK JUST LIKE OUR DADDY, BUT YOU'RE NOT HIM!
WHERE IS OUR REAL DADDY?
I THOUGHT YOU WERE GOING TO DEAL WITH THE KIDS. SMOOTH THINGS OVER...
THANKS. WHAT DO I SAY? "YOUR POP WENT OFF WITH A PAIR OF COBRA ASSASSINS AND GOT HIMSELF KILLED? BUT THAT'S ALL RIGHT, BECAUSE HE WAS REALLY AN UNDERCOVER COBRA AGENT ALL ALONG"?
"AND GUESS WHAT, KIDS? COBRA IS REPLACING OLD DAD WITH ANOTHER DAD THAT LOOKS AND SOUNDS JUST LIKE THE OLD ONE!"
IS THAT WHAT I TELL THEM?
YOU CAN TELL 'EM I COME FROM MARS FOR ALL I--
I THINK YOUR FRIEND'S BEEN CHEWIN' ON LOCO WEED!
HEY! WHERE--?

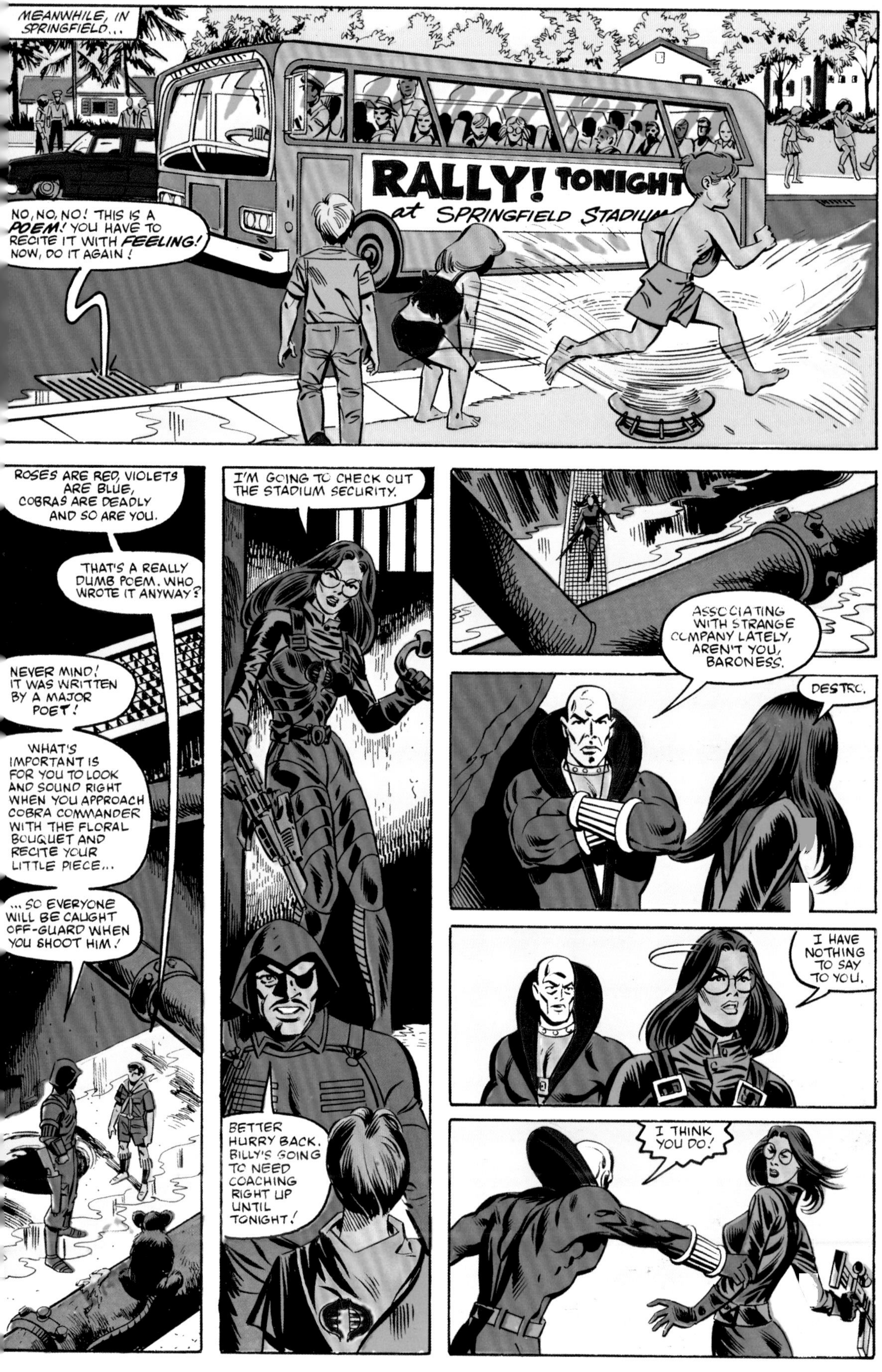
MEANWHILE, IN SPRINGFIELD...
RALLY! TONIGHT at SPRINGFIELD STADIUM
NO, NO, NO! THIS IS A POEM! YOU HAVE TO RECITE IT WITH FEELING! NOW, DO IT AGAIN!
ROSES ARE RED, VIOLETS ARE BLUE, COBRAS ARE DEADLY AND SO ARE YOU.
THAT'S A REALLY DUMB POEM. WHO WROTE IT ANYWAY?
NEVER MIND! IT WAS WRITTEN BY A MAJOR POET!
WHAT'S IMPORTANT IS FOR YOU TO LOOK AND SOUND RIGHT WHEN YOU APPROACH COBRA COMMANDER WITH THE FLORAL BOUQUET AND RECITE YOUR LITTLE PIECE...
...SO EVERYONE WILL BE CAUGHT OFF-GUARD WHEN YOU SHOOT HIM!
I'M GOING TO CHECK OUT THE STADIUM SECURITY.
BETTER HURRY BACK. BILLY'S GOING TO NEED COACHING RIGHT UP UNTIL TONIGHT!
ASSOCIATING WITH STRANGE COMPANY LATELY, AREN'T YOU, BARONESS.
DESTRO.
I HAVE NOTHING TO SAY TO YOU.
I THINK YOU DO!

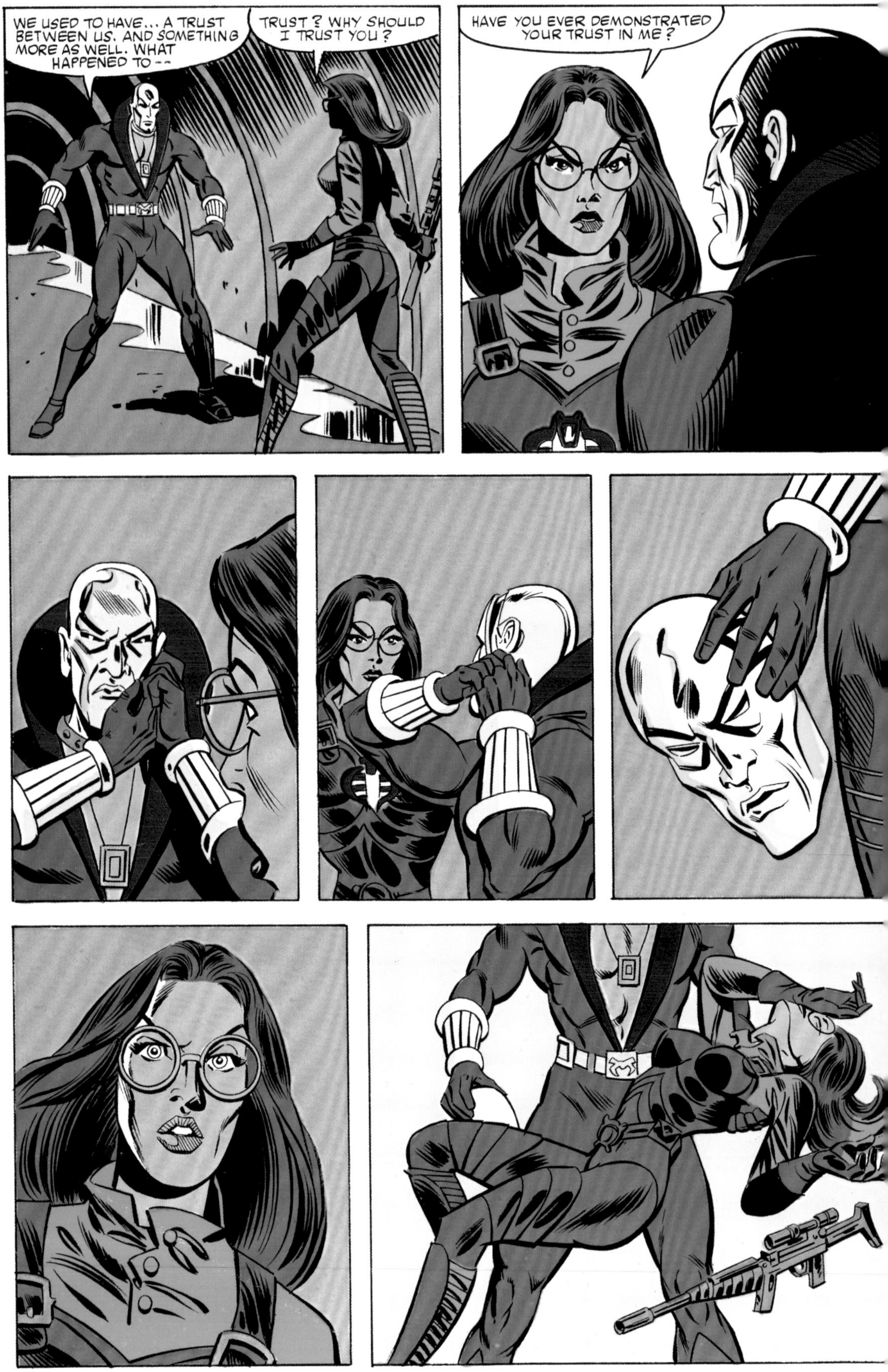
WE USED TO HAVE... A TRUST BETWEEN US. AND SOMETHING MORE AS WELL. WHAT HAPPENED TO --
TRUST? WHY SHOULD I TRUST YOU?
HAVE YOU EVER DEMONSTRATED YOUR TRUST IN ME?

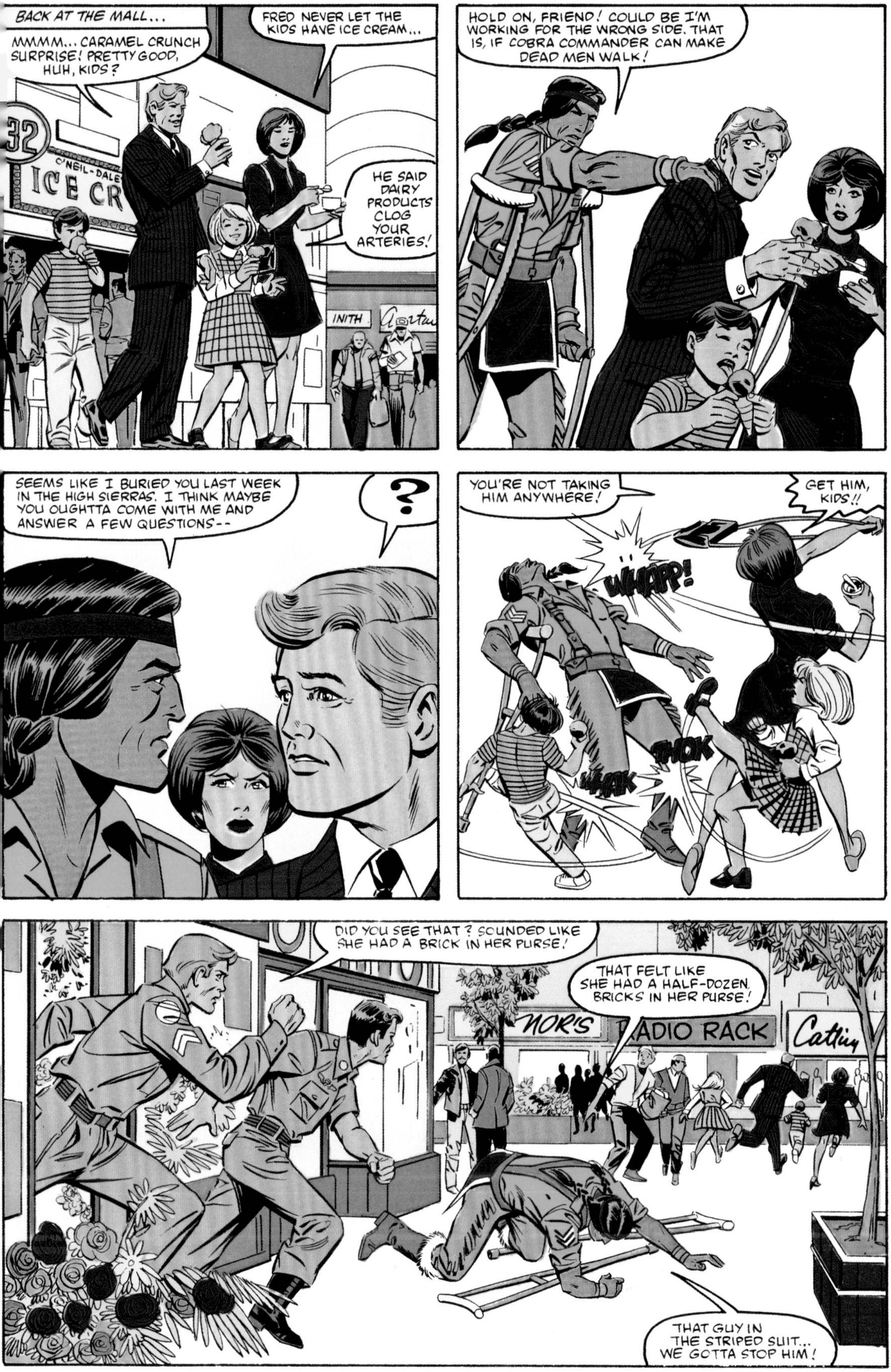
BACK AT THE MALL...
MMMM... CARAMEL CRUNCH SURPRISE! PRETTY GOOD, HUH, KIDS?
FRED NEVER LET THE KIDS HAVE ICE CREAM...
HE SAID DAIRY PRODUCTS CLOG YOUR ARTERIES!
32
O'NEIL-DALE
ICE CR
INITH
HOLD ON, FRIEND! COULD BE I'M WORKING FOR THE WRONG SIDE. THAT IS, IF COBRA COMMANDER CAN MAKE DEAD MEN WALK!
SEEMS LIKE I BURIED YOU LAST WEEK IN THE HIGH SIERRAS. I THINK MAYBE YOU OUGHTTA COME WITH ME AND ANSWER A FEW QUESTIONS--
?
YOU'RE NOT TAKING HIM ANYWHERE!
GET HIM, KIDS!!
WHAPP!
THOK
WHAK
DID YOU SEE THAT? SOUNDED LIKE SHE HAD A BRICK IN HER PURSE!
THAT FELT LIKE SHE HAD A HALF-DOZEN BRICKS IN HER PURSE!
NOR'S
RADIO RACK
THAT GUY IN THE STRIPED SUIT... WE GOTTA STOP HIM!

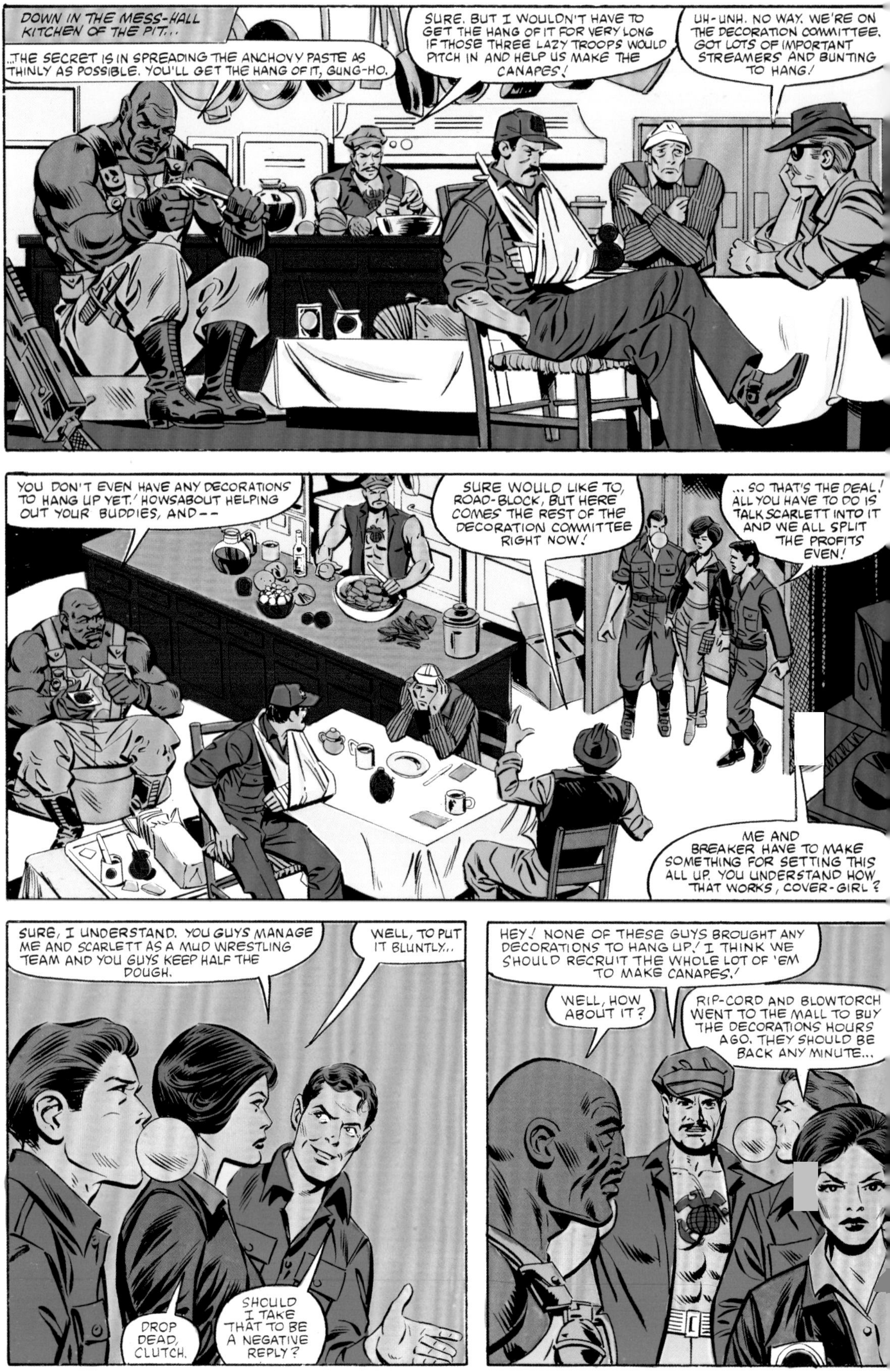
DOWN IN THE MESS-HALL KITCHEN OF THE PIT...
...THE SECRET IS IN SPREADING THE ANCHOVY PASTE AS THINLY AS POSSIBLE. YOU'LL GET THE HANG OF IT, GUNG-HO.
SURE. BUT I WOULDN'T HAVE TO GET THE HANG OF IT FOR VERY LONG IF THOSE THREE LAZY TROOPS WOULD PITCH IN AND HELP US MAKE THE CANAPES!
UH-UNH. NO WAY. WE'RE ON THE DECORATION COMMITTEE. GOT LOTS OF IMPORTANT STREAMERS AND BUNTING TO HANG!
YOU DON'T EVEN HAVE ANY DECORATIONS TO HANG UP YET! HOWSABOUT HELPING OUT YOUR BUDDIES, AND--
SURE WOULD LIKE TO, ROAD-BLOCK, BUT HERE COMES THE REST OF THE DECORATION COMMITTEE RIGHT NOW!
...SO THAT'S THE DEAL! ALL YOU HAVE TO DO IS TALK SCARLETT INTO IT AND WE ALL SPLIT THE PROFITS EVEN!
ME AND BREAKER HAVE TO MAKE SOMETHING FOR SETTING THIS ALL UP. YOU UNDERSTAND HOW THAT WORKS, COVER-GIRL?
SURE, I UNDERSTAND. YOU GUYS MANAGE ME AND SCARLETT AS A MUD WRESTLING TEAM AND YOU GUYS KEEP HALF THE DOUGH.
WELL, TO PUT IT BLUNTLY...
DROP DEAD, CLUTCH.
SHOULD I TAKE THAT TO BE A NEGATIVE REPLY?
HEY! NONE OF THESE GUYS BROUGHT ANY DECORATIONS TO HANG UP! I THINK WE SHOULD RECRUIT THE WHOLE LOT OF 'EM TO MAKE CANAPES!
WELL, HOW ABOUT IT?
RIP-CORD AND BLOWTORCH WENT TO THE MALL TO BUY THE DECORATIONS HOURS AGO. THEY SHOULD BE BACK ANY MINUTE...

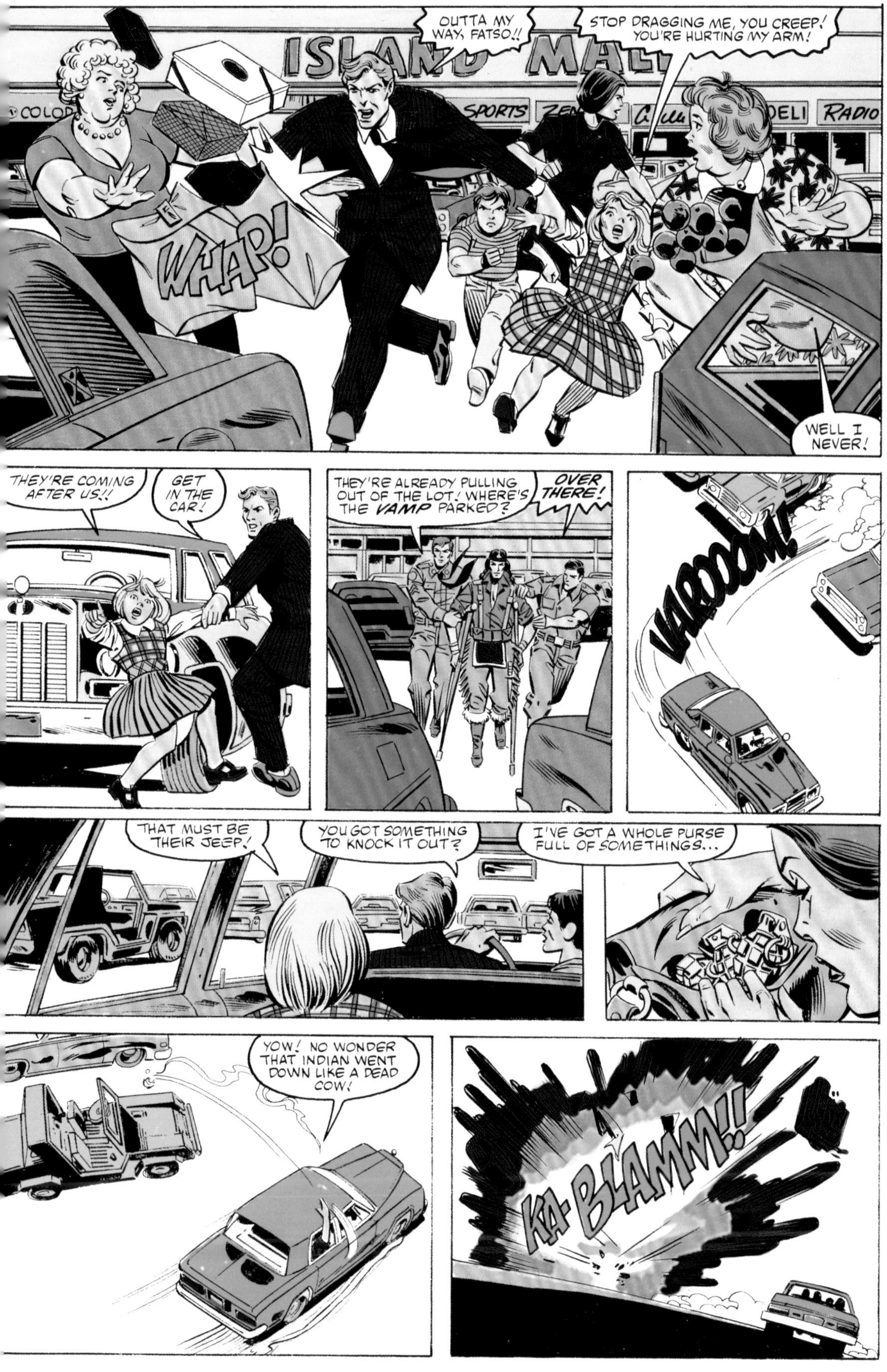

ISLAND MALL
COLOR
SPORTS
DELI
RADIO
OUTTA MY WAY, FATSO!!
STOP DRAGGING ME, YOU CREEP! YOU'RE HURTING MY ARM!
WHAP!
WELL I NEVER!
THEY'RE COMING AFTER US!!
GET IN THE CAR!
THEY'RE ALREADY PULLING OUT OF THE LOT! WHERE'S THE VAMP PARKED?
OVER THERE!
VAROOOM!
THAT MUST BE THEIR JEEP!
YOU GOT SOMETHING TO KNOCK IT OUT?
I'VE GOT A WHOLE PURSE FULL OF SOMETHINGS...
YOW! NO WONDER THAT INDIAN WENT DOWN LIKE A DEAD COW!
KA-BLAMM!!

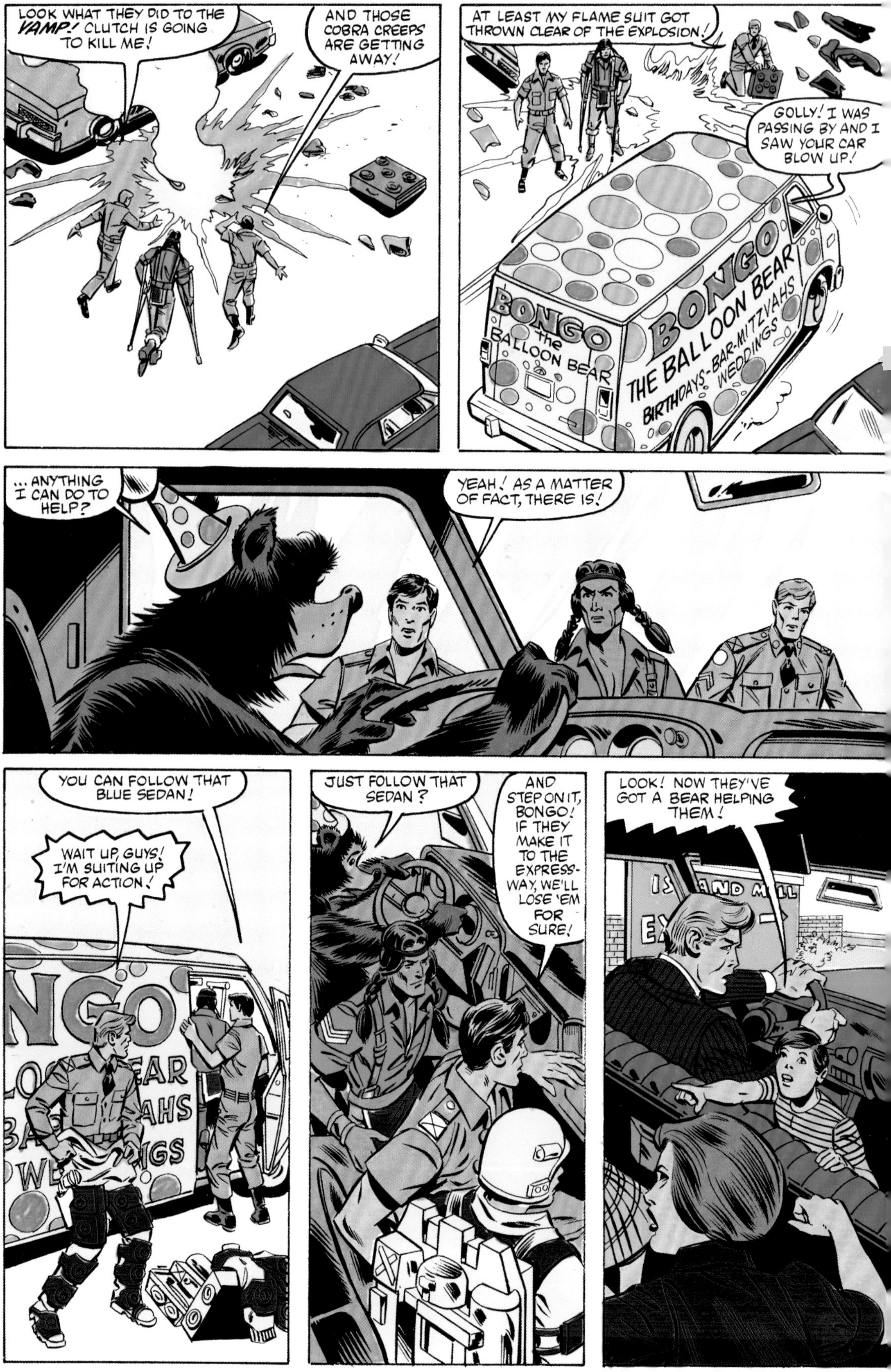

LOOK WHAT THEY DID TO THE VAMP! CLUTCH IS GOING TO KILL ME!
AND THOSE COBRA CREEPS ARE GETTING AWAY!
AT LEAST MY FLAME SUIT GOT THROWN CLEAR OF THE EXPLOSION!
GOLLY! I WAS PASSING BY AND I SAW YOUR CAR BLOW UP!
BONGO the BALLOON BEAR
BONGO THE BALLOON BEAR
BIRTHDAYS-BAR-MITZVAHS WEDDINGS
...ANYTHING I CAN DO TO HELP?
YEAH! AS A MATTER OF FACT, THERE IS!
YOU CAN FOLLOW THAT BLUE SEDAN!
WAIT UP, GUYS! I'M SUITING UP FOR ACTION!
JUST FOLLOW THAT SEDAN?
AND STEP ON IT, BONGO! IF THEY MAKE IT TO THE EXPRESS-WAY, WE'LL LOSE 'EM FOR SURE!
LOOK! NOW THEY'VE GOT A BEAR HELPING THEM!

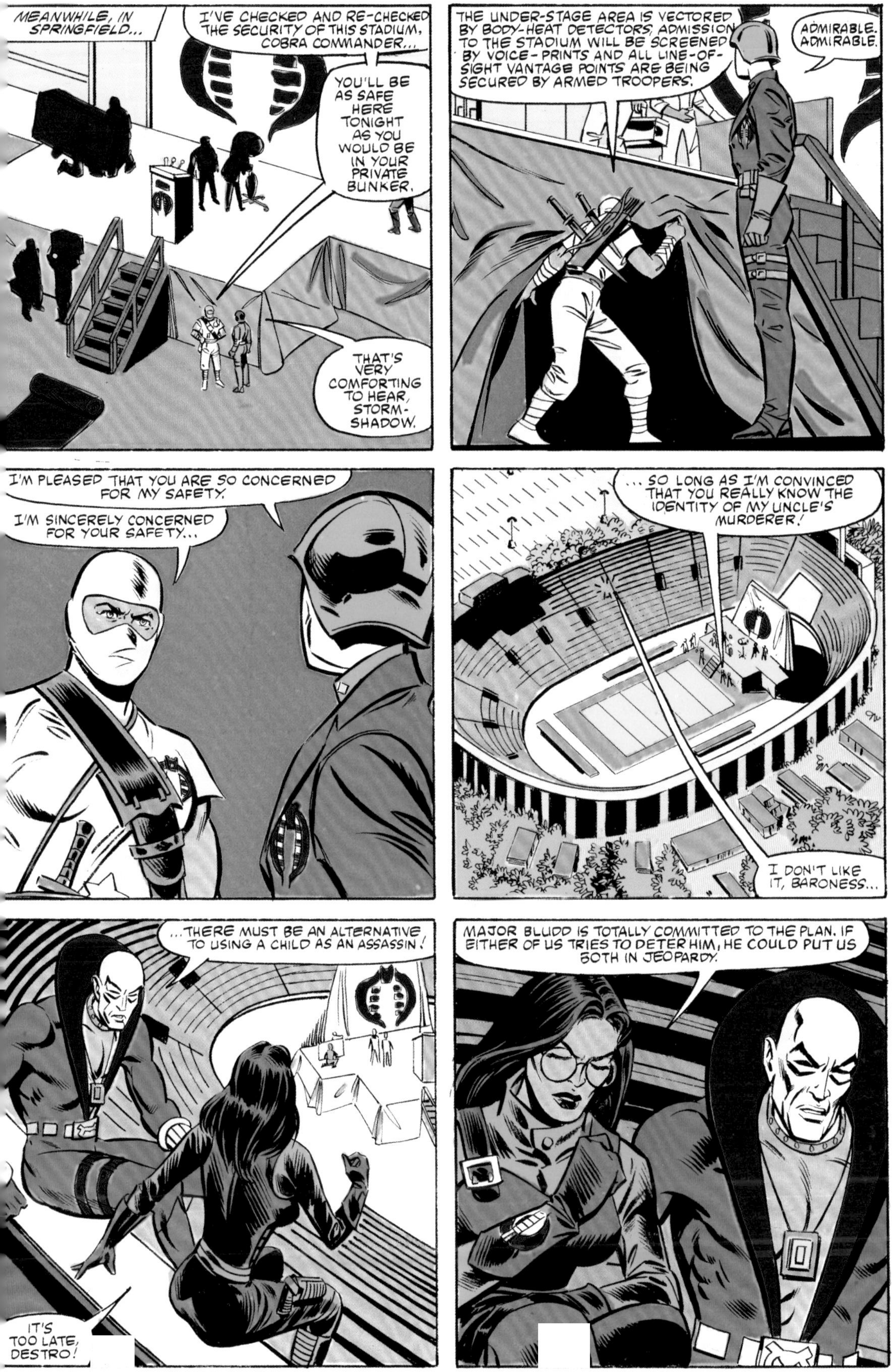
MEANWHILE, IN SPRINGFIELD...
I'VE CHECKED AND RE-CHECKED THE SECURITY OF THIS STADIUM, COBRA COMMANDER...
YOU'LL BE AS SAFE HERE TONIGHT AS YOU WOULD BE IN YOUR PRIVATE BUNKER.
THAT'S VERY COMFORTING TO HEAR, STORM-SHADOW.
THE UNDER-STAGE AREA IS VECTORED BY BODY-HEAT DETECTORS; ADMISSION TO THE STADIUM WILL BE SCREENED BY VOICE-PRINTS AND ALL LINE-OF-SIGHT VANTAGE POINTS ARE BEING SECURED BY ARMED TROOPERS.
ADMIRABLE. ADMIRABLE.
I'M PLEASED THAT YOU ARE SO CONCERNED FOR MY SAFETY.
I'M SINCERELY CONCERNED FOR YOUR SAFETY...
...SO LONG AS I'M CONVINCED THAT YOU REALLY KNOW THE IDENTITY OF MY UNCLE'S MURDERER!
I DON'T LIKE IT, BARONESS...
...THERE MUST BE AN ALTERNATIVE TO USING A CHILD AS AN ASSASSIN!
IT'S TOO LATE, DESTRO!
MAJOR BLUDD IS TOTALLY COMMITTED TO THE PLAN. IF EITHER OF US TRIES TO DETER HIM, HE COULD PUT US BOTH IN JEOPARDY.

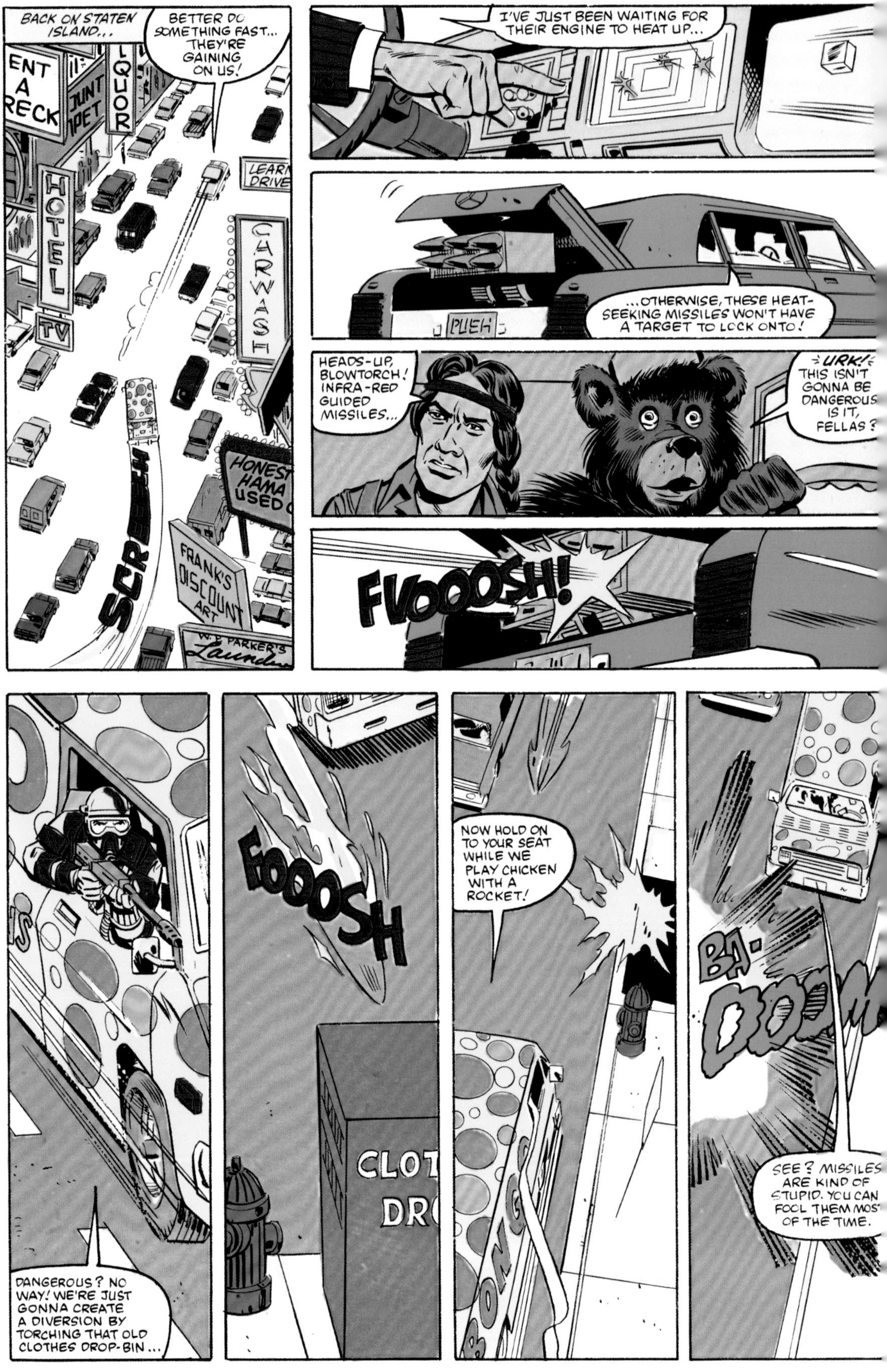
BACK ON STATEN ISLAND...
BETTER DO SOMETHING FAST... THEY'RE GAINING ON US!
ENT A RECK
LIQUOR
HOTEL
TV
CARWASH
LEARN DRIVE
HONEST HAMA USED
FRANK'S DISCOUNT ART
W.D. PARKER'S
SCREEECH
I'VE JUST BEEN WAITING FOR THEIR ENGINE TO HEAT UP...
...OTHERWISE, THESE HEAT-SEEKING MISSILES WON'T HAVE A TARGET TO LOCK ONTO!
HEADS-UP, BLOWTORCH! INFRA-RED GUIDED MISSILES...
URK! THIS ISN'T GONNA BE DANGEROUS IS IT, FELLAS?
FVOOOSH!
DANGEROUS? NO WAY! WE'RE JUST GONNA CREATE A DIVERSION BY TORCHING THAT OLD CLOTHES DROP-BIN...
FOOOSH
NOW HOLD ON TO YOUR SEAT WHILE WE PLAY CHICKEN WITH A ROCKET!
BA-
SEE? MISSILES ARE KIND OF STUPID. YOU CAN FOOL THEM MOST OF THE TIME.

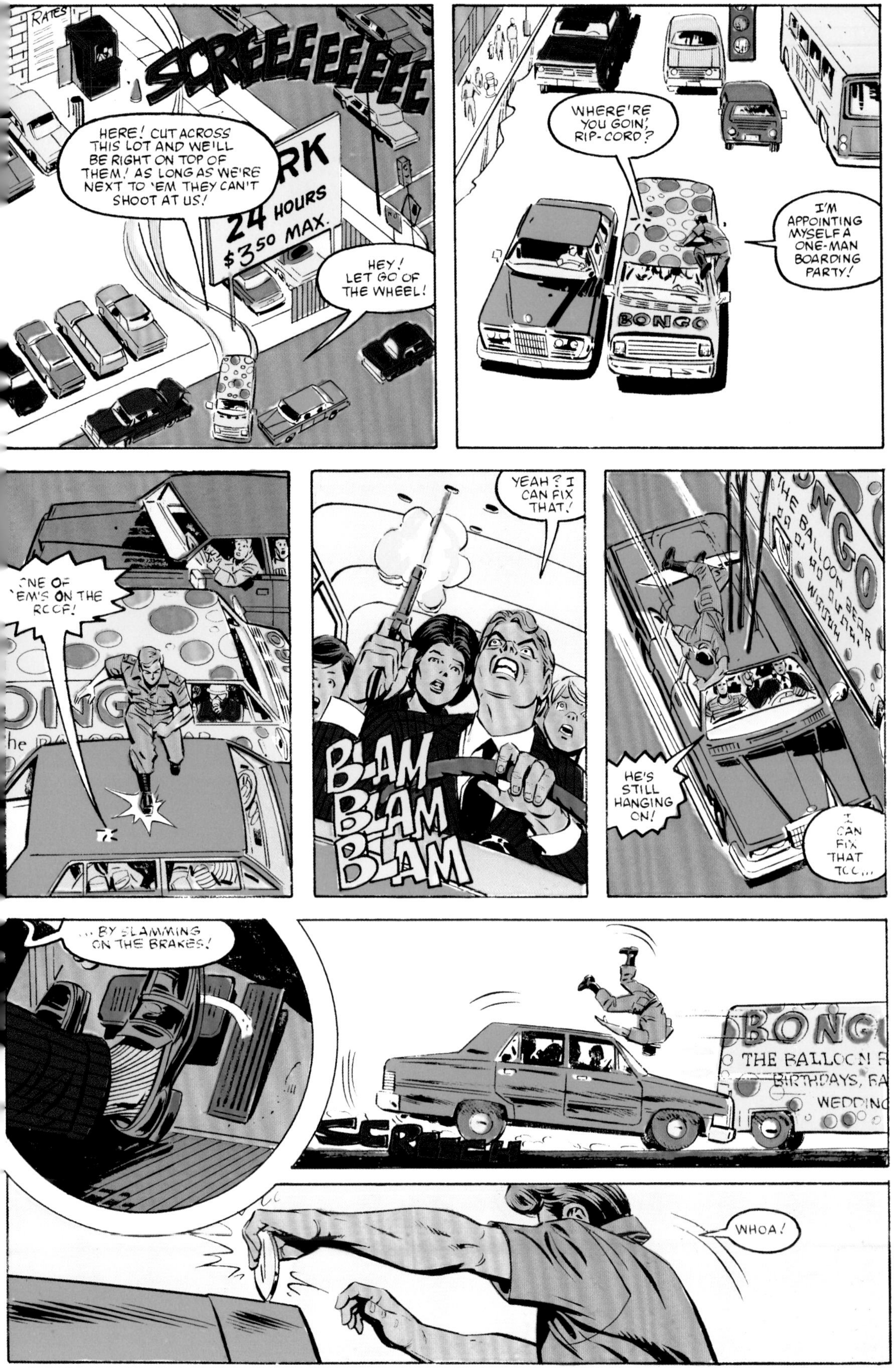
SCREEEEEEEEEE
HERE! CUT ACROSS THIS LOT AND WE'LL BE RIGHT ON TOP OF THEM! AS LONG AS WE'RE NEXT TO 'EM THEY CAN'T SHOOT AT US!
RK
24 HOURS
$3.50 MAX.
HEY! LET GO OF THE WHEEL!
WHERE'RE YOU GOIN', RIP-CORD?
I'M APPOINTING MYSELF A ONE-MAN BOARDING PARTY!
BONGO
ONE OF 'EM'S ON THE ROOF!
YEAH? I CAN FIX THAT!
BLAM BLAM BLAM
HE'S STILL HANGING ON!
I CAN FIX THAT TOO...
...BY SLAMMING ON THE BRAKES!
BONG
THE BALLOON
BIRTHDAYS, FA
WEDDING
WHOA!

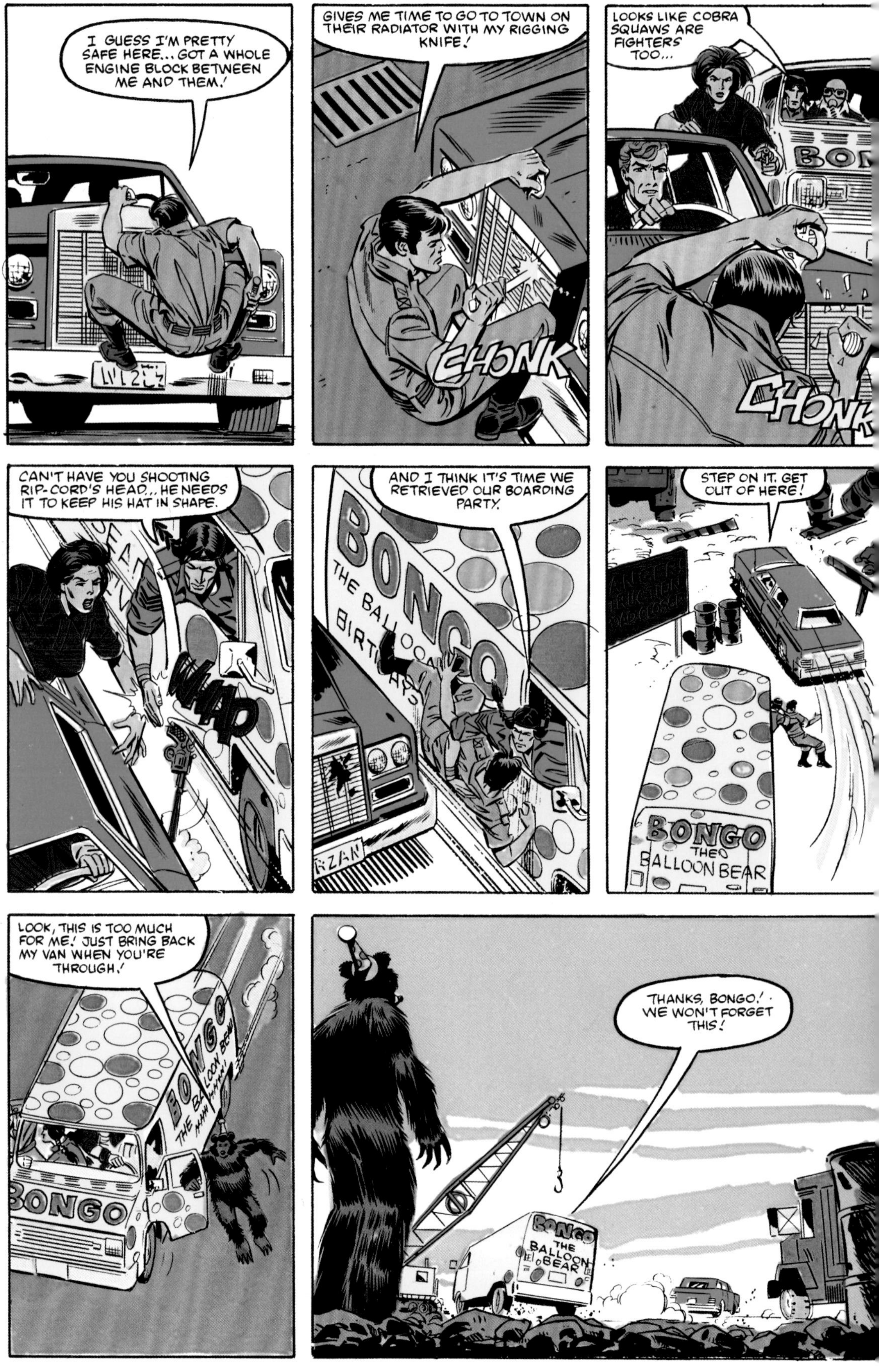
I GUESS I'M PRETTY SAFE HERE... GOT A WHOLE ENGINE BLOCK BETWEEN ME AND THEM!
GIVES ME TIME TO GO TO TOWN ON THEIR RADIATOR WITH MY RIGGING KNIFE!
CHONK
LOOKS LIKE COBRA SQUAWS ARE FIGHTERS TOO...
CHONK
CAN'T HAVE YOU SHOOTING RIP-CORD'S HEAD... HE NEEDS IT TO KEEP HIS HAT IN SHAPE.
WHAP
AND I THINK IT'S TIME WE RETRIEVED OUR BOARDING PARTY.
BONGO
STEP ON IT. GET OUT OF HERE!
BONGO THE BALLOON BEAR
LOOK, THIS IS TOO MUCH FOR ME! JUST BRING BACK MY VAN WHEN YOU'RE THROUGH!
BONGO
THANKS, BONGO! WE WON'T FORGET THIS!
BONGO THE BALLOON BEAR

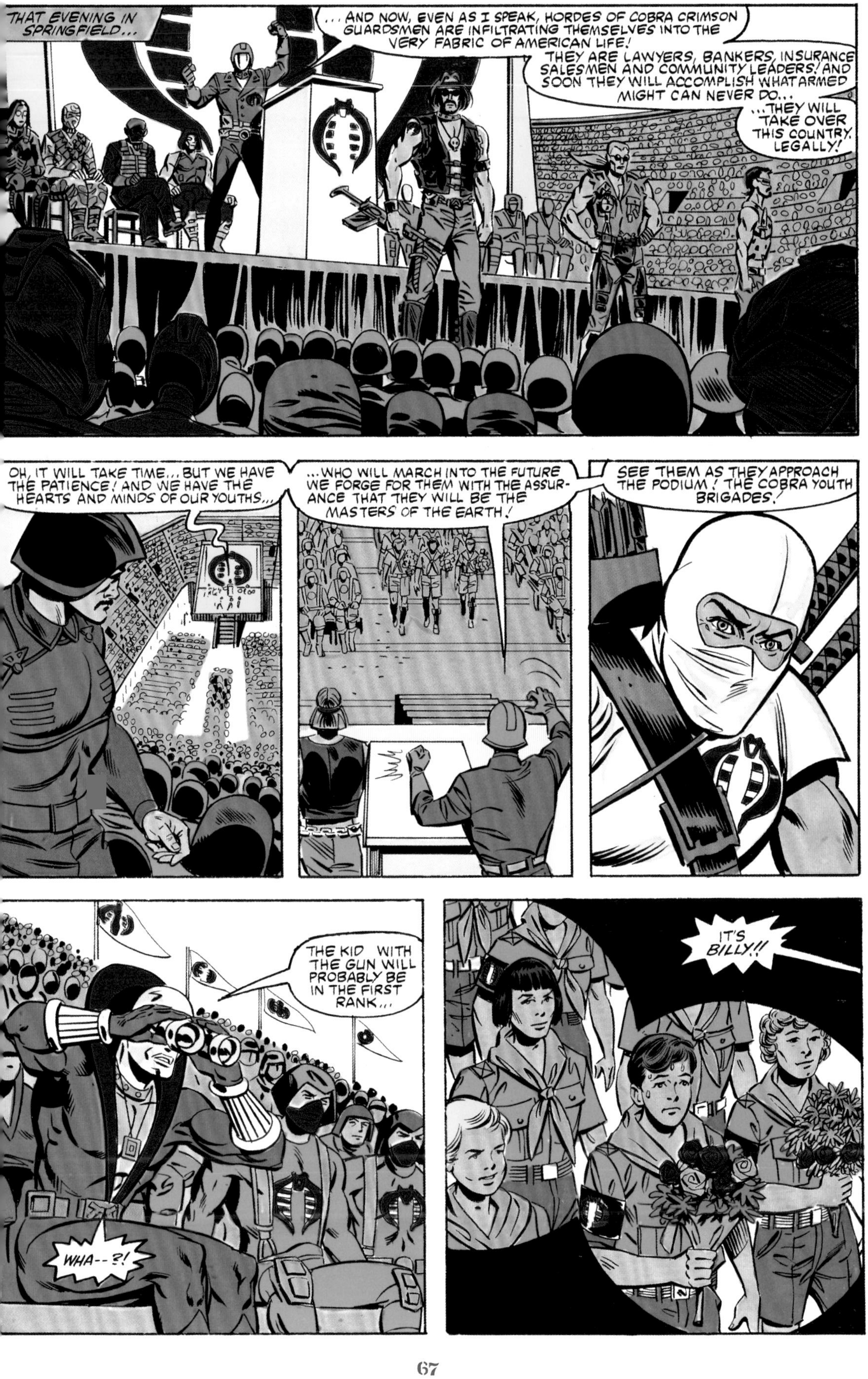
THAT EVENING IN SPRINGFIELD...
...AND NOW, EVEN AS I SPEAK, HORDES OF COBRA CRIMSON GUARDSMEN ARE INFILTRATING THEMSELVES INTO THE VERY FABRIC OF AMERICAN LIFE!
THEY ARE LAWYERS, BANKERS, INSURANCE SALESMEN AND COMMUNITY LEADERS! AND SOON THEY WILL ACCOMPLISH WHAT ARMED MIGHT CAN NEVER DO...
...THEY WILL TAKE OVER THIS COUNTRY. LEGALLY!
OH, IT WILL TAKE TIME... BUT WE HAVE THE PATIENCE! AND WE HAVE THE HEARTS AND MINDS OF OUR YOUTHS...
...WHO WILL MARCH INTO THE FUTURE WE FORGE FOR THEM WITH THE ASSURANCE THAT THEY WILL BE THE MASTERS OF THE EARTH!
SEE THEM AS THEY APPROACH THE PODIUM! THE COBRA YOUTH BRIGADES!
THE KID WITH THE GUN WILL PROBABLY BE IN THE FIRST RANK...
WHA--?!
IT'S BILLY!!

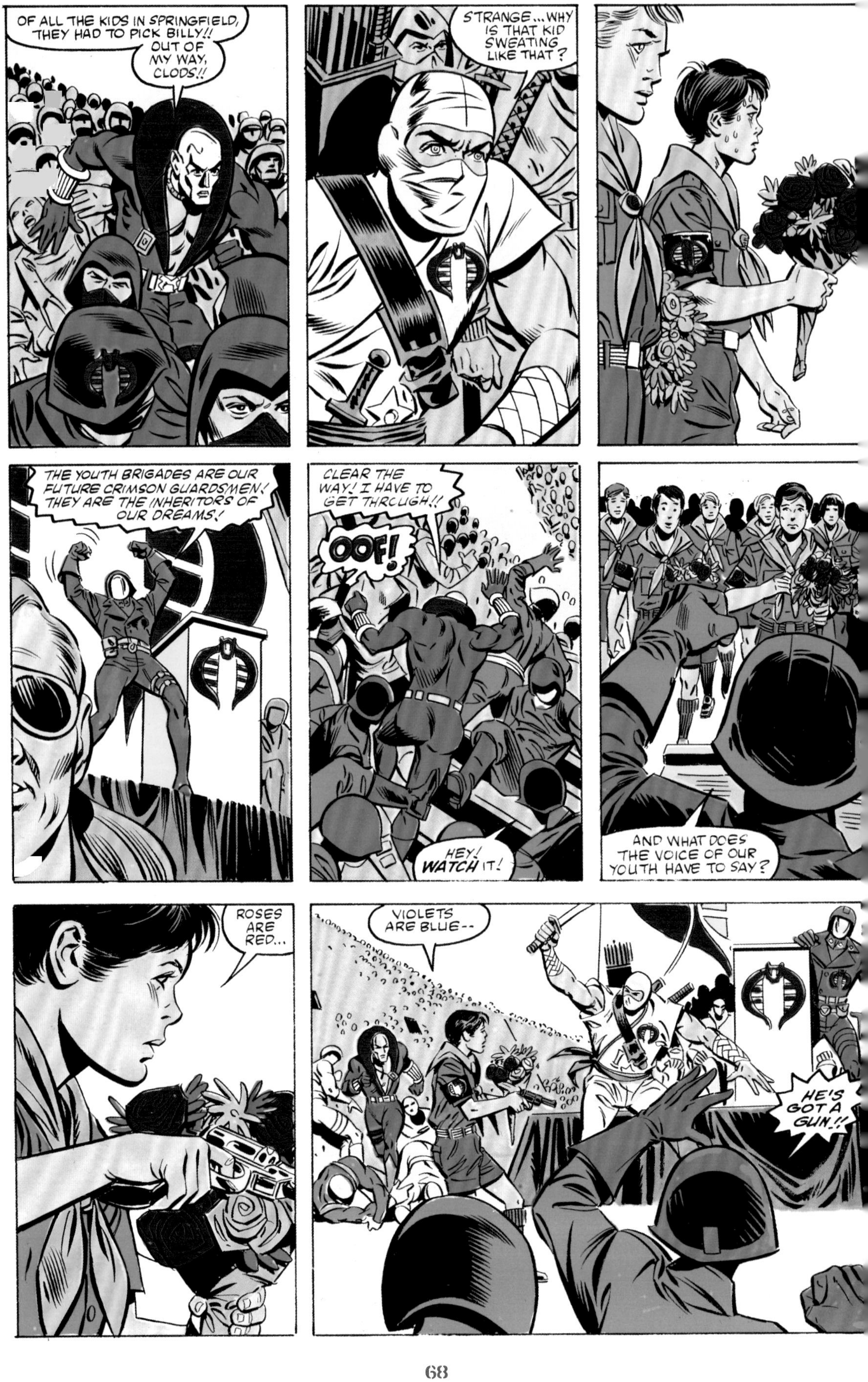
OF ALL THE KIDS IN SPRINGFIELD, THEY HAD TO PICK BILLY!!
OUT OF MY WAY, CLODS!!
STRANGE... WHY IS THAT KID SWEATING LIKE THAT?
THE YOUTH BRIGADES ARE OUR FUTURE CRIMSON GUARDSMEN! THEY ARE THE INHERITORS OF OUR DREAMS!
CLEAR THE WAY! I HAVE TO GET THROUGH!!
OOF!
HEY! WATCH IT!
AND WHAT DOES THE VOICE OF OUR YOUTH HAVE TO SAY?
ROSES ARE RED...
VIOLETS ARE BLUE--
HE'S GOT A GUN!!

NO! I WON'T LET THIS HAPPEN!!

BLAM

DROP IT, BILLY. IT'S ALL OVER.

WHAT'S GOING ON HERE? TAKE THIS LITTLE ASSASSIN OUT BACK AND GET RID OF HIM!

YOU SHOULD HAVE LET STORM-SHADOW MAKE AN EXAMPLE OUT OF HIM!

IS THAT SO?

I THINK YOU SHOULD TAKE A GOOD LOOK AT HIM FIRST...

WE MAY HAVE SOME DIFFER-ENCES OF OPINION AND EVEN HOSTILITY BETWEEN US BUT THERE ARE STILL SOME THINGS I WILL NOT ABIDE BY. PATRICIDE IS ONE OF THEM.

PATRICIDE?

BILLY?

D-D-DAD??

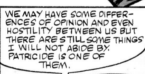

ON STATEN ISLAND...

THAT'S IT, GUYS... WE LOST 'EM!

WHAT'S THE DRILL? INITIATE A CIRCULAR SEARCH PATTERN?

BONGO
LLOON BEAR
AYS, MITZV/
DDING

BONGO

YOU CAN'T RUN AN EFFECTIVE SEARCH WITH JUST ONE VEHICLE....

... AND CHANCES ARE GOOD THAT THE PREY HAS GONE TO GROUND.

THEN, WHAT DO WE DO NOW?

AT THE PIT...

WELL, DUKE?

WE'VE GOT THREE JOES STILL MISSING, SIR. I SUGGEST WE PROCEED WITHOUT THEM.

GRAND OPENI

GRAND OPENING

GOOD. LET'S GET THE BALL ROLLING.

TEN-HUT!!

AT-EASE...

≥AHEM≤ I'VE PREPARED A SHORT SPEECH ON THE OCCASION OF--

THE LIFT IS COMING DOWN.

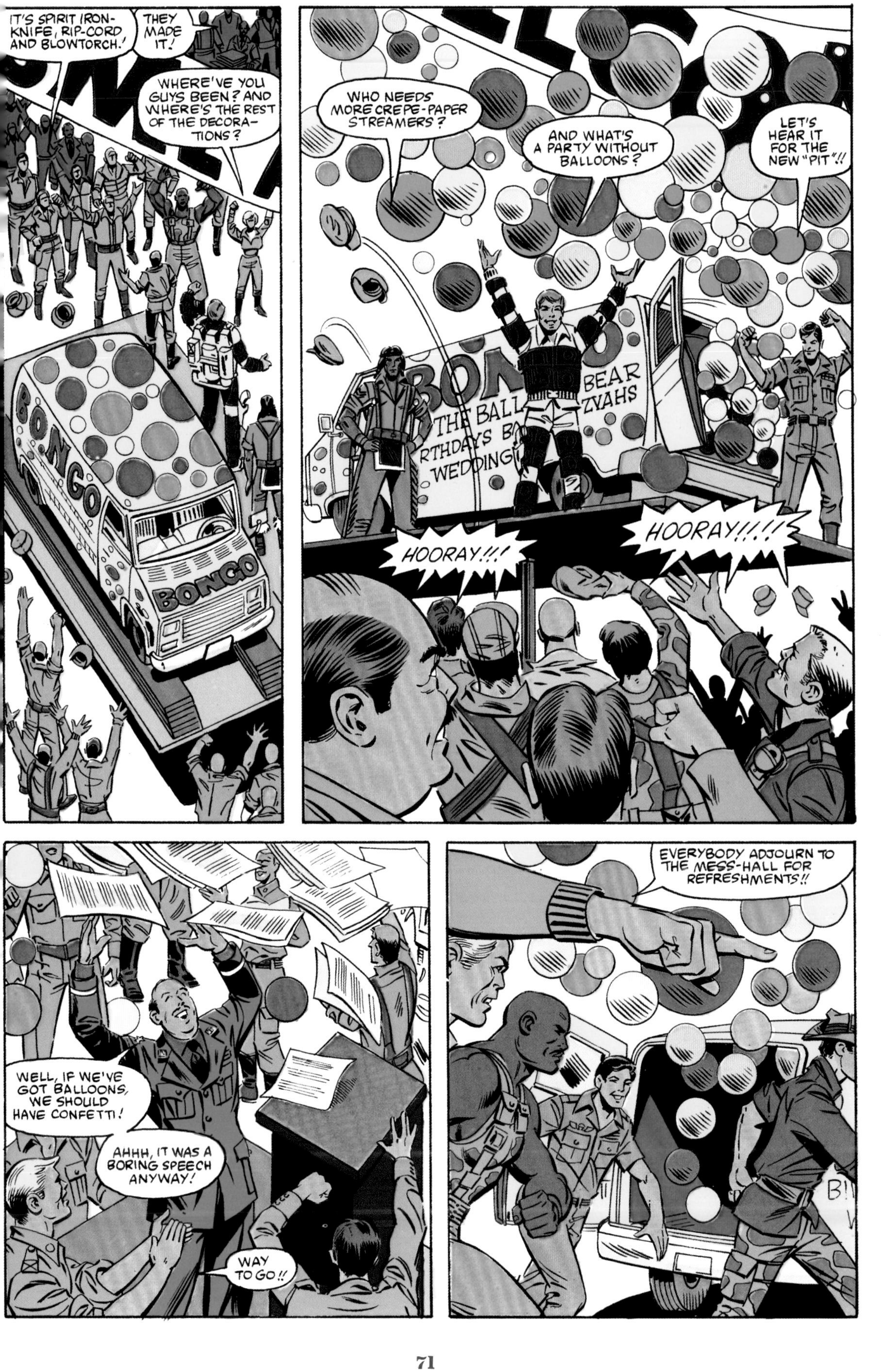
IT'S SPIRIT IRON-KNIFE, RIP-CORD AND BLOWTORCH.'
THEY MADE IT.'
WHERE'VE YOU GUYS BEEN? AND WHERE'S THE REST OF THE DECORA-TIONS?
WHO NEEDS MORE CREPE-PAPER STREAMERS?
AND WHAT'S A PARTY WITHOUT BALLOONS?
LET'S HEAR IT FOR THE NEW "PIT"!!
BONGO
HOORAY!!!
HOORAY!!!!!
WELL, IF WE'VE GOT BALLOONS, WE SHOULD HAVE CONFETTI!
AHHH, IT WAS A BORING SPEECH ANYWAY!
WAY TO GO!!
EVERYBODY ADJOURN TO THE MESS-HALL FOR REFRESHMENTS!!

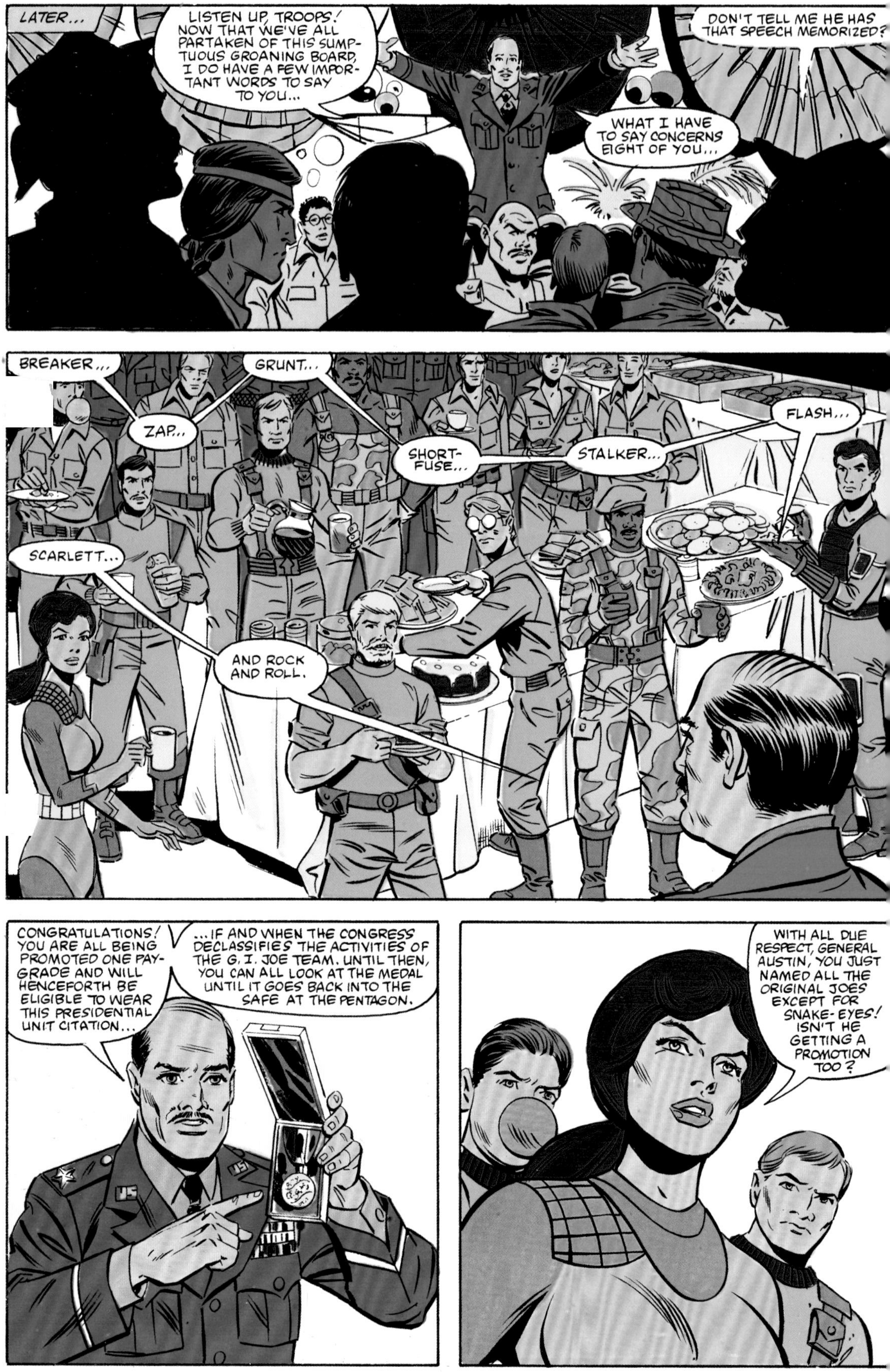
LATER...
LISTEN UP, TROOPS! NOW THAT WE'VE ALL PARTAKEN OF THIS SUMPTUOUS GROANING BOARD, I DO HAVE A FEW IMPORTANT WORDS TO SAY TO YOU...
DON'T TELL ME HE HAS THAT SPEECH MEMORIZED?
WHAT I HAVE TO SAY CONCERNS EIGHT OF YOU...
BREAKER...
ZAP...
GRUNT...
SHORT-FUSE...
STALKER...
FLASH...
SCARLETT...
AND ROCK AND ROLL.
CONGRATULATIONS! YOU ARE ALL BEING PROMOTED ONE PAY-GRADE AND WILL HENCEFORTH BE ELIGIBLE TO WEAR THIS PRESIDENTIAL UNIT CITATION...
...IF AND WHEN THE CONGRESS DECLASSIFIES THE ACTIVITIES OF THE G. I. JOE TEAM. UNTIL THEN, YOU CAN ALL LOOK AT THE MEDAL UNTIL IT GOES BACK INTO THE SAFE AT THE PENTAGON.
WITH ALL DUE RESPECT, GENERAL AUSTIN, YOU JUST NAMED ALL THE ORIGINAL JOES EXCEPT FOR SNAKE-EYES! ISN'T HE GETTING A PROMOTION TOO?

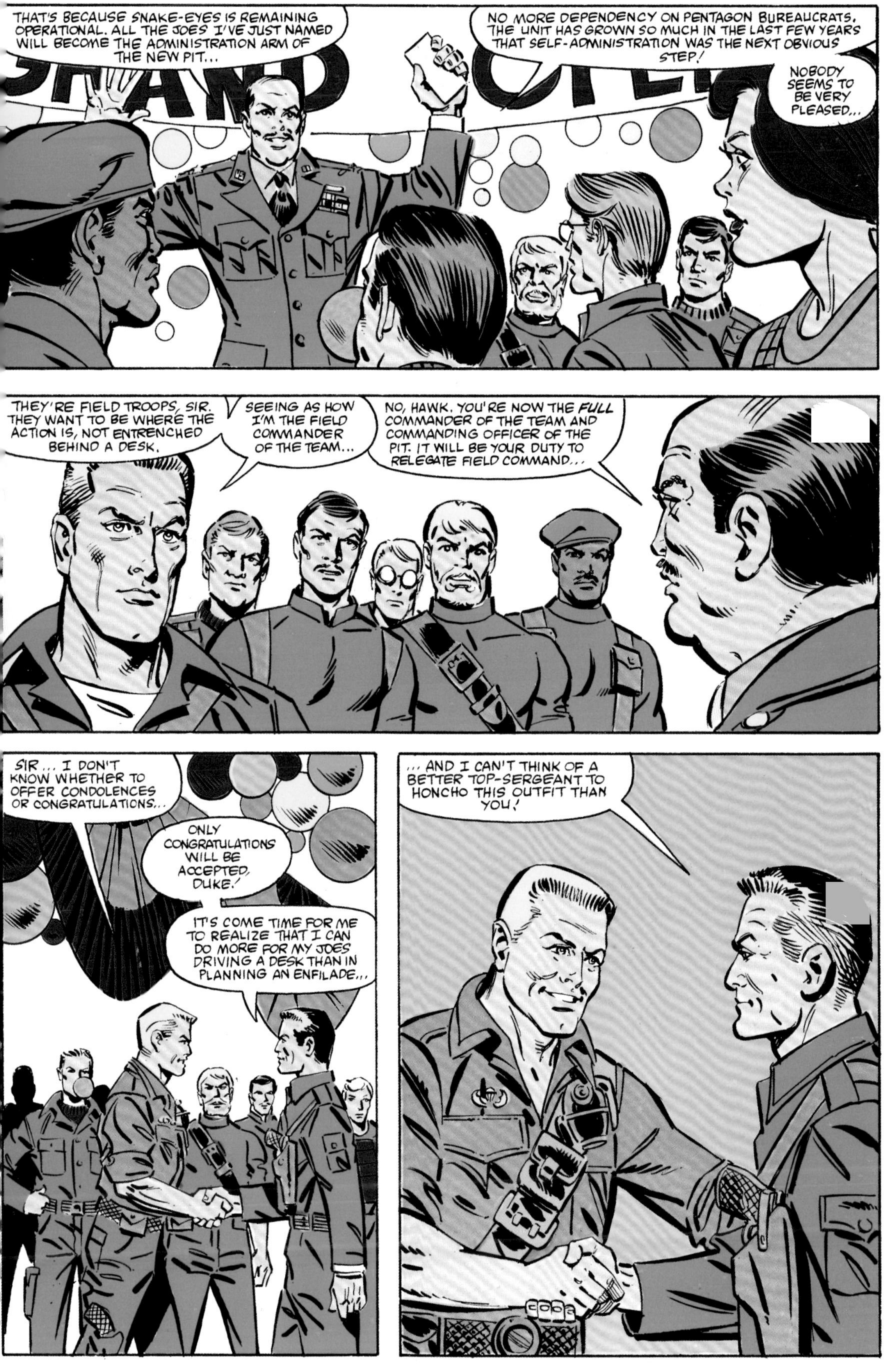
THAT'S BECAUSE SNAKE-EYES IS REMAINING OPERATIONAL. ALL THE JOES I'VE JUST NAMED WILL BECOME THE ADMINISTRATION ARM OF THE NEW PIT...
NO MORE DEPENDENCY ON PENTAGON BUREAUCRATS. THE UNIT HAS GROWN SO MUCH IN THE LAST FEW YEARS THAT SELF-ADMINISTRATION WAS THE NEXT OBVIOUS STEP!
NOBODY SEEMS TO BE VERY PLEASED...
THEY'RE FIELD TROOPS, SIR. THEY WANT TO BE WHERE THE ACTION IS, NOT ENTRENCHED BEHIND A DESK.
SEEING AS HOW I'M THE FIELD COMMANDER OF THE TEAM...
NO, HAWK. YOU'RE NOW THE FULL COMMANDER OF THE TEAM AND COMMANDING OFFICER OF THE PIT. IT WILL BE YOUR DUTY TO RELEGATE FIELD COMMAND...
SIR... I DON'T KNOW WHETHER TO OFFER CONDOLENCES OR CONGRATULATIONS...
ONLY CONGRATULATIONS WILL BE ACCEPTED, DUKE!
IT'S COME TIME FOR ME TO REALIZE THAT I CAN DO MORE FOR MY JOES DRIVING A DESK THAN IN PLANNING AN ENFILADE...
...AND I CAN'T THINK OF A BETTER TOP-SERGEANT TO HONCHO THIS OUTFIT THAN YOU!

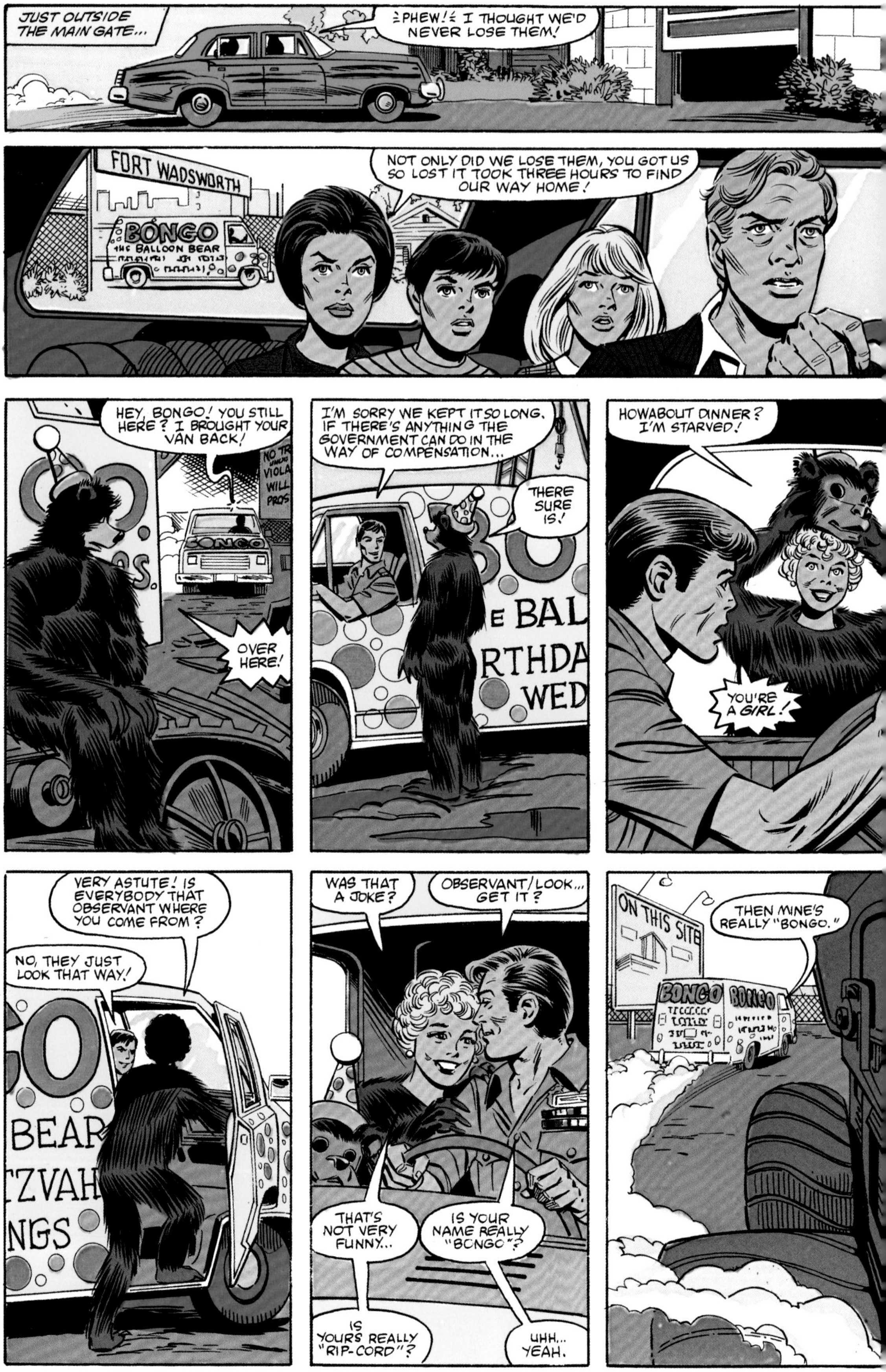
JUST OUTSIDE THE MAIN GATE...
PHEW! I THOUGHT WE'D NEVER LOSE THEM!
FORT WADSWORTH
BONGO THE BALLOON BEAR
NOT ONLY DID WE LOSE THEM, YOU GOT US SO LOST IT TOOK THREE HOURS TO FIND OUR WAY HOME!
HEY, BONGO! YOU STILL HERE? I BROUGHT YOUR VAN BACK!
OVER HERE!
I'M SORRY WE KEPT IT SO LONG. IF THERE'S ANYTHING THE GOVERNMENT CAN DO IN THE WAY OF COMPENSATION...
THERE SURE IS!
HOWABOUT DINNER? I'M STARVED!
YOU'RE A GIRL!
VERY ASTUTE! IS EVERYBODY THAT OBSERVANT WHERE YOU COME FROM?
NO, THEY JUST LOOK THAT WAY!
WAS THAT A JOKE?
OBSERVANT/LOOK... GET IT?
THAT'S NOT VERY FUNNY...
IS YOUR NAME REALLY "BONGO"?
IS YOURS REALLY "RIP-CORD"?
UHH... YEAH.
ON THIS SITE
THEN MINE'S REALLY "BONGO."

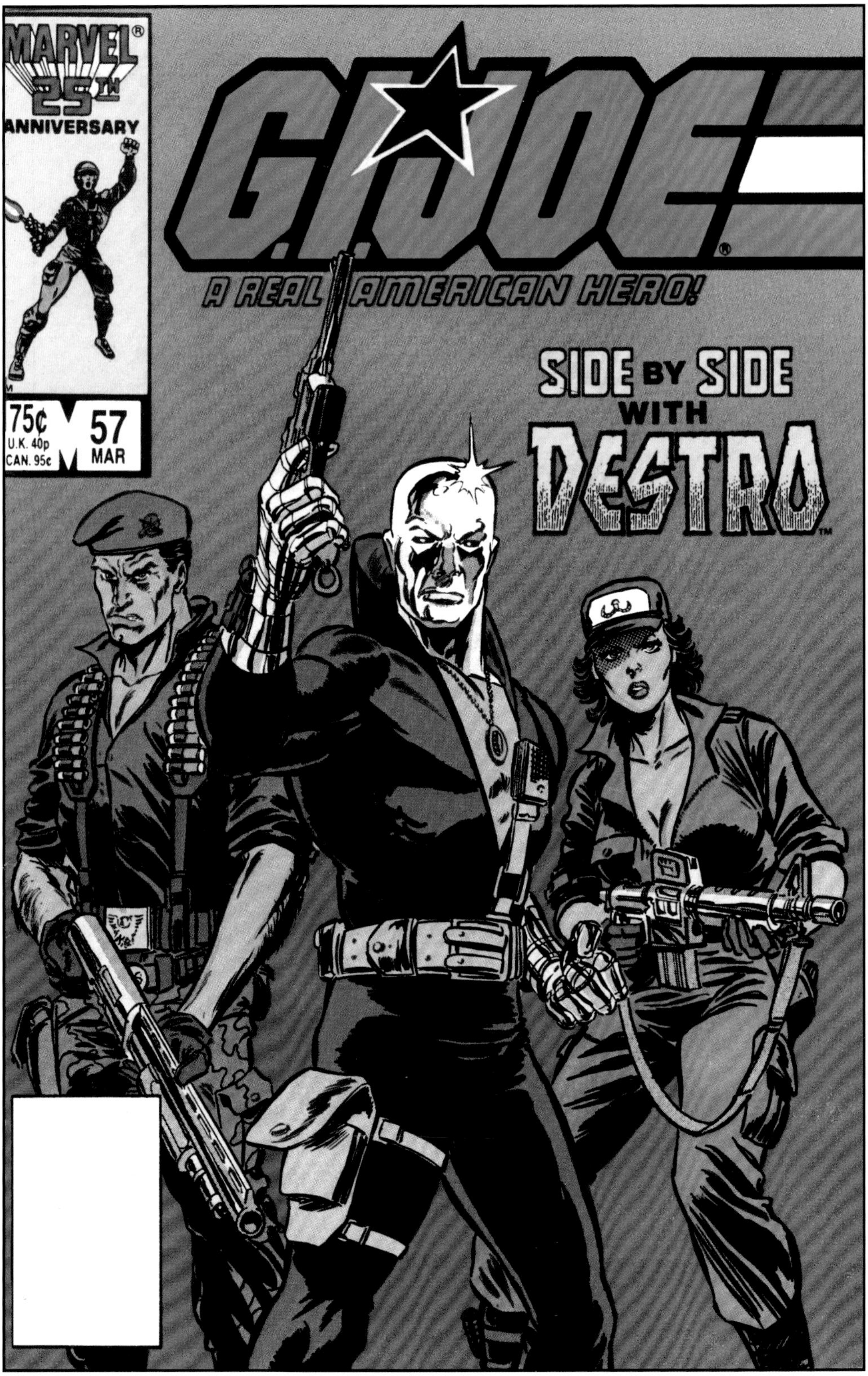

MARVEL
25TH
ANNIVERSARY
G.I. JOE
A REAL AMERICAN HERO!
SIDE BY SIDE
WITH
DESTRO
75¢
U.K. 40p
CAN. 95¢
57
MAR

STAN LEE PRESENTS

STRANGE BEDFELLOWS

| LARRY HAMA | RON WAGNER | KIM DeMULDER | GEORGE ROUSSOS | JOE ROSEN | BOB HARRAS | JIM SHOOTER |
| SCRIPT | PENCILER | INKS | COLORS | LETTERING | EDITOR | ED. IN CHIEF |

ON THE HANGAR DECK OF THE AIRCRAFT CARRIER USS FLAGG...

OUR TECH BOYS HAVE BEEN GOING OVER THESE TERROR-DROME SEGMENTS EVER SINCE YOU HAULED THEM BACK FROM SIERRA GORDO *...

...THERE ARE SEVERAL COMPONENTS THAT DEFY ANALYSIS, WE DON'T HAVE A CLUE AS TO WHAT THEY DO AND WE'VE TRACED THEM ALL TO THE SAME MANUFACTURER: M.A.R.S.!

I KNOW ALL ABOUT THEM, HAWK, THE MILITARY ARMAMENTS RESEARCH SYNDICATE IS AN INTERNATIONAL WEAPONS FIRM WITH CORPORATE HEADQUARTERS IN SCOTLAND. EVER HEAR OF THEM, FLINT?

M.A.R.S.: ORIGINALLY ESTABLISHED IN 1752 AS A NAVAL GUN FOUNDRY BY JAMES McCULLEN DESTRO, ANCESTOR OF THE LATE DESTRO WE ALL KNEW, WHO, BY THE WAY, WAS THE FIFTEENTH EARL OF SOMETHING OR THE OTHER...

YES, I'VE HEARD OF THEM, LADY JAYE.

*LAST ISSUE!

77

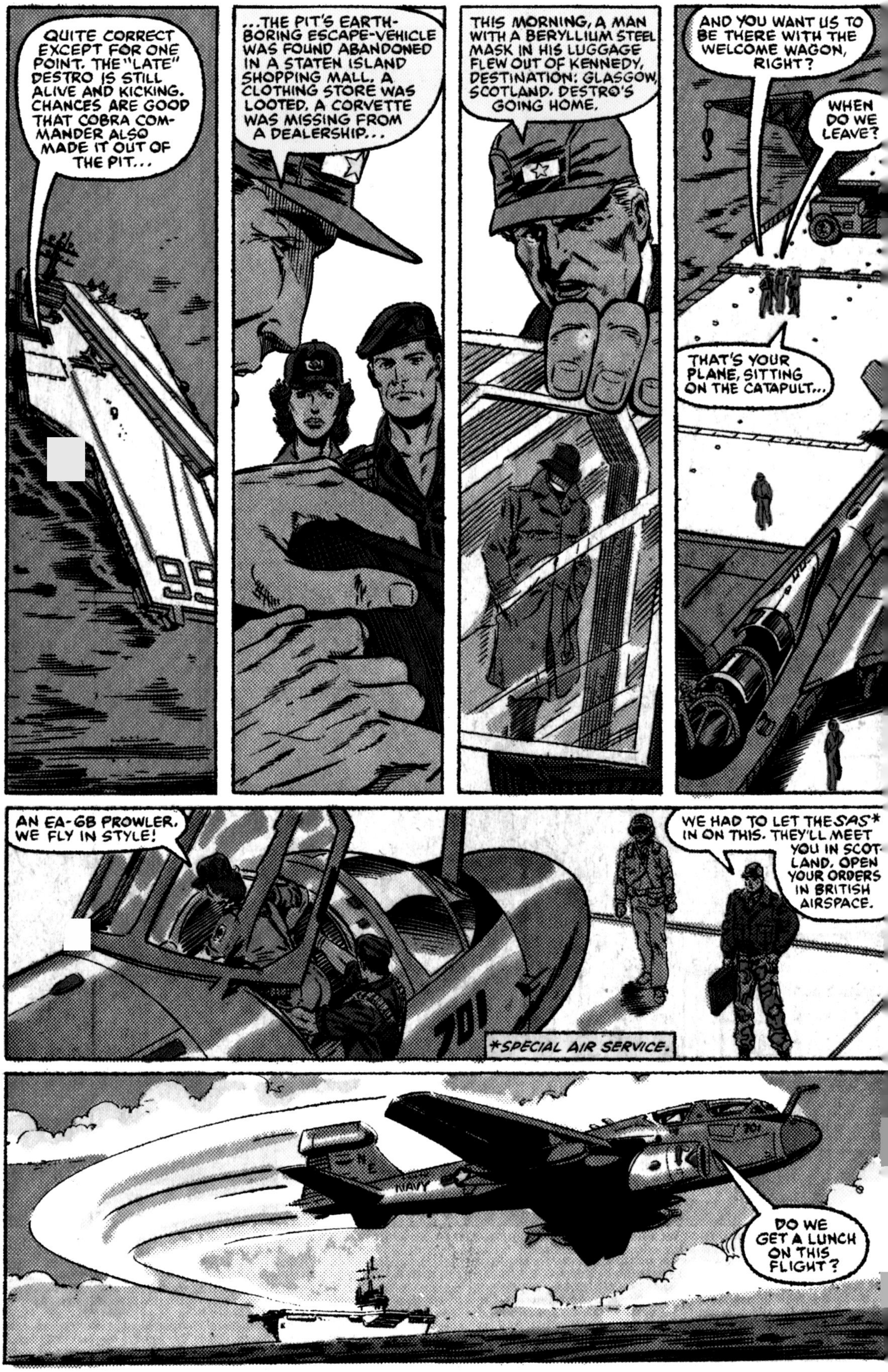
QUITE CORRECT EXCEPT FOR ONE POINT. THE "LATE" DESTRO IS STILL ALIVE AND KICKING. CHANCES ARE GOOD THAT COBRA COMMANDER ALSO MADE IT OUT OF THE PIT...
...THE PIT'S EARTH-BORING ESCAPE-VEHICLE WAS FOUND ABANDONED IN A STATEN ISLAND SHOPPING MALL. A CLOTHING STORE WAS LOOTED. A CORVETTE WAS MISSING FROM A DEALERSHIP...
THIS MORNING, A MAN WITH A BERYLLIUM STEEL MASK IN HIS LUGGAGE FLEW OUT OF KENNEDY. DESTINATION: GLASGOW, SCOTLAND. DESTRO'S GOING HOME.
AND YOU WANT US TO BE THERE WITH THE WELCOME WAGON, RIGHT?
WHEN DO WE LEAVE?
THAT'S YOUR PLANE, SITTING ON THE CATAPULT...
AN EA-6B PROWLER. WE FLY IN STYLE!
WE HAD TO LET THE SAS* IN ON THIS. THEY'LL MEET YOU IN SCOTLAND. OPEN YOUR ORDERS IN BRITISH AIRSPACE.
*SPECIAL AIR SERVICE.
701
NAVY
DO WE GET A LUNCH ON THIS FLIGHT?

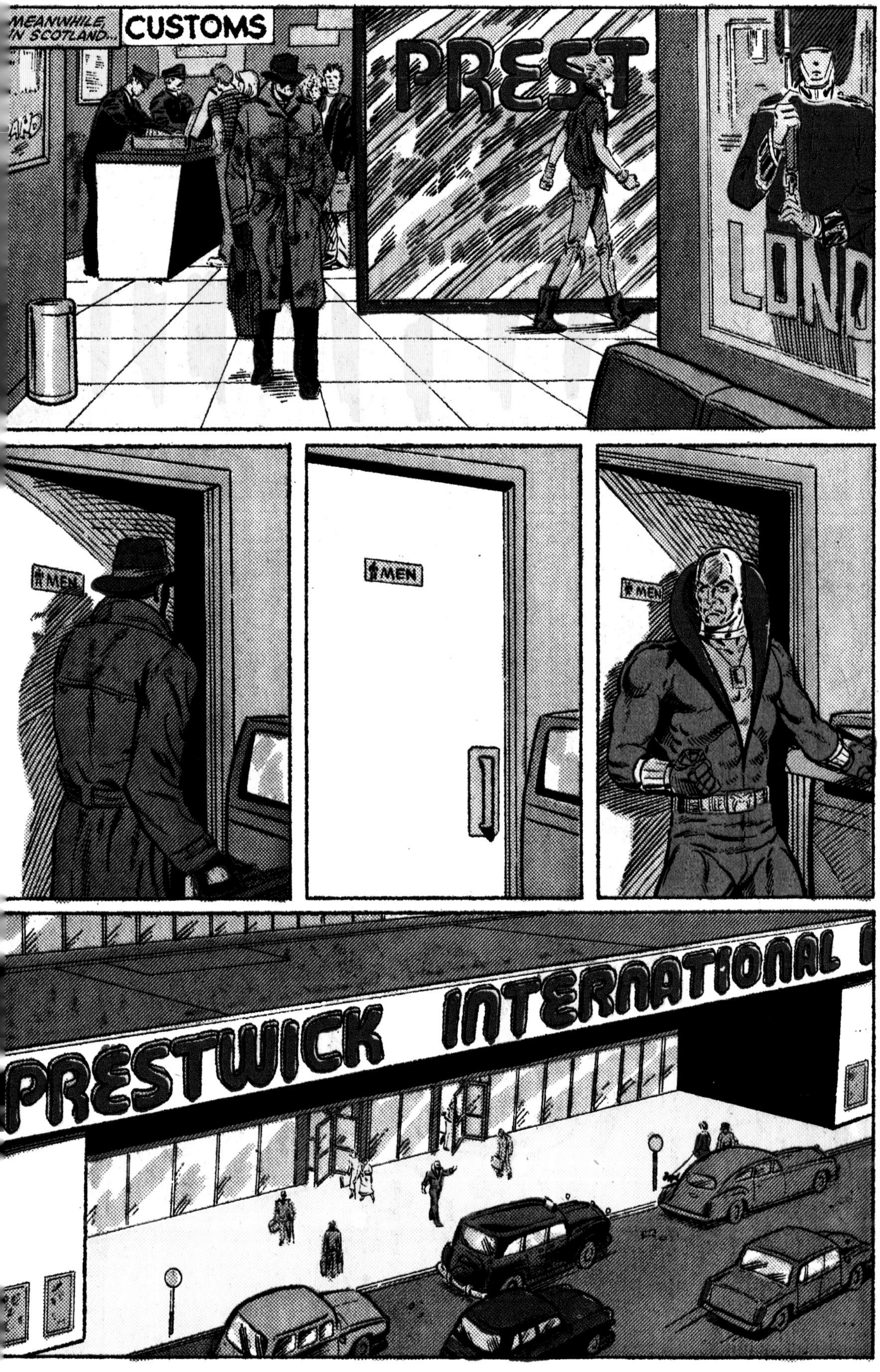

MEANWHILE, IN SCOTLAND...
CUSTOMS
PREST
LOND
MEN
MEN
MEN
PRESTWICK INTERNATIONAL

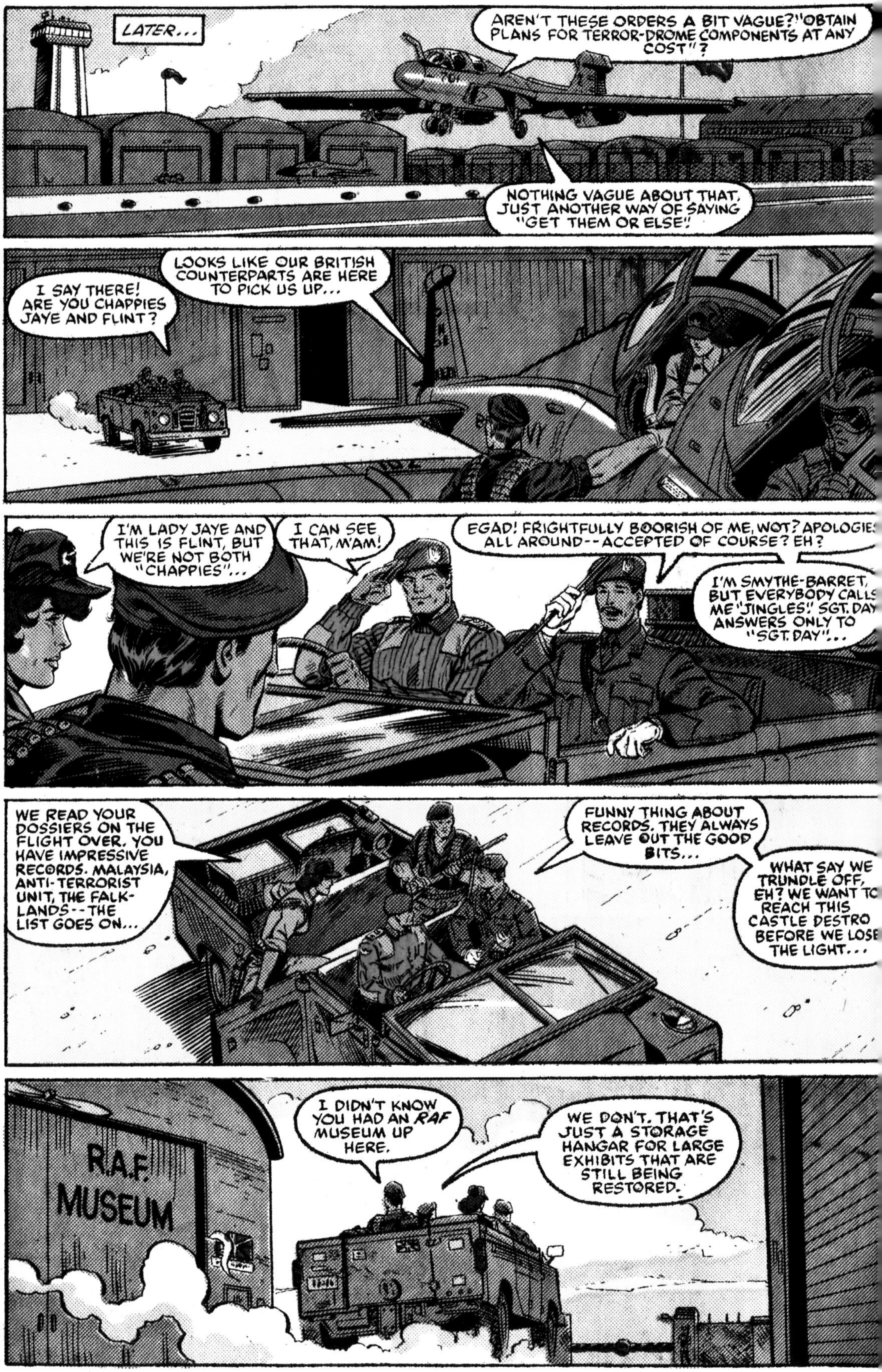
LATER...
AREN'T THESE ORDERS A BIT VAGUE? "OBTAIN PLANS FOR TERROR-DROME COMPONENTS AT ANY COST"?
NOTHING VAGUE ABOUT THAT. JUST ANOTHER WAY OF SAYING "GET THEM OR ELSE!"
I SAY THERE! ARE YOU CHAPPIES JAYE AND FLINT?
LOOKS LIKE OUR BRITISH COUNTERPARTS ARE HERE TO PICK US UP...
I'M LADY JAYE AND THIS IS FLINT, BUT WE'RE NOT BOTH "CHAPPIES"...
I CAN SEE THAT, M'AM!
EGAD! FRIGHTFULLY BOORISH OF ME, WOT? APOLOGIES ALL AROUND--ACCEPTED OF COURSE? EH?
I'M SMYTHE-BARRET, BUT EVERYBODY CALLS ME "JINGLES." SGT. DAY ANSWERS ONLY TO "SGT. DAY"...
WE READ YOUR DOSSIERS ON THE FLIGHT OVER. YOU HAVE IMPRESSIVE RECORDS. MALAYSIA, ANTI-TERRORIST UNIT, THE FALK-LANDS--THE LIST GOES ON...
FUNNY THING ABOUT RECORDS. THEY ALWAYS LEAVE OUT THE GOOD BITS...
WHAT SAY WE TRUNDLE OFF, EH? WE WANT TO REACH THIS CASTLE DESTRO BEFORE WE LOSE THE LIGHT...
R.A.F. MUSEUM
I DIDN'T KNOW YOU HAD AN *RAF* MUSEUM UP HERE.
WE DON'T. THAT'S JUST A STORAGE HANGAR FOR LARGE EXHIBITS THAT ARE STILL BEING RESTORED.

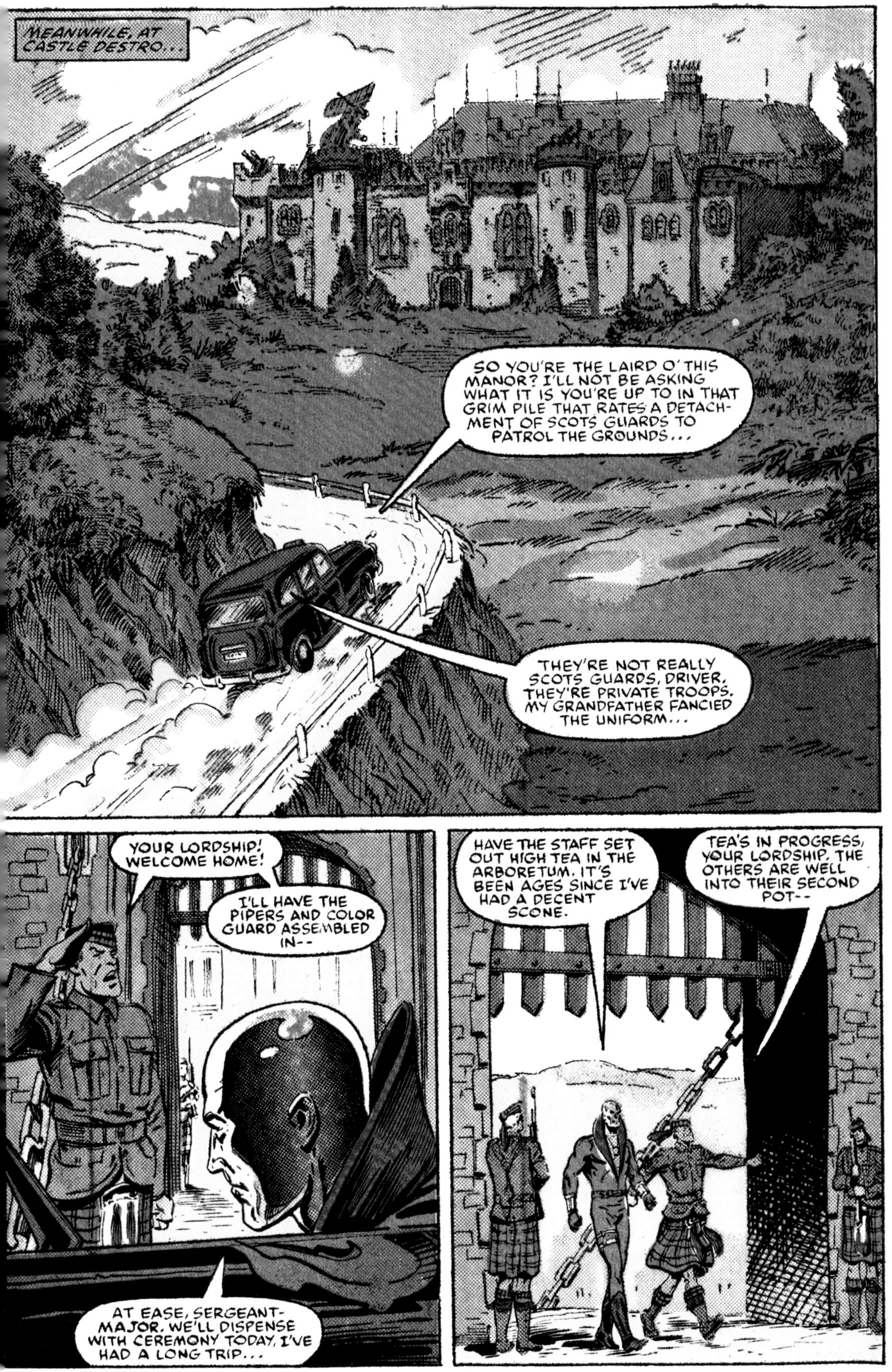
MEANWHILE, AT CASTLE DESTRO...
SO YOU'RE THE LAIRD O' THIS MANOR? I'LL NOT BE ASKING WHAT IT IS YOU'RE UP TO IN THAT GRIM PILE THAT RATES A DETACHMENT OF SCOTS GUARDS TO PATROL THE GROUNDS...
THEY'RE NOT REALLY SCOTS GUARDS, DRIVER. THEY'RE PRIVATE TROOPS. MY GRANDFATHER FANCIED THE UNIFORM...
YOUR LORDSHIP! WELCOME HOME!
I'LL HAVE THE PIPERS AND COLOR GUARD ASSEMBLED IN--
AT EASE, SERGEANT-MAJOR. WE'LL DISPENSE WITH CEREMONY TODAY. I'VE HAD A LONG TRIP...
HAVE THE STAFF SET OUT HIGH TEA IN THE ARBORETUM. IT'S BEEN AGES SINCE I'VE HAD A DECENT SCONE.
TEA'S IN PROGRESS, YOUR LORDSHIP. THE OTHERS ARE WELL INTO THEIR SECOND POT--

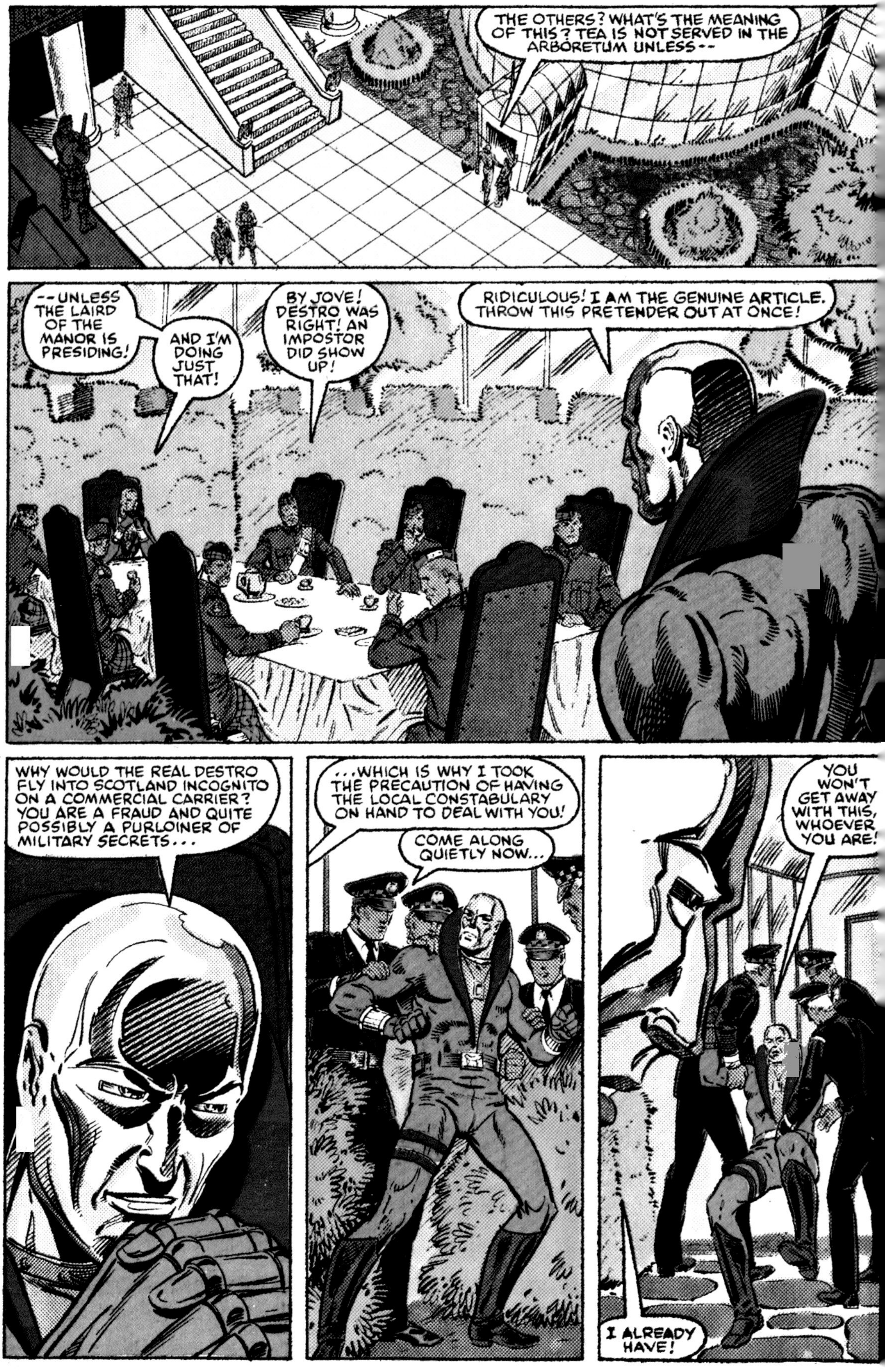

THE OTHERS? WHAT'S THE MEANING OF THIS? TEA IS NOT SERVED IN THE ARBORETUM UNLESS--
--UNLESS THE LAIRD OF THE MANOR IS PRESIDING!
AND I'M DOING JUST THAT!
BY JOVE! DESTRO WAS RIGHT! AN IMPOSTOR DID SHOW UP!
RIDICULOUS! I AM THE GENUINE ARTICLE. THROW THIS PRETENDER OUT AT ONCE!
WHY WOULD THE REAL DESTRO FLY INTO SCOTLAND INCOGNITO ON A COMMERCIAL CARRIER? YOU ARE A FRAUD AND QUITE POSSIBLY A PURLOINER OF MILITARY SECRETS...
...WHICH IS WHY I TOOK THE PRECAUTION OF HAVING THE LOCAL CONSTABULARY ON HAND TO DEAL WITH YOU!
COME ALONG QUIETLY NOW...
YOU WON'T GET AWAY WITH THIS, WHOEVER YOU ARE!
I ALREADY HAVE!

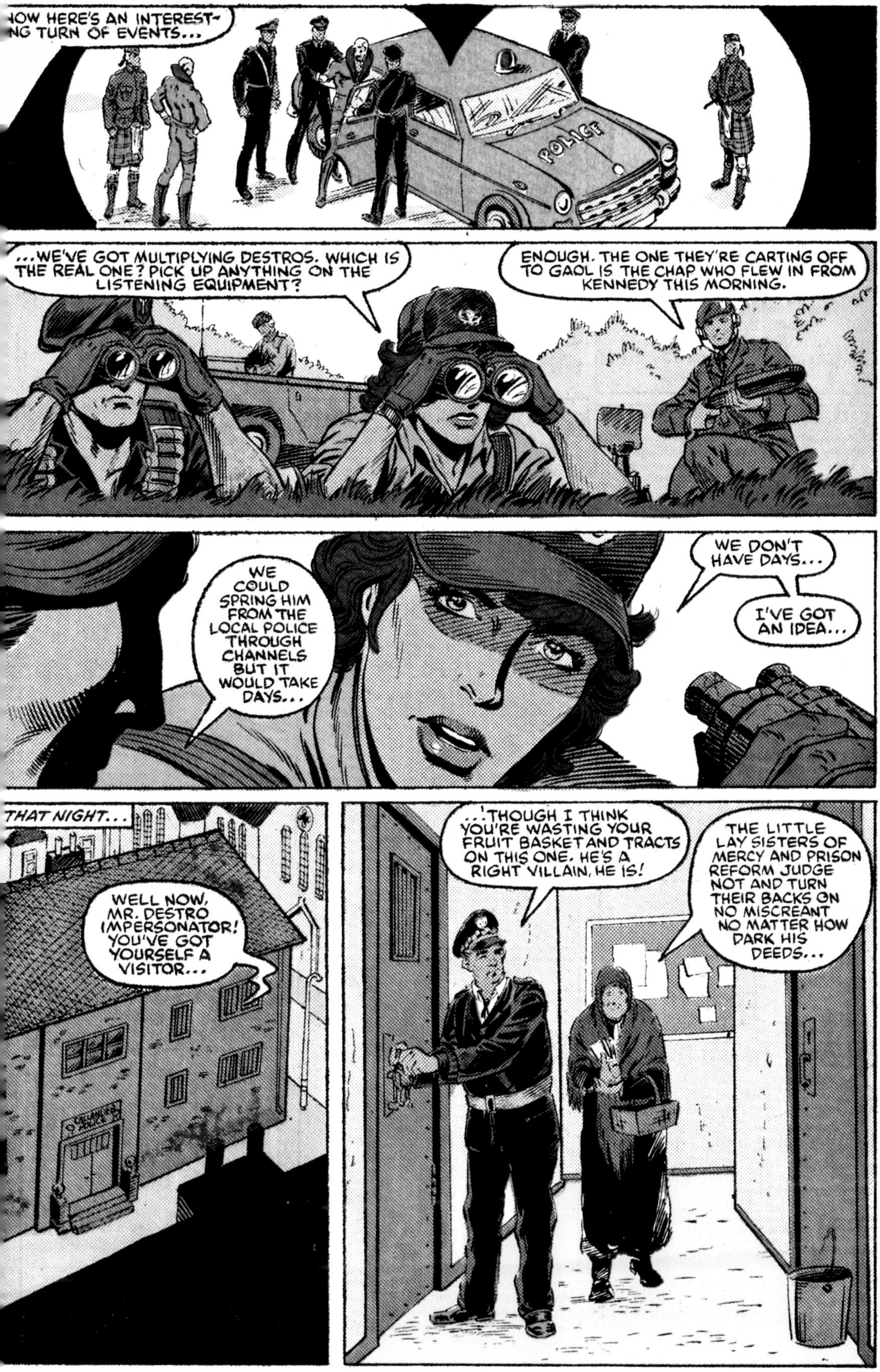
NOW HERE'S AN INTERESTING TURN OF EVENTS...
...WE'VE GOT MULTIPLYING DESTROS. WHICH IS THE REAL ONE? PICK UP ANYTHING ON THE LISTENING EQUIPMENT?
ENOUGH. THE ONE THEY'RE CARTING OFF TO GAOL IS THE CHAP WHO FLEW IN FROM KENNEDY THIS MORNING.
WE COULD SPRING HIM FROM THE LOCAL POLICE THROUGH CHANNELS BUT IT WOULD TAKE DAYS...
WE DON'T HAVE DAYS...
I'VE GOT AN IDEA...
THAT NIGHT...
WELL NOW, MR. DESTRO IMPERSONATOR! YOU'VE GOT YOURSELF A VISITOR...
...THOUGH I THINK YOU'RE WASTING YOUR FRUIT BASKET AND TRACTS ON THIS ONE. HE'S A RIGHT VILLAIN, HE IS!
THE LITTLE LAY SISTERS OF MERCY AND PRISON REFORM JUDGE NOT AND TURN THEIR BACKS ON NO MISCREANT NO MATTER HOW DARK HIS DEEDS...

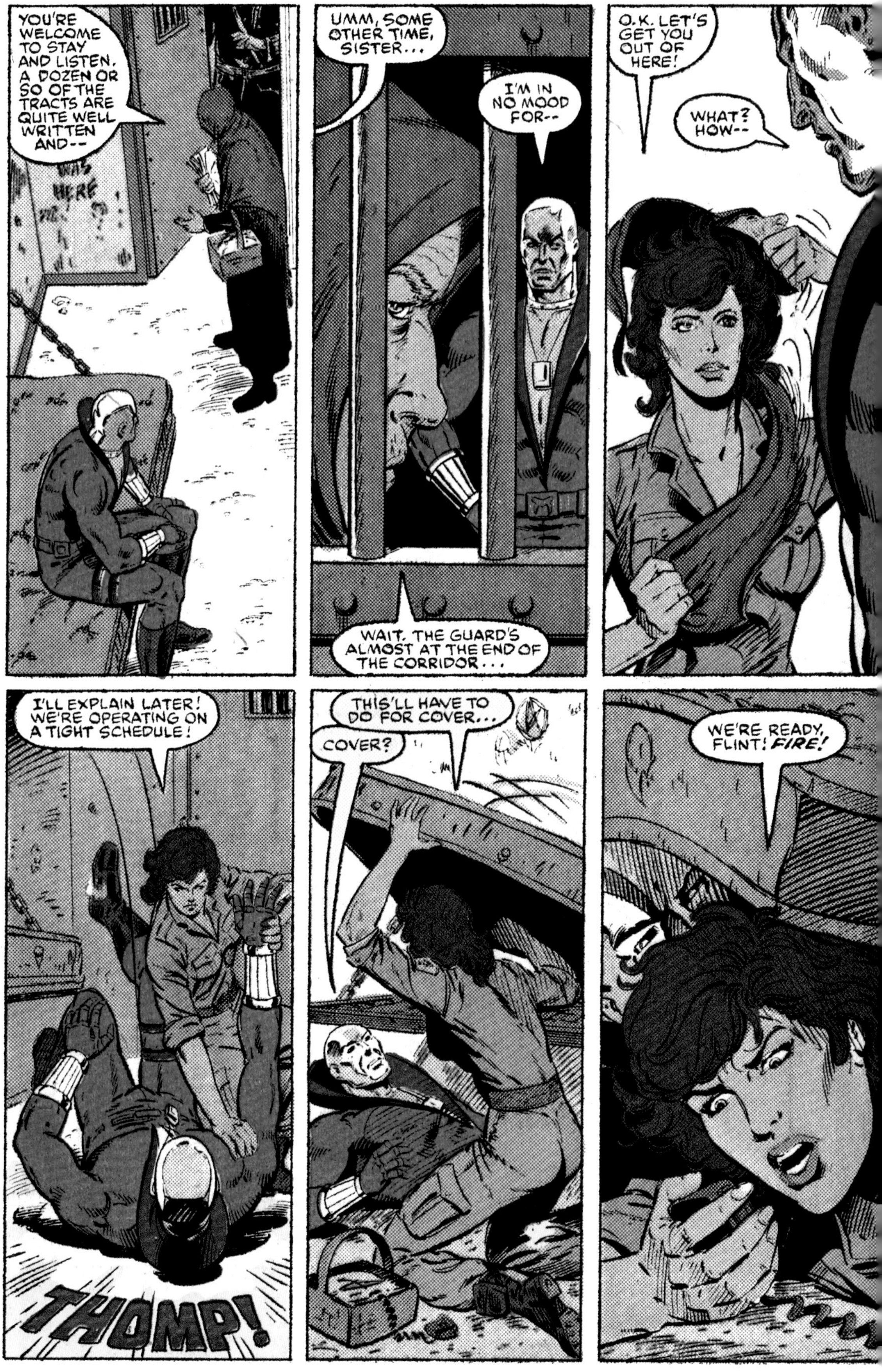
YOU'RE WELCOME TO STAY AND LISTEN. A DOZEN OR SO OF THE TRACTS ARE QUITE WELL WRITTEN AND--
UMM, SOME OTHER TIME, SISTER...
I'M IN NO MOOD FOR--
WAIT. THE GUARD'S ALMOST AT THE END OF THE CORRIDOR...
O.K. LET'S GET YOU OUT OF HERE!
WHAT? HOW--
I'LL EXPLAIN LATER! WE'RE OPERATING ON A TIGHT SCHEDULE!
THOMP!
THIS'LL HAVE TO DO FOR COVER...
COVER?
WE'RE READY, FLINT! FIRE!

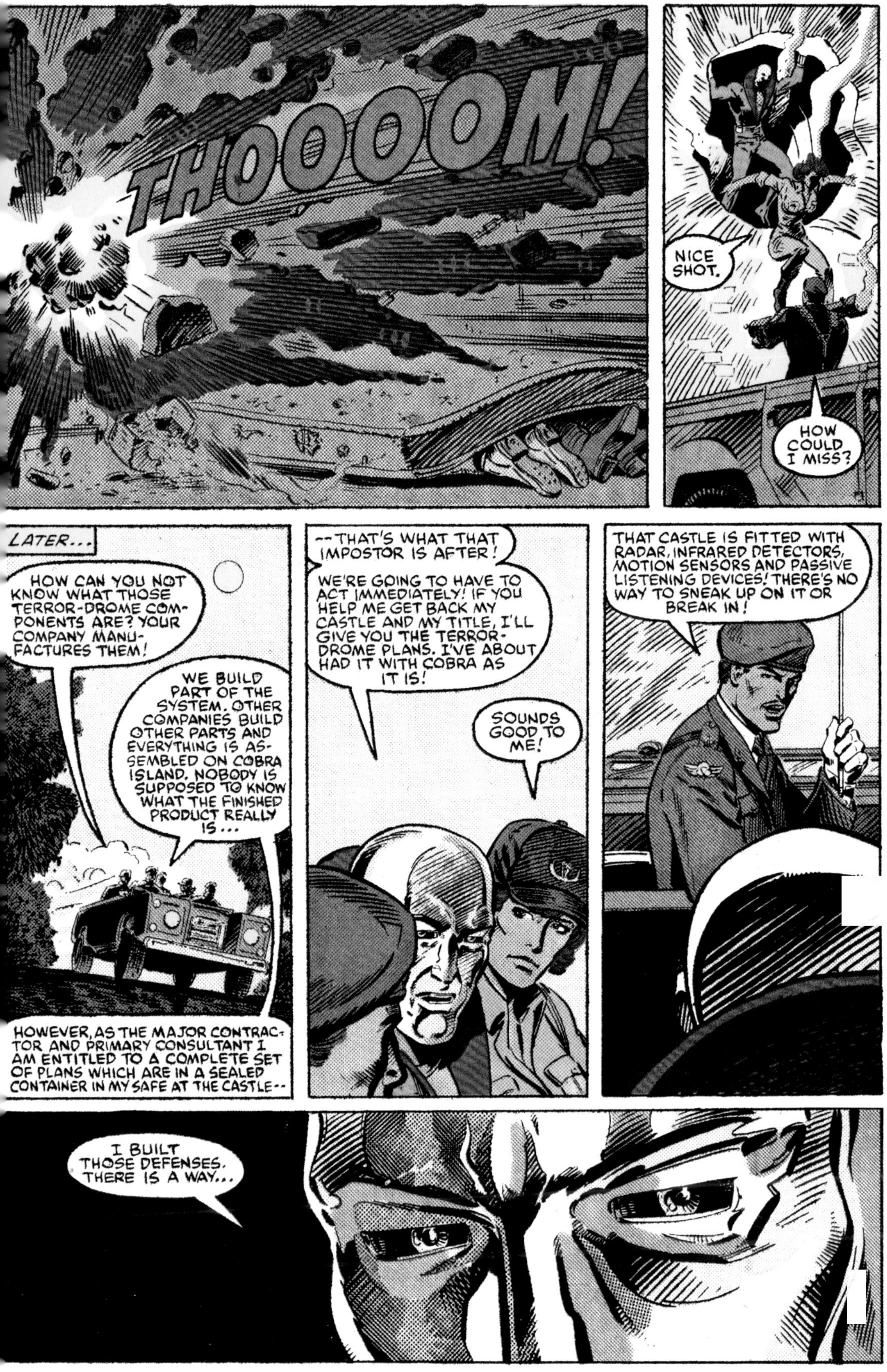
THOOOOM!
NICE SHOT.
HOW COULD I MISS?
LATER...
HOW CAN YOU NOT KNOW WHAT THOSE TERROR-DROME COMPONENTS ARE? YOUR COMPANY MANUFACTURES THEM!
WE BUILD PART OF THE SYSTEM. OTHER COMPANIES BUILD OTHER PARTS AND EVERYTHING IS ASSEMBLED ON COBRA ISLAND. NOBODY IS SUPPOSED TO KNOW WHAT THE FINISHED PRODUCT REALLY IS...
HOWEVER, AS THE MAJOR CONTRACTOR AND PRIMARY CONSULTANT I AM ENTITLED TO A COMPLETE SET OF PLANS WHICH ARE IN A SEALED CONTAINER IN MY SAFE AT THE CASTLE--
--THAT'S WHAT THAT IMPOSTOR IS AFTER!
WE'RE GOING TO HAVE TO ACT IMMEDIATELY! IF YOU HELP ME GET BACK MY CASTLE AND MY TITLE, I'LL GIVE YOU THE TERROR-DROME PLANS. I'VE ABOUT HAD IT WITH COBRA AS IT IS!
SOUNDS GOOD TO ME!
THAT CASTLE IS FITTED WITH RADAR, INFRARED DETECTORS, MOTION SENSORS AND PASSIVE LISTENING DEVICES! THERE'S NO WAY TO SNEAK UP ON IT OR BREAK IN!
I BUILT THOSE DEFENSES. THERE IS A WAY...

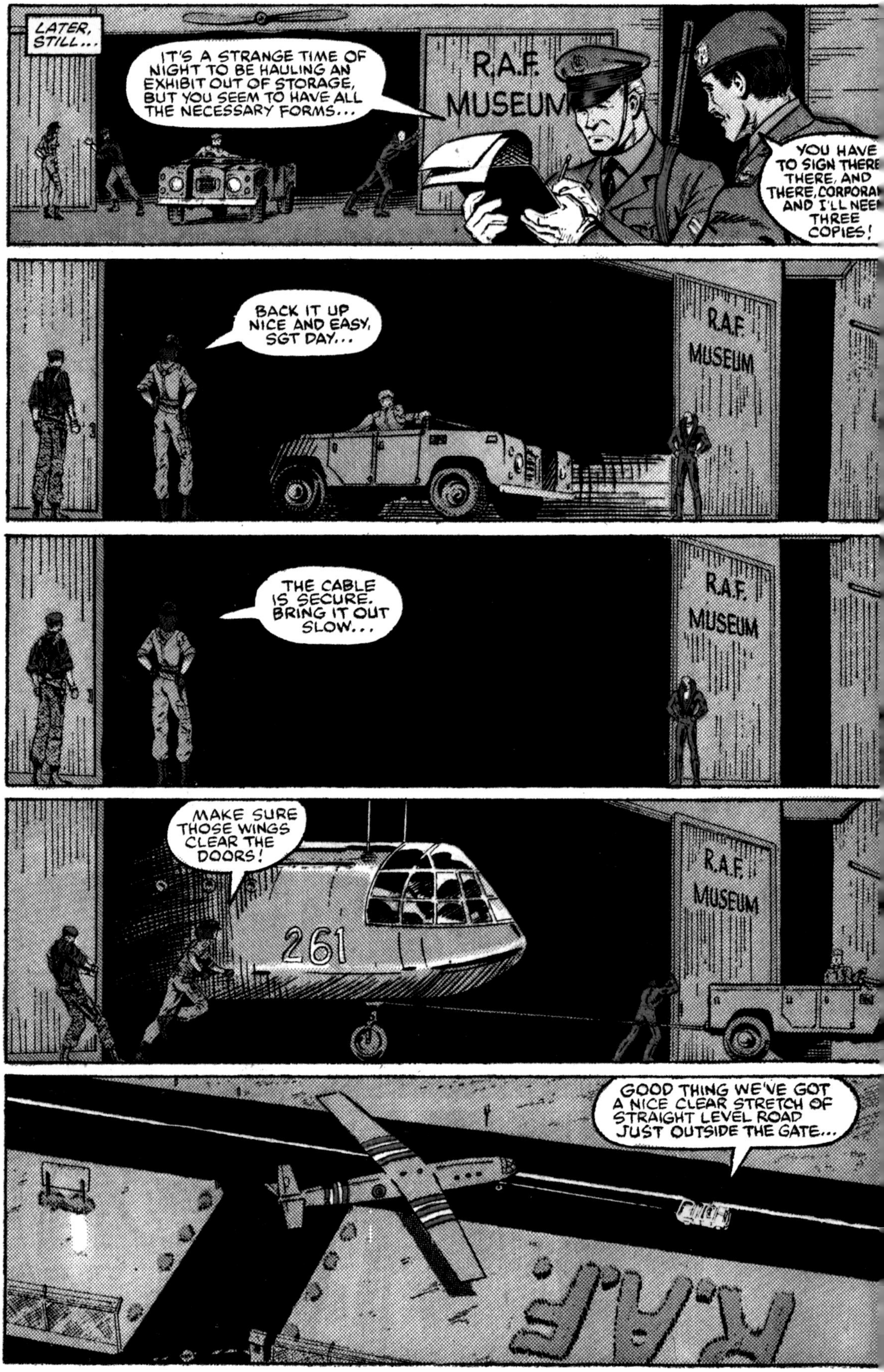
LATER, STILL...
IT'S A STRANGE TIME OF NIGHT TO BE HAULING AN EXHIBIT OUT OF STORAGE, BUT YOU SEEM TO HAVE ALL THE NECESSARY FORMS...
R.A.F. MUSEUM
YOU HAVE TO SIGN THERE THERE, AND THERE, CORPORAL AND I'LL NEED THREE COPIES!
BACK IT UP NICE AND EASY, SGT DAY...
R.A.F. MUSEUM
THE CABLE IS SECURE. BRING IT OUT SLOW...
R.A.F. MUSEUM
MAKE SURE THOSE WINGS CLEAR THE DOORS!
261
R.A.F. MUSEUM
GOOD THING WE'VE GOT A NICE CLEAR STRETCH OF STRAIGHT LEVEL ROAD JUST OUTSIDE THE GATE...

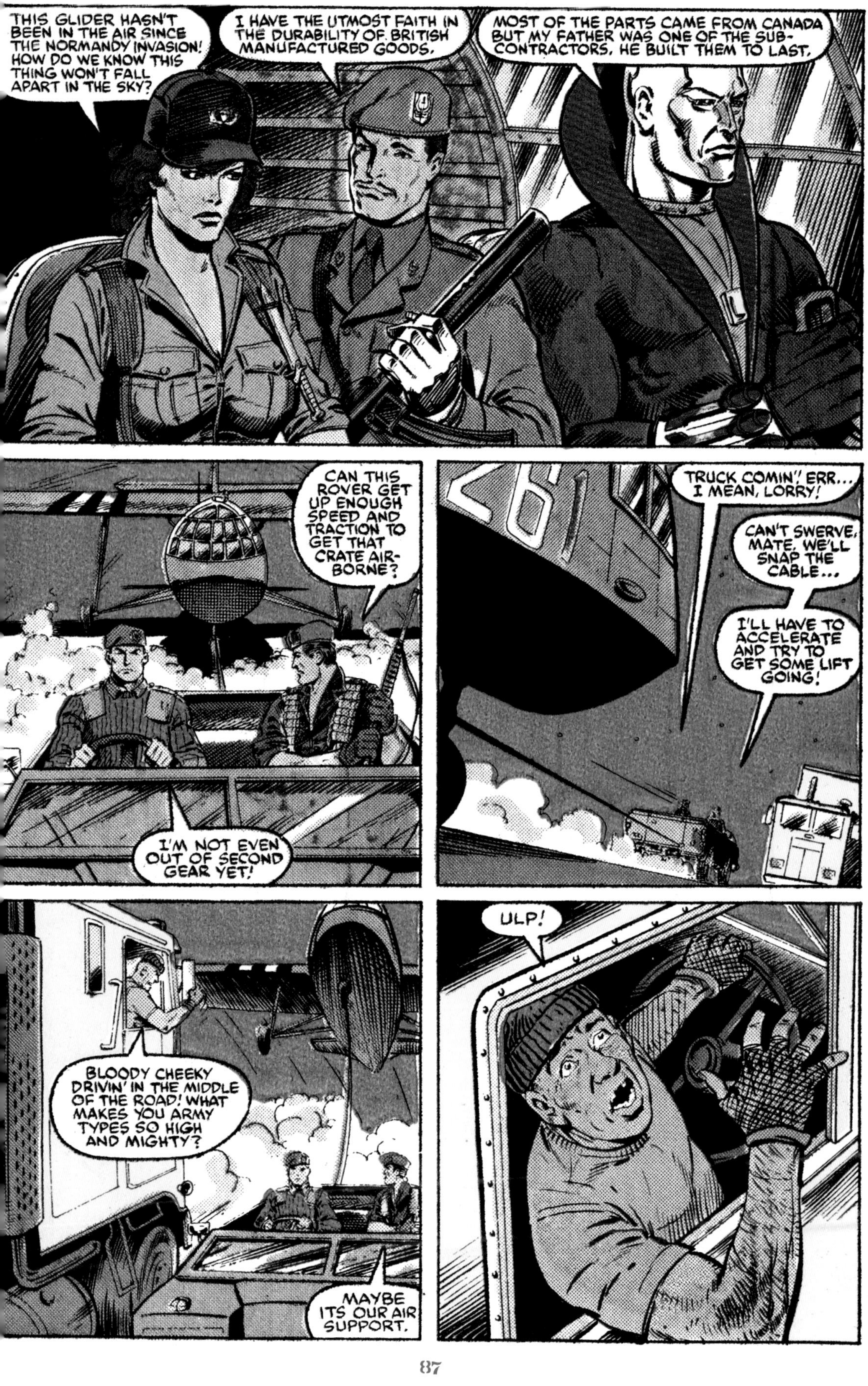
THIS GLIDER HASN'T BEEN IN THE AIR SINCE THE NORMANDY INVASION! HOW DO WE KNOW THIS THING WON'T FALL APART IN THE SKY?
I HAVE THE UTMOST FAITH IN THE DURABILITY OF BRITISH MANUFACTURED GOODS.
MOST OF THE PARTS CAME FROM CANADA BUT MY FATHER WAS ONE OF THE SUB-CONTRACTORS. HE BUILT THEM TO LAST.
CAN THIS ROVER GET UP ENOUGH SPEED AND TRACTION TO GET THAT CRATE AIR-BORNE?
I'M NOT EVEN OUT OF SECOND GEAR YET!
TRUCK COMIN'! ERR... I MEAN, LORRY!
CAN'T SWERVE, MATE. WE'LL SNAP THE CABLE...
I'LL HAVE TO ACCELERATE AND TRY TO GET SOME LIFT GOING!
BLOODY CHEEKY DRIVIN' IN THE MIDDLE OF THE ROAD! WHAT MAKES YOU ARMY TYPES SO HIGH AND MIGHTY?
MAYBE ITS OUR AIR SUPPORT.
ULP!

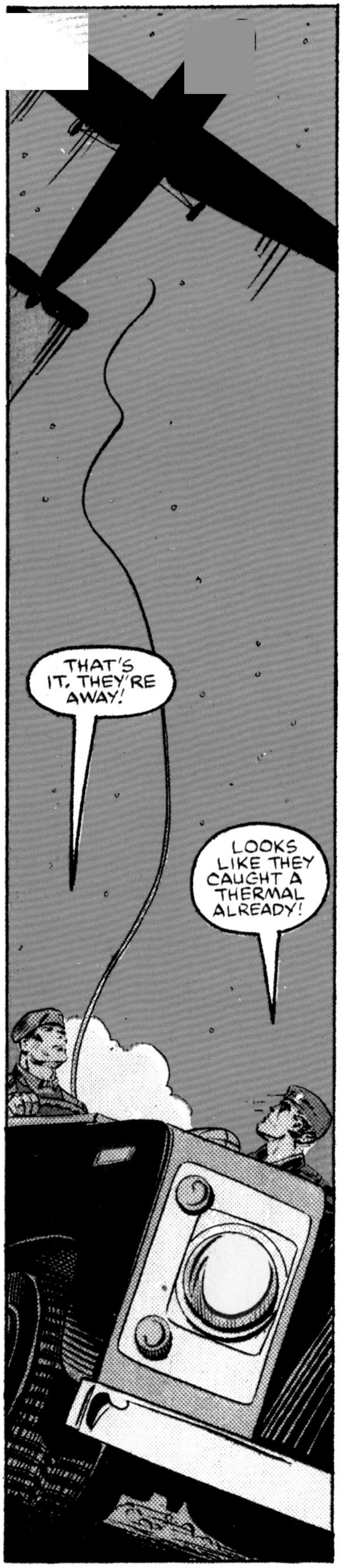
THAT'S IT. THEY'RE AWAY!
LOOKS LIKE THEY CAUGHT A THERMAL ALREADY!

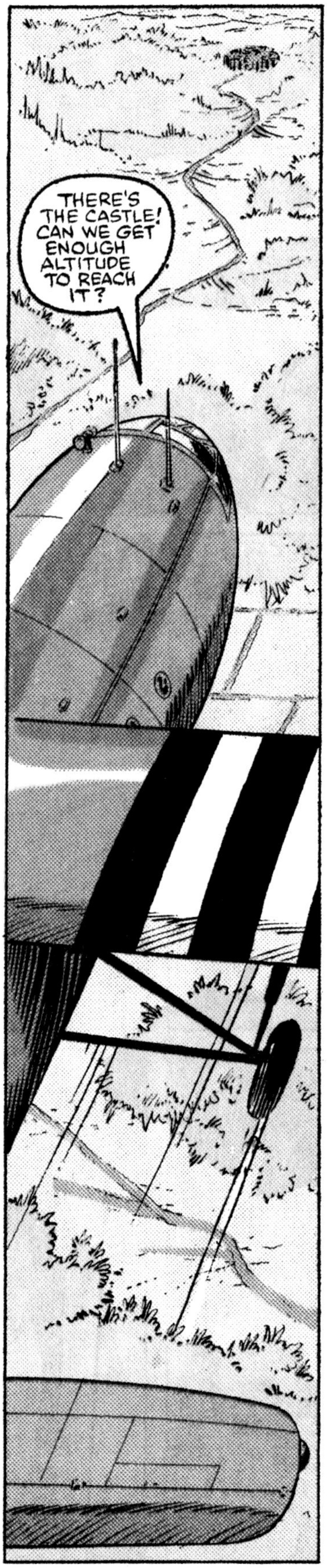
THERE'S THE CASTLE! CAN WE GET ENOUGH ALTITUDE TO REACH IT?

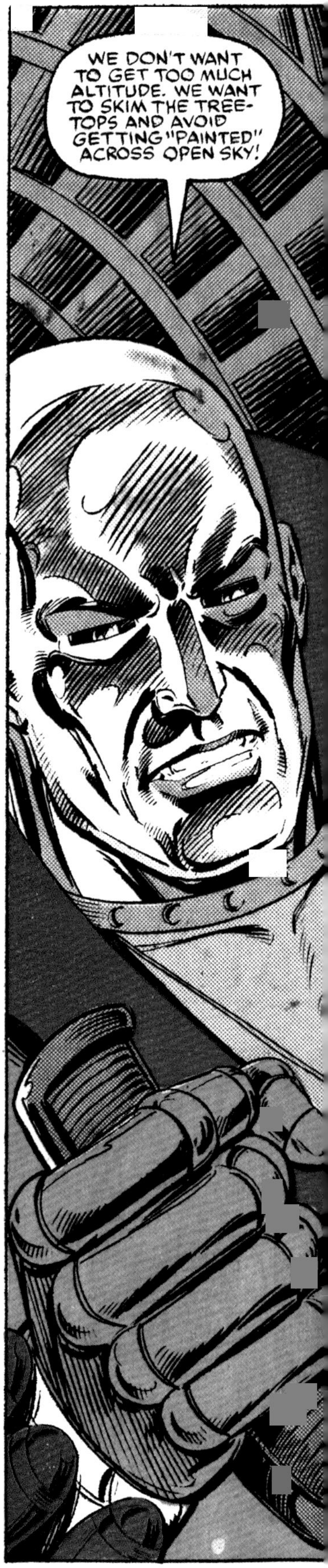
WE DON'T WANT TO GET TOO MUCH ALTITUDE. WE WANT TO SKIM THE TREE-TOPS AND AVOID GETTING "PAINTED" ACROSS OPEN SKY!

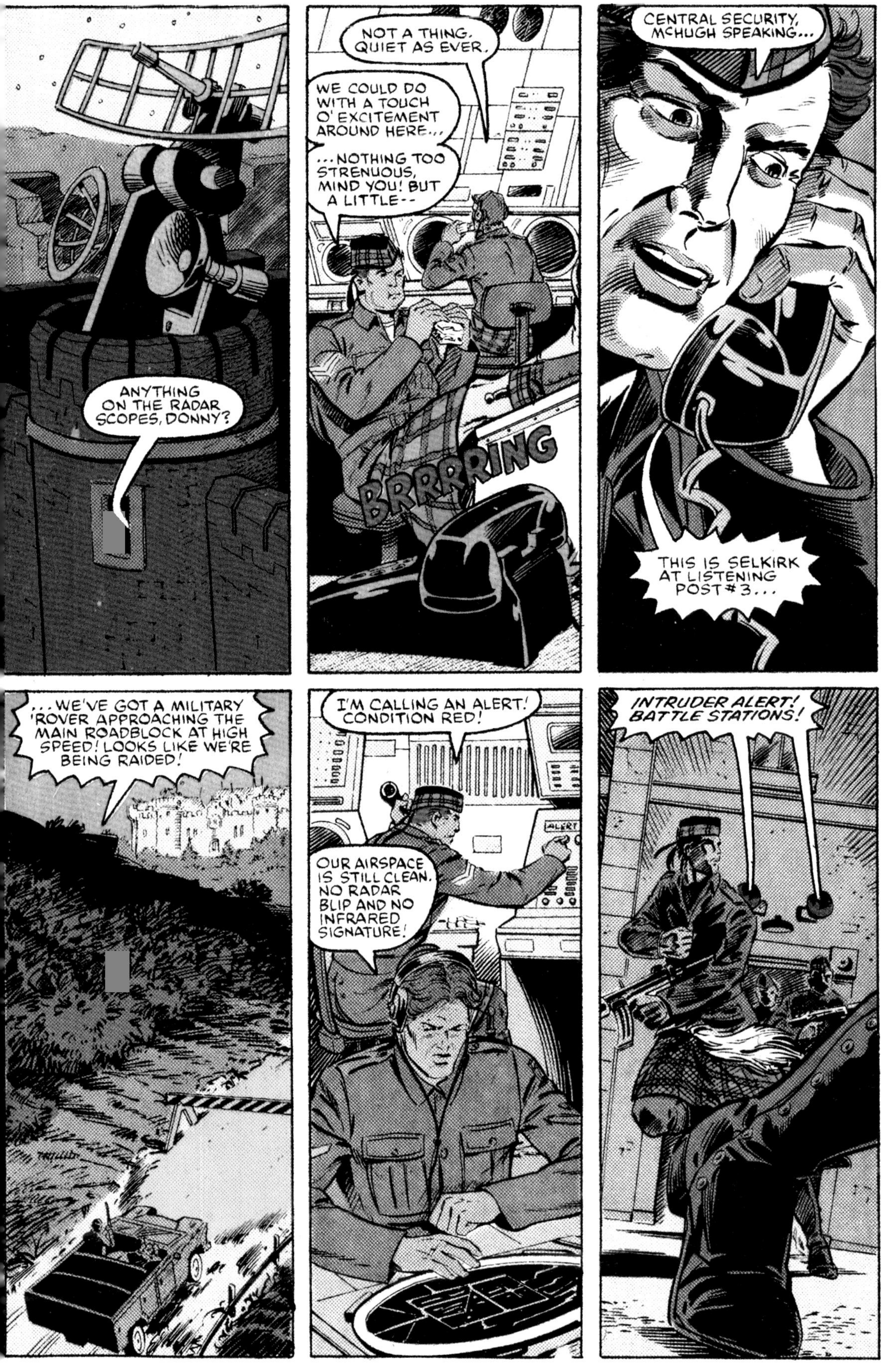

ANYTHING ON THE RADAR SCOPES, DONNY?
NOT A THING. QUIET AS EVER.
WE COULD DO WITH A TOUCH O' EXCITEMENT AROUND HERE...
...NOTHING TOO STRENUOUS, MIND YOU! BUT A LITTLE--
BRRRRING
CENTRAL SECURITY, McHUGH SPEAKING...
THIS IS SELKIRK AT LISTENING POST #3...
...WE'VE GOT A MILITARY 'ROVER APPROACHING THE MAIN ROADBLOCK AT HIGH SPEED! LOOKS LIKE WE'RE BEING RAIDED!
I'M CALLING AN ALERT! CONDITION RED!
ALERT
OUR AIRSPACE IS STILL CLEAN. NO RADAR BLIP AND NO INFRARED SIGNATURE!
INTRUDER ALERT! BATTLE STATIONS!

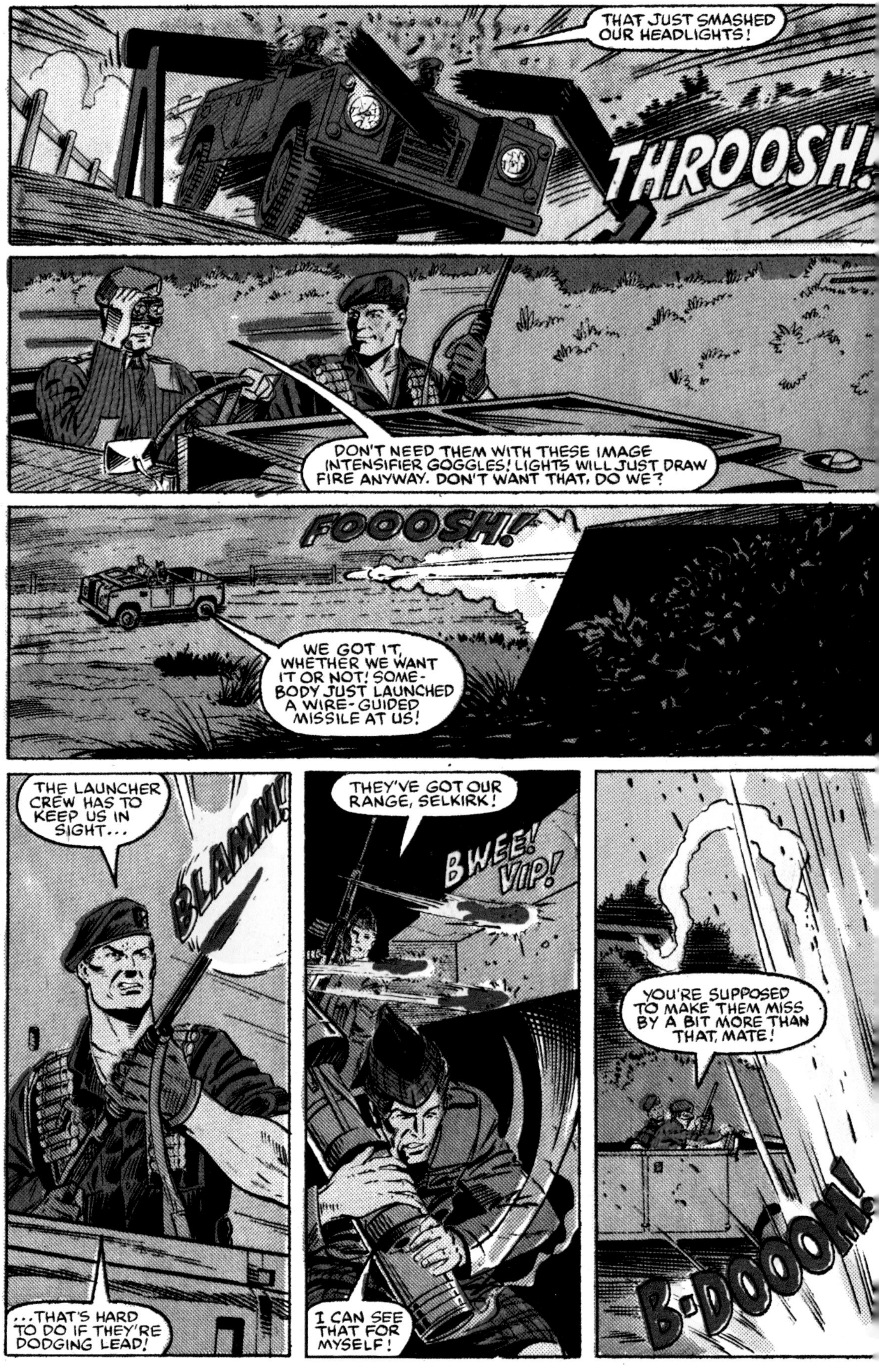

THAT JUST SMASHED OUR HEADLIGHTS!
THROOSH!
DON'T NEED THEM WITH THESE IMAGE INTENSIFIER GOGGLES! LIGHTS WILL JUST DRAW FIRE ANYWAY. DON'T WANT THAT, DO WE?
FOOOSH!
WE GOT IT, WHETHER WE WANT IT OR NOT! SOME-BODY JUST LAUNCHED A WIRE-GUIDED MISSILE AT US!
THE LAUNCHER CREW HAS TO KEEP US IN SIGHT...
BLAMM!
...THAT'S HARD TO DO IF THEY'RE DODGING LEAD!
THEY'VE GOT OUR RANGE, SELKIRK!
BWEE! VIP!
I CAN SEE THAT FOR MYSELF!
YOU'RE SUPPOSED TO MAKE THEM MISS BY A BIT MORE THAN THAT, MATE!
B-DOOOM!

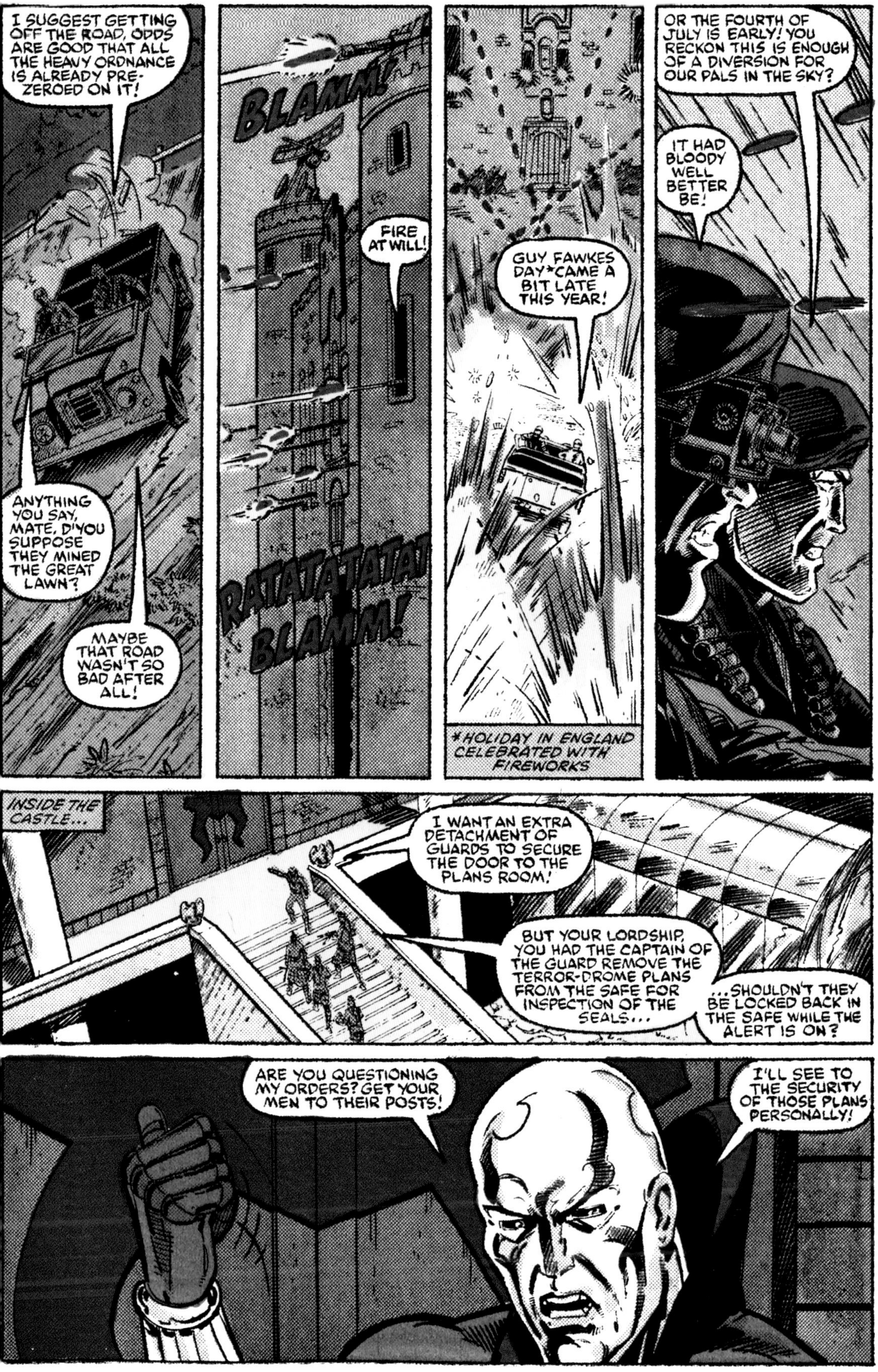

I SUGGEST GETTING OFF THE ROAD. ODDS ARE GOOD THAT ALL THE HEAVY ORDNANCE IS ALREADY PRE-ZEROED ON IT!
ANYTHING YOU SAY, MATE. D'YOU SUPPOSE THEY MINED THE GREAT LAWN?
MAYBE THAT ROAD WASN'T SO BAD AFTER ALL!
BLAMM!
FIRE AT WILL!
RATATATATAT
BLAMM!
GUY FAWKES DAY*CAME A BIT LATE THIS YEAR!
*HOLIDAY IN ENGLAND CELEBRATED WITH FIREWORKS
OR THE FOURTH OF JULY IS EARLY! YOU RECKON THIS IS ENOUGH OF A DIVERSION FOR OUR PALS IN THE SKY?
IT HAD BLOODY WELL BETTER BE!
INSIDE THE CASTLE...
I WANT AN EXTRA DETACHMENT OF GUARDS TO SECURE THE DOOR TO THE PLANS ROOM!
BUT YOUR LORDSHIP, YOU HAD THE CAPTAIN OF THE GUARD REMOVE THE TERROR-DROME PLANS FROM THE SAFE FOR INSPECTION OF THE SEALS...
...SHOULDN'T THEY BE LOCKED BACK IN THE SAFE WHILE THE ALERT IS ON?
ARE YOU QUESTIONING MY ORDERS? GET YOUR MEN TO THEIR POSTS!
I'LL SEE TO THE SECURITY OF THOSE PLANS PERSONALLY!

WE'D BETTER DO SOMETHING FAST! THEY'RE BRACKETING FLINT AND DAY PRETTY CLOSE!

CAN YOU SPOT A CLEAR SPOT TO LAND INSIDE THE CASTLE WALLS?

THERE ISN'T A PLAUSIBLE LANDING SITE ON THOSE GROUNDS! DESTRO MUST HAVE KNOWN THAT! WHAT WAS THE USE OF STEALING THIS GLIDER?

I NEVER SAID I WAS GOING TO LAND INSIDE THE CASTLE GROUNDS...

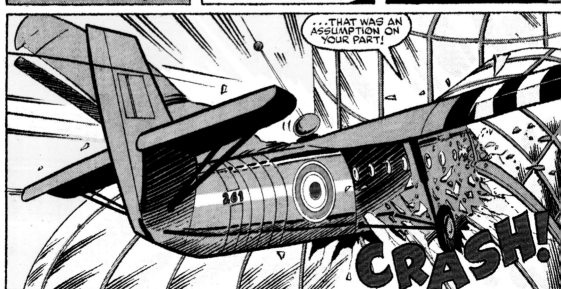

...THAT WAS AN ASSUMPTION ON YOUR PART!

CRASH!

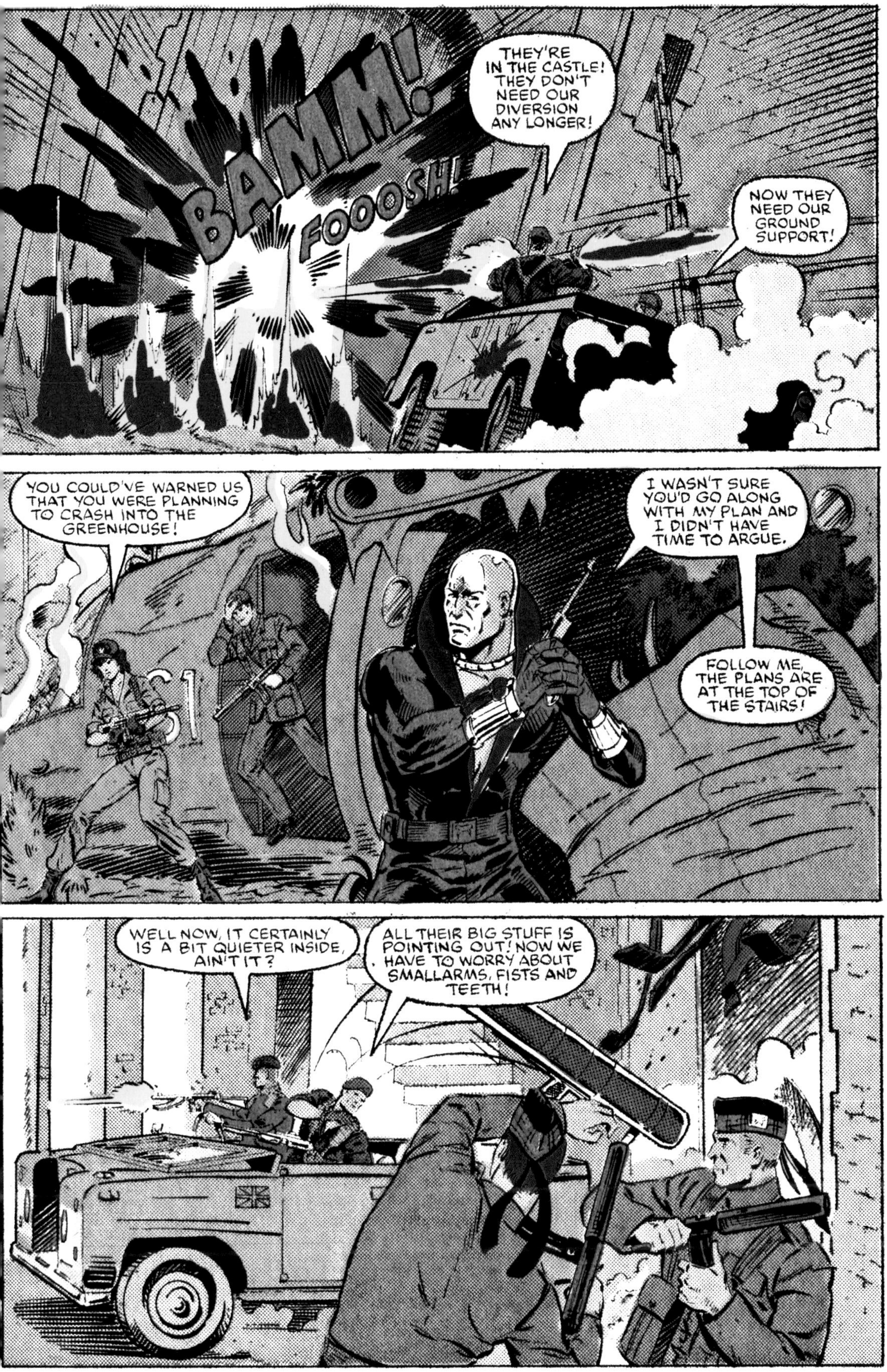
BAMM!
FOOOSH!
THEY'RE IN THE CASTLE! THEY DON'T NEED OUR DIVERSION ANY LONGER!
NOW THEY NEED OUR GROUND SUPPORT!
YOU COULD'VE WARNED US THAT YOU WERE PLANNING TO CRASH INTO THE GREENHOUSE!
I WASN'T SURE YOU'D GO ALONG WITH MY PLAN AND I DIDN'T HAVE TIME TO ARGUE.
FOLLOW ME, THE PLANS ARE AT THE TOP OF THE STAIRS!
WELL NOW, IT CERTAINLY IS A BIT QUIETER INSIDE, AIN'T IT?
ALL THEIR BIG STUFF IS POINTING OUT! NOW WE HAVE TO WORRY ABOUT SMALLARMS, FISTS AND TEETH!

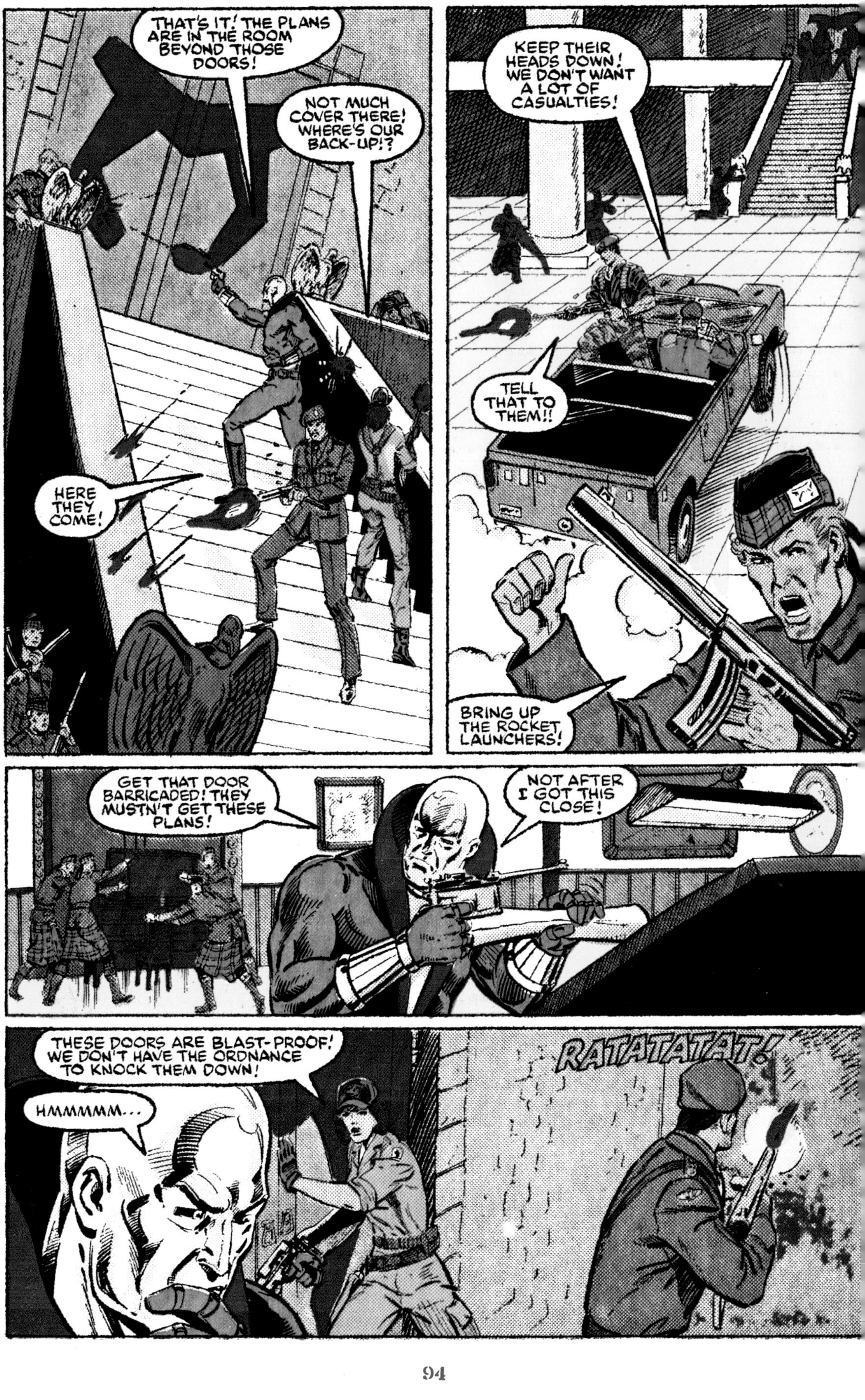

THAT'S IT! THE PLANS ARE IN THE ROOM BEYOND THOSE DOORS!
NOT MUCH COVER THERE! WHERE'S OUR BACK-UP!?
HERE THEY COME!
KEEP THEIR HEADS DOWN! WE DON'T WANT A LOT OF CASUALTIES!
TELL THAT TO THEM!!
BRING UP THE ROCKET LAUNCHERS!
GET THAT DOOR BARRICADED! THEY MUSTN'T GET THESE PLANS!
NOT AFTER I GOT THIS CLOSE!
THESE DOORS ARE BLAST-PROOF! WE DON'T HAVE THE ORDNANCE TO KNOCK THEM DOWN!
HMMMMM...
RATATATAT!

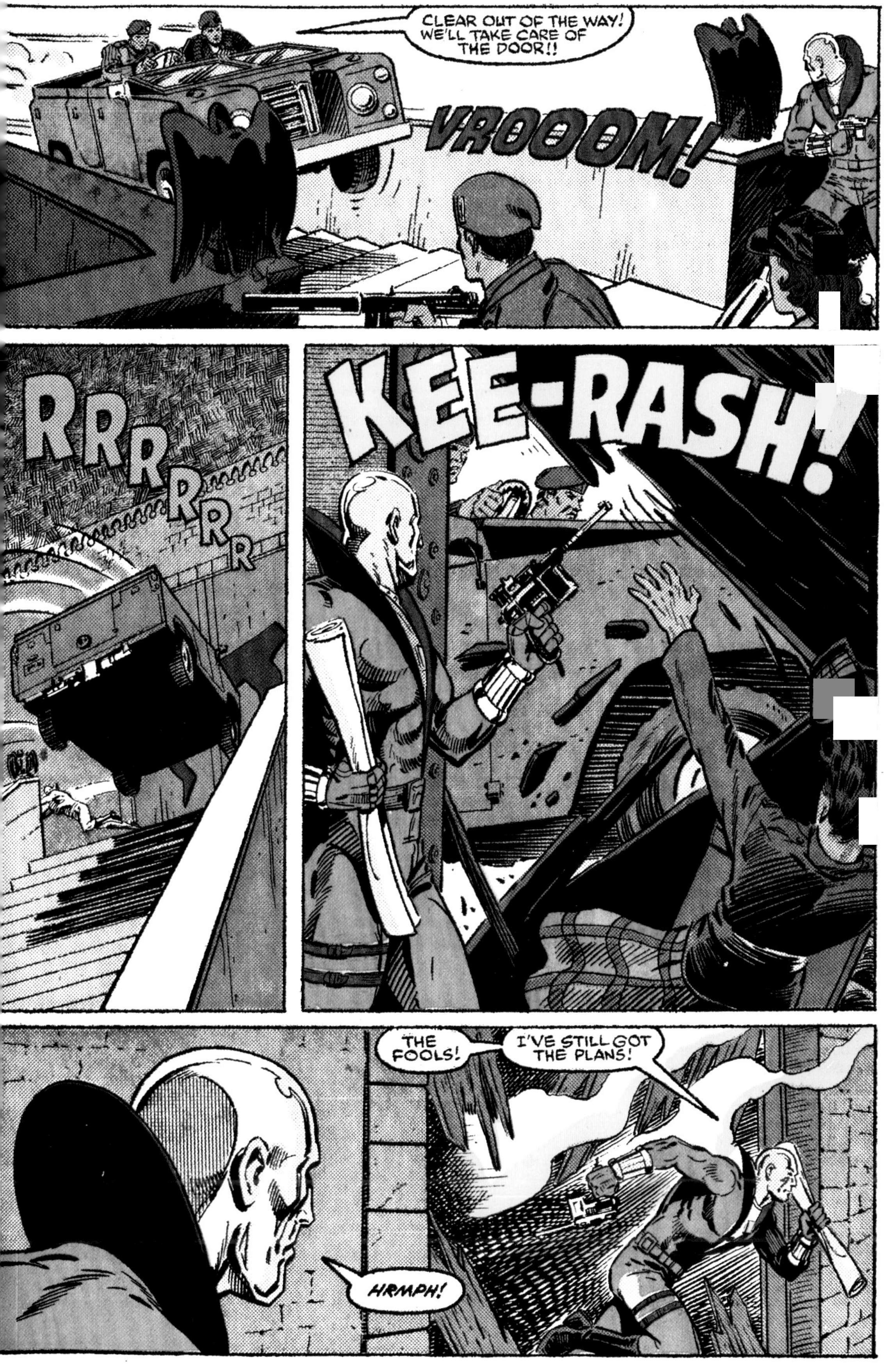
CLEAR OUT OF THE WAY! WE'LL TAKE CARE OF THE DOOR!!
VROOOM!
RRRRRRR
KEE-RASH!
THE FOOLS!
I'VE STILL GOT THE PLANS!
HRMPH!

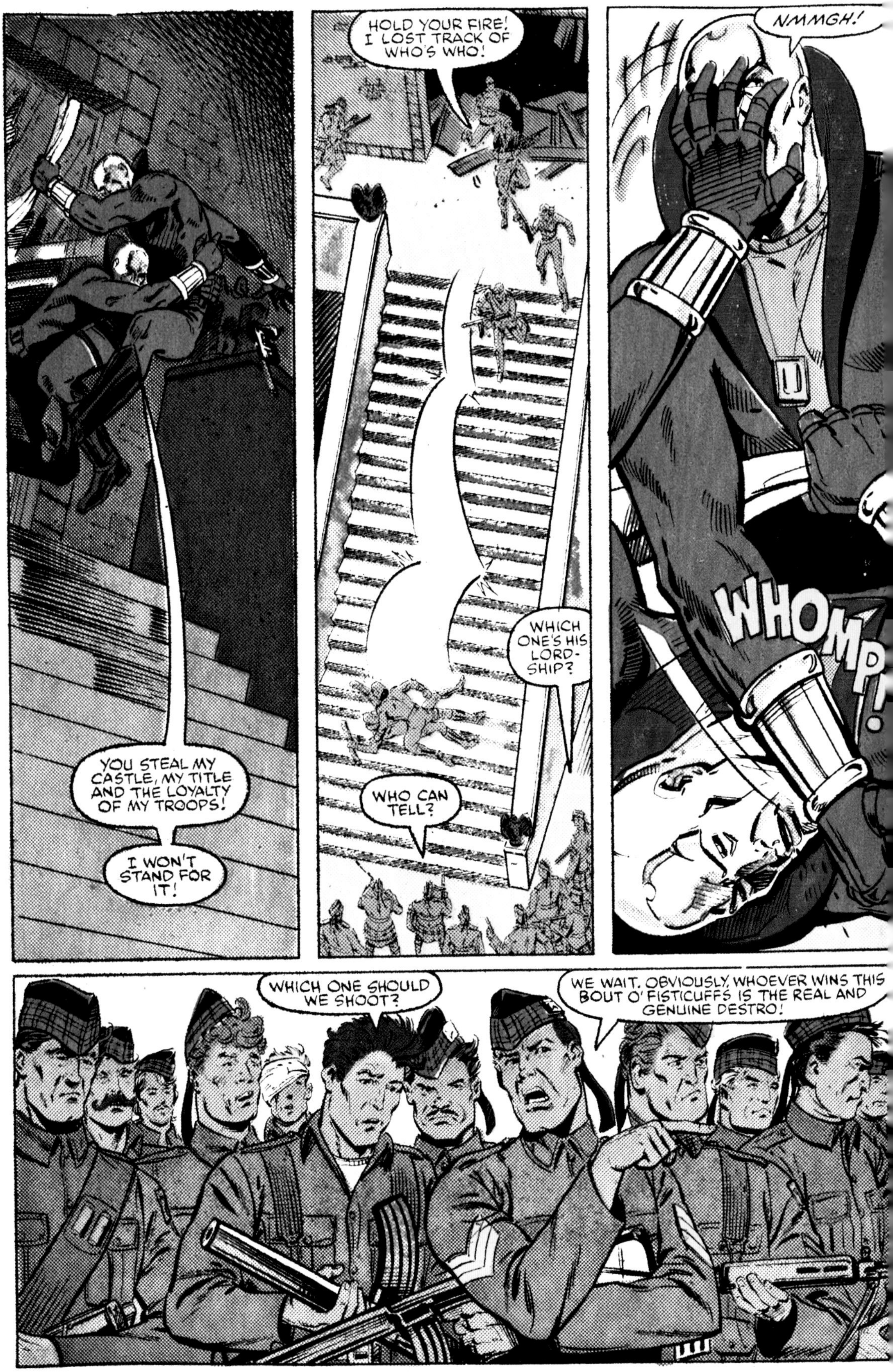

YOU STEAL MY CASTLE, MY TITLE AND THE LOYALTY OF MY TROOPS!
I WON'T STAND FOR IT!
HOLD YOUR FIRE! I LOST TRACK OF WHO'S WHO!
WHICH ONE'S HIS LORDSHIP?
WHO CAN TELL?
NMMGH!
WHOMP!
WHICH ONE SHOULD WE SHOOT?
WE WAIT. OBVIOUSLY, WHOEVER WINS THIS BOUT O' FISTICUFFS IS THE REAL AND GENUINE DESTRO!

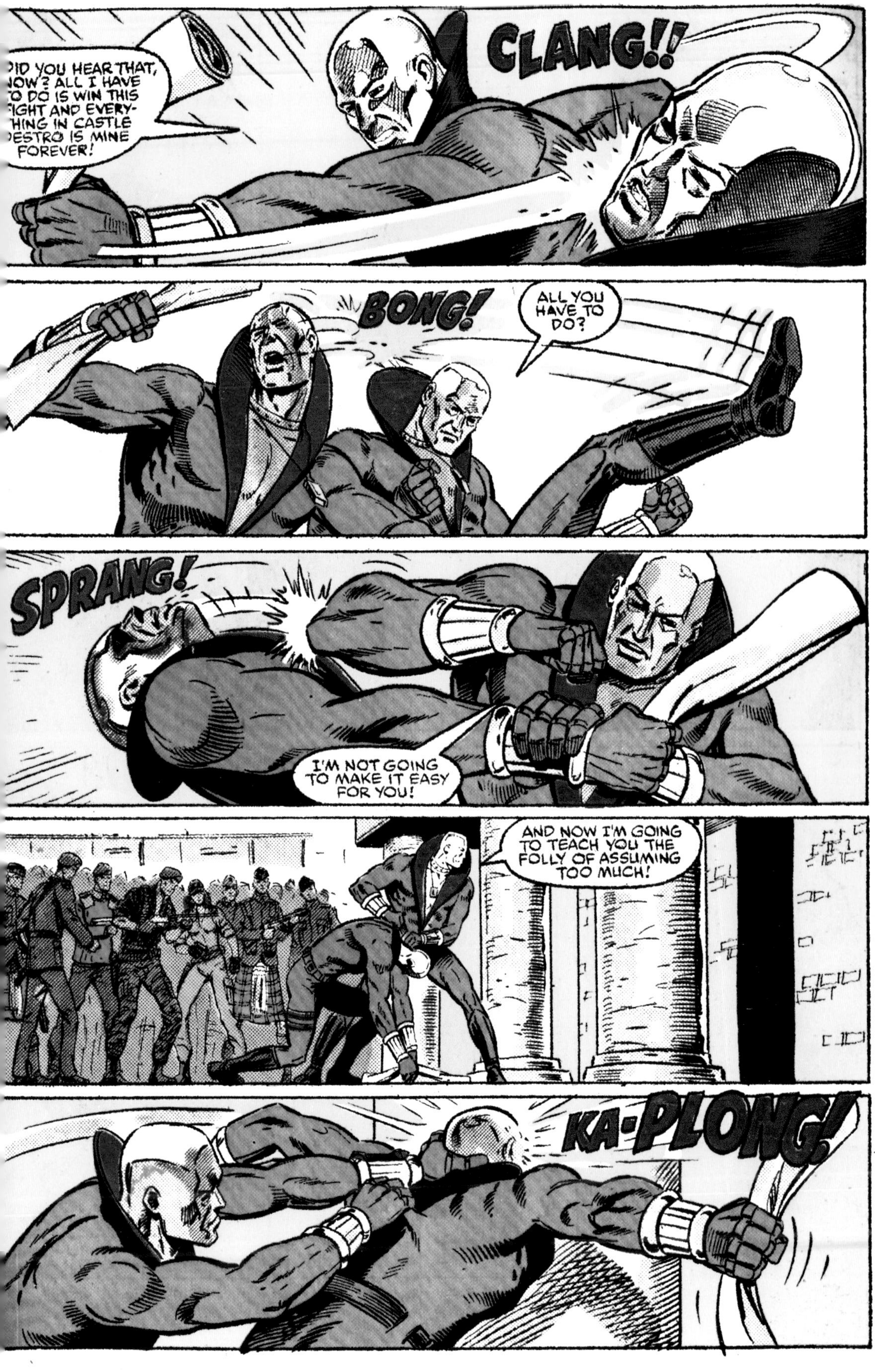
DID YOU HEAR THAT, NOW? ALL I HAVE TO DO IS WIN THIS FIGHT AND EVERYTHING IN CASTLE DESTRO IS MINE FOREVER!
CLANG!!
BONG!
ALL YOU HAVE TO DO?
SPRANG!
I'M NOT GOING TO MAKE IT EASY FOR YOU!
AND NOW I'M GOING TO TEACH YOU THE FOLLY OF ASSUMING TOO MUCH!
KA-PLONG!

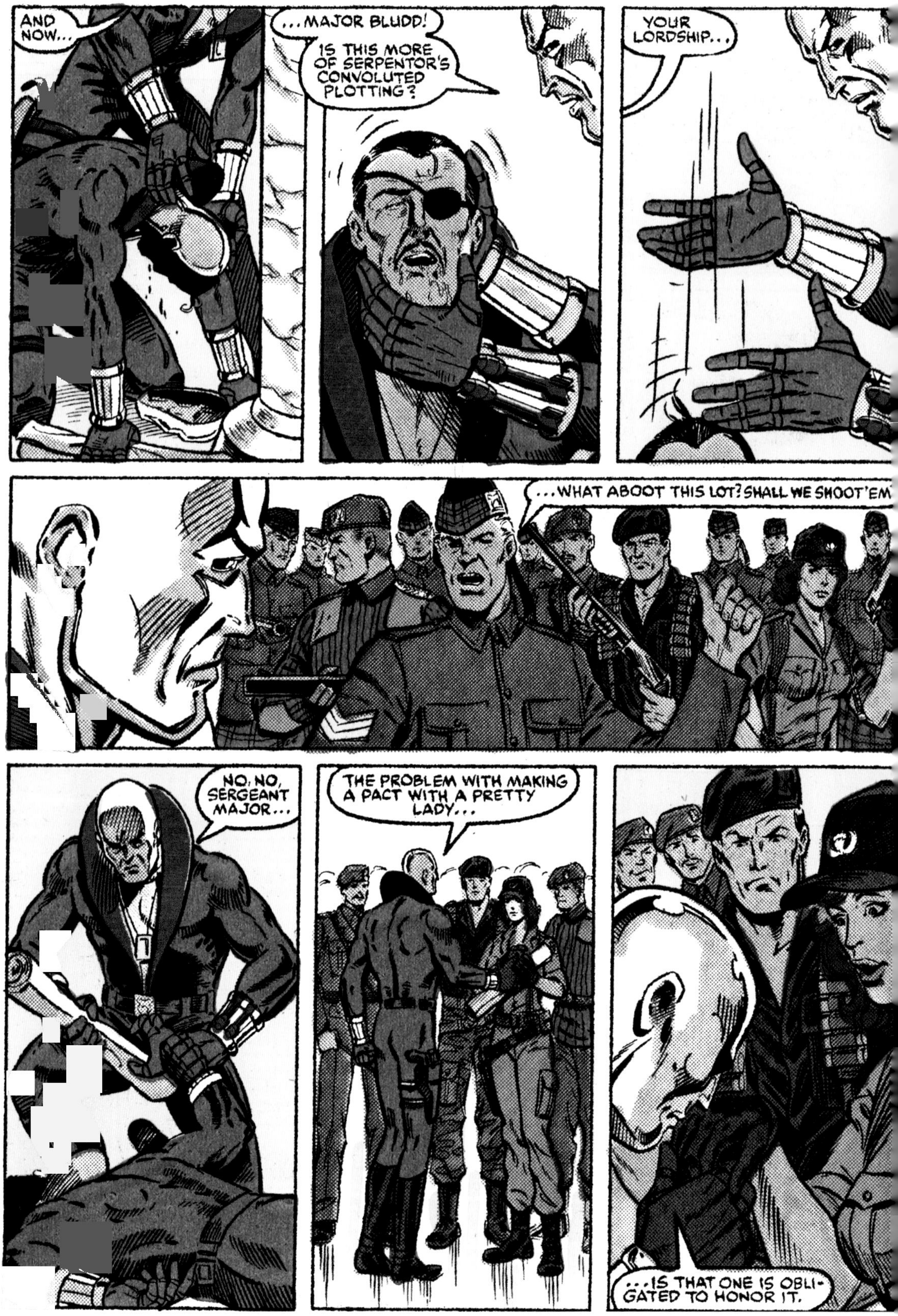
AND NOW...
...MAJOR BLUDD!
IS THIS MORE OF SERPENTOR'S CONVOLUTED PLOTTING?
YOUR LORDSHIP...
...WHAT ABOOT THIS LOT? SHALL WE SHOOT 'EM
NO, NO, SERGEANT MAJOR...
THE PROBLEM WITH MAKING A PACT WITH A PRETTY LADY...
...IS THAT ONE IS OBLIGATED TO HONOR IT.

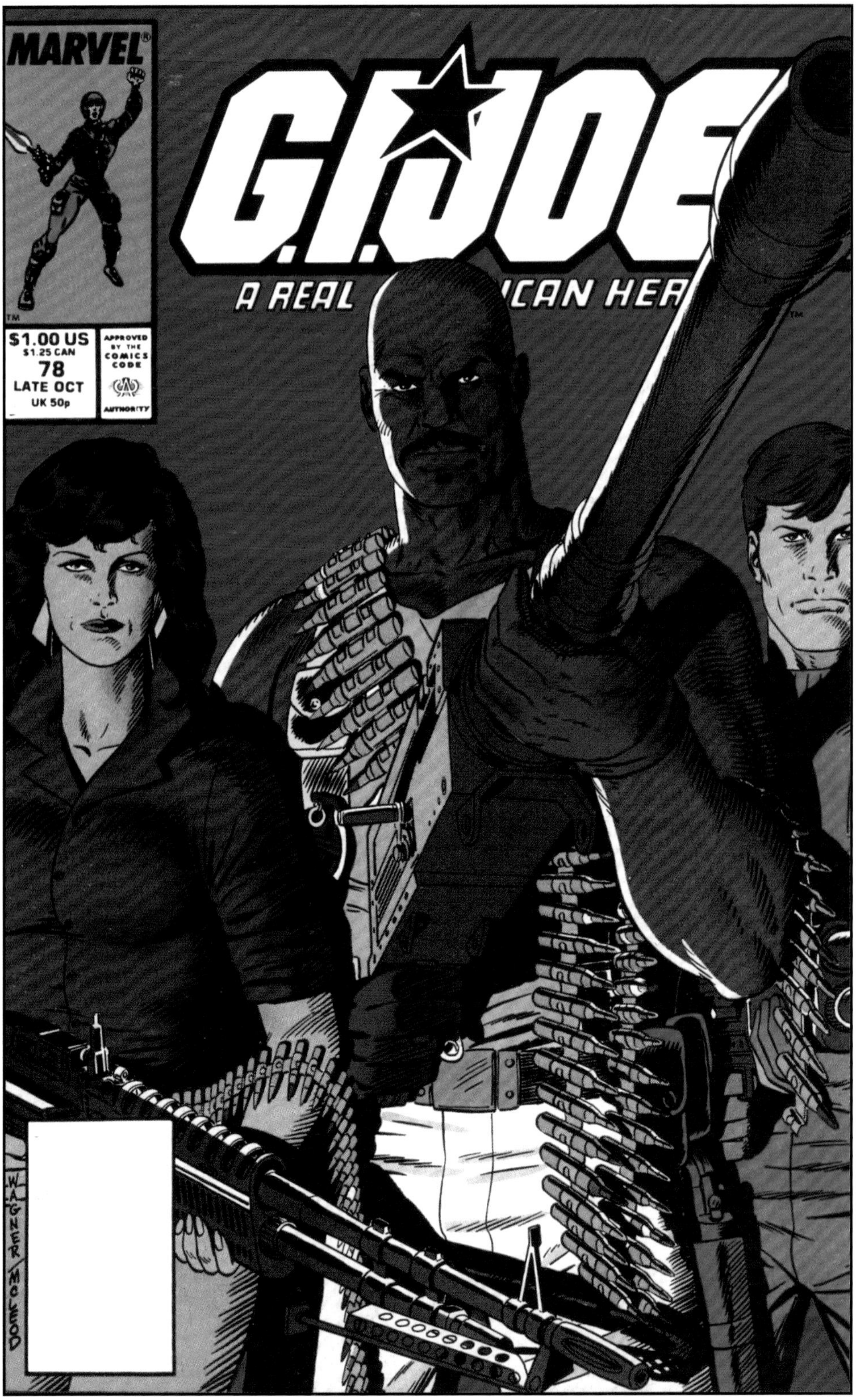
MARVEL
G.I. JOE
A REAL ICAN HER
$1.00 US
$1.25 CAN
78
LATE OCT
UK 50p
APPROVED BY THE COMICS CODE AUTHORITY
WAGNER McLEOD

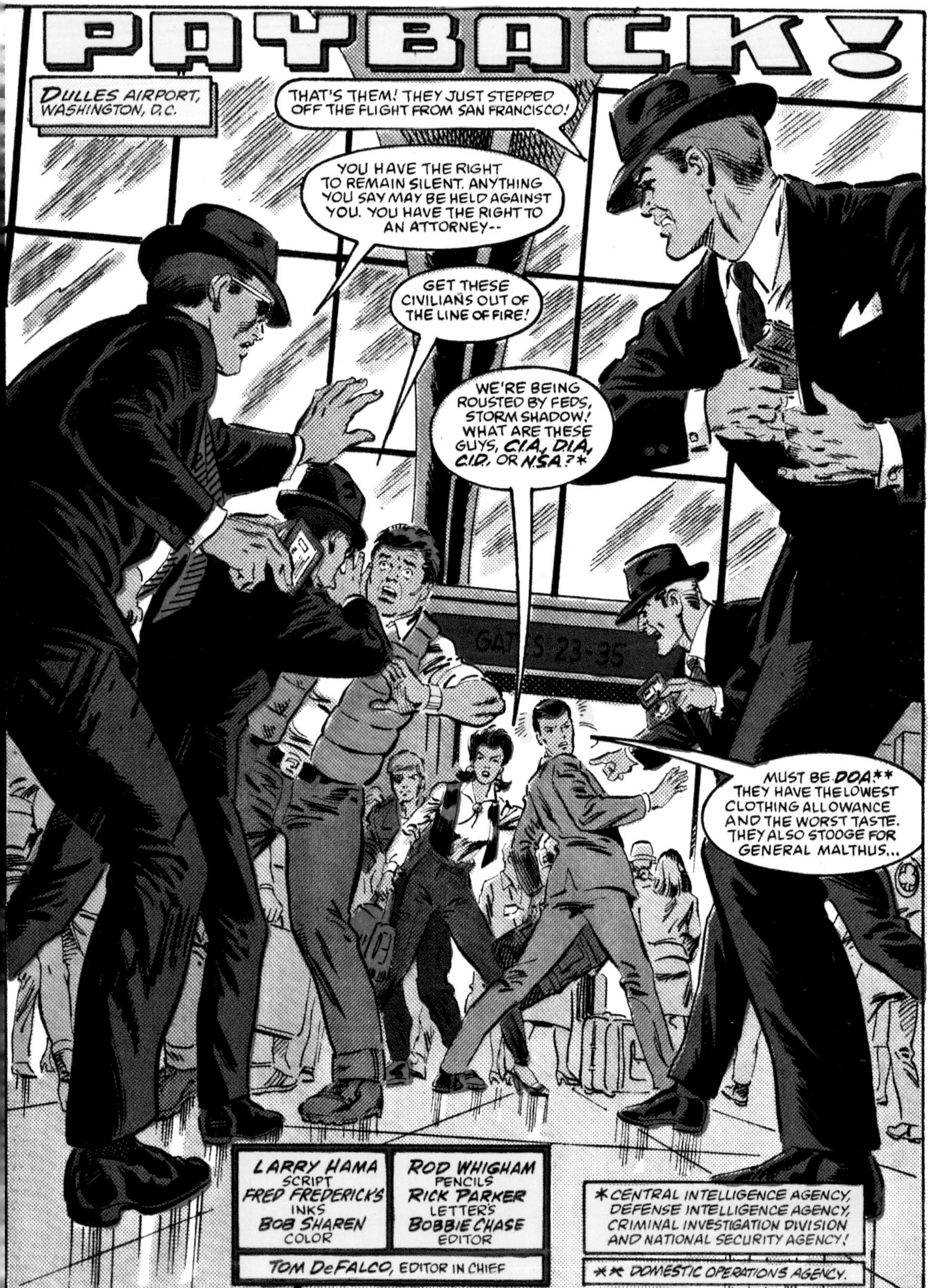
PAYBACK!
DULLES AIRPORT, WASHINGTON, D.C.
THAT'S THEM! THEY JUST STEPPED OFF THE FLIGHT FROM SAN FRANCISCO!
YOU HAVE THE RIGHT TO REMAIN SILENT. ANYTHING YOU SAY MAY BE HELD AGAINST YOU. YOU HAVE THE RIGHT TO AN ATTORNEY--
GET THESE CIVILIANS OUT OF THE LINE OF FIRE!
WE'RE BEING ROUSTED BY FEDS, STORM SHADOW! WHAT ARE THESE GUYS, C.I.A., D.I.A., C.I.D. OR N.S.A.?*
GATES 23-35
MUST BE DOA** THEY HAVE THE LOWEST CLOTHING ALLOWANCE AND THE WORST TASTE. THEY ALSO STOOGE FOR GENERAL MALTHUS...
LARRY HAMA SCRIPT
FRED FREDERICKS INKS
BOB SHAREN COLOR
ROD WHIGHAM PENCILS
RICK PARKER LETTERS
BOBBIE CHASE EDITOR
TOM DeFALCO, EDITOR IN CHIEF
*CENTRAL INTELLIGENCE AGENCY, DEFENSE INTELLIGENCE AGENCY, CRIMINAL INVESTIGATION DIVISION AND NATIONAL SECURITY AGENCY!
** DOMESTIC OPERATIONS AGENCY.

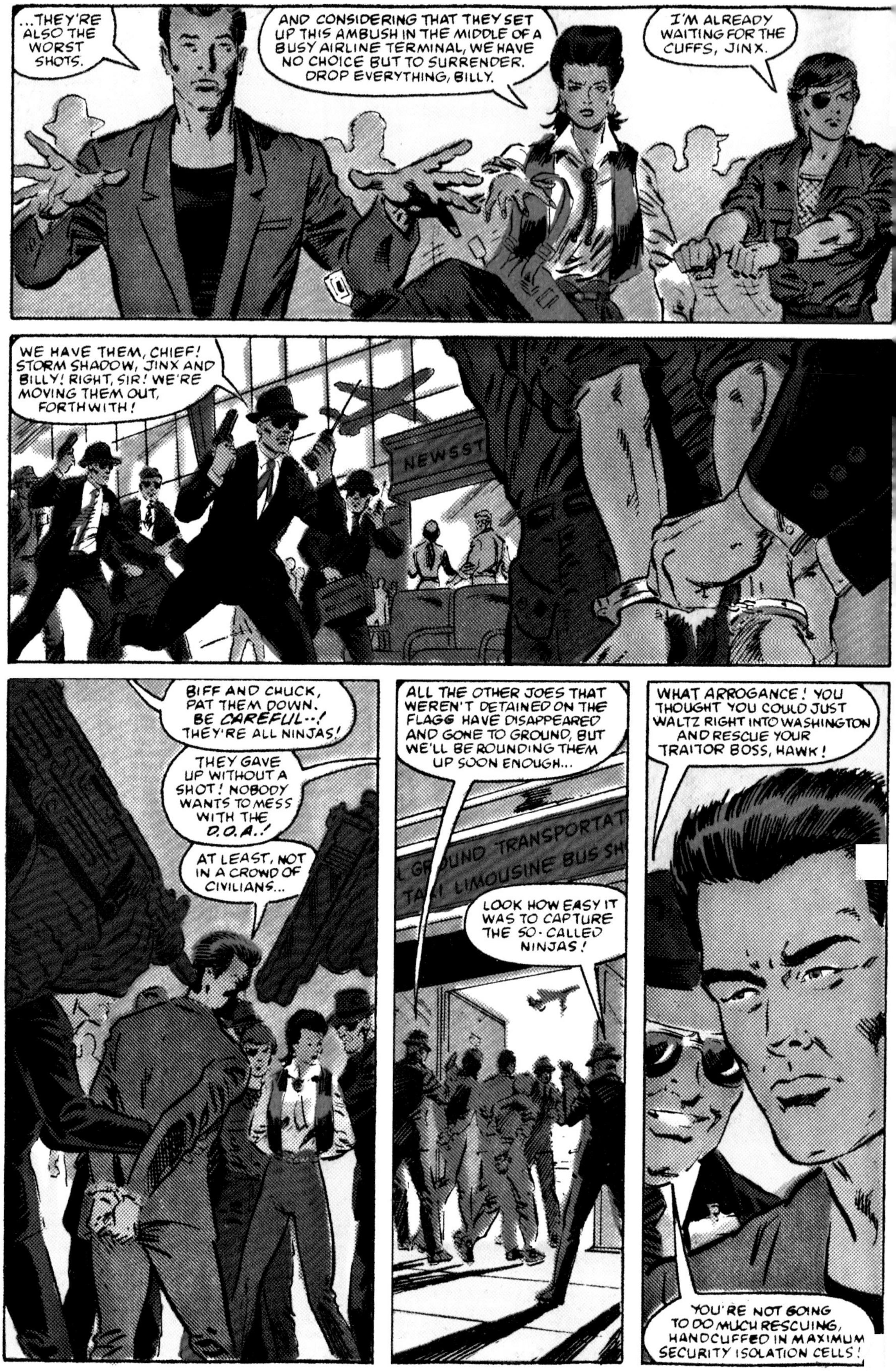
...THEY'RE ALSO THE WORST SHOTS.
AND CONSIDERING THAT THEY SET UP THIS AMBUSH IN THE MIDDLE OF A BUSY AIRLINE TERMINAL, WE HAVE NO CHOICE BUT TO SURRENDER. DROP EVERYTHING, BILLY.
I'M ALREADY WAITING FOR THE CUFFS, JINX.
WE HAVE THEM, CHIEF! STORM SHADOW, JINX AND BILLY! RIGHT, SIR! WE'RE MOVING THEM OUT, FORTHWITH!
NEWSST
BIFF AND CHUCK, PAT THEM DOWN. BE CAREFUL--! THEY'RE ALL NINJAS!
THEY GAVE UP WITHOUT A SHOT! NOBODY WANTS TO MESS WITH THE D.O.A.!
AT LEAST, NOT IN A CROWD OF CIVILIANS...
ALL THE OTHER JOES THAT WEREN'T DETAINED ON THE FLAGG HAVE DISAPPEARED AND GONE TO GROUND, BUT WE'LL BE ROUNDING THEM UP SOON ENOUGH...
GROUND TRANSPORTAT
TAXI LIMOUSINE BUS SH
LOOK HOW EASY IT WAS TO CAPTURE THE SO-CALLED NINJAS!
WHAT ARROGANCE! YOU THOUGHT YOU COULD JUST WALTZ RIGHT INTO WASHINGTON AND RESCUE YOUR TRAITOR BOSS, HAWK!
YOU'RE NOT GOING TO DO MUCH RESCUING, HANDCUFFED IN MAXIMUM SECURITY ISOLATION CELLS!

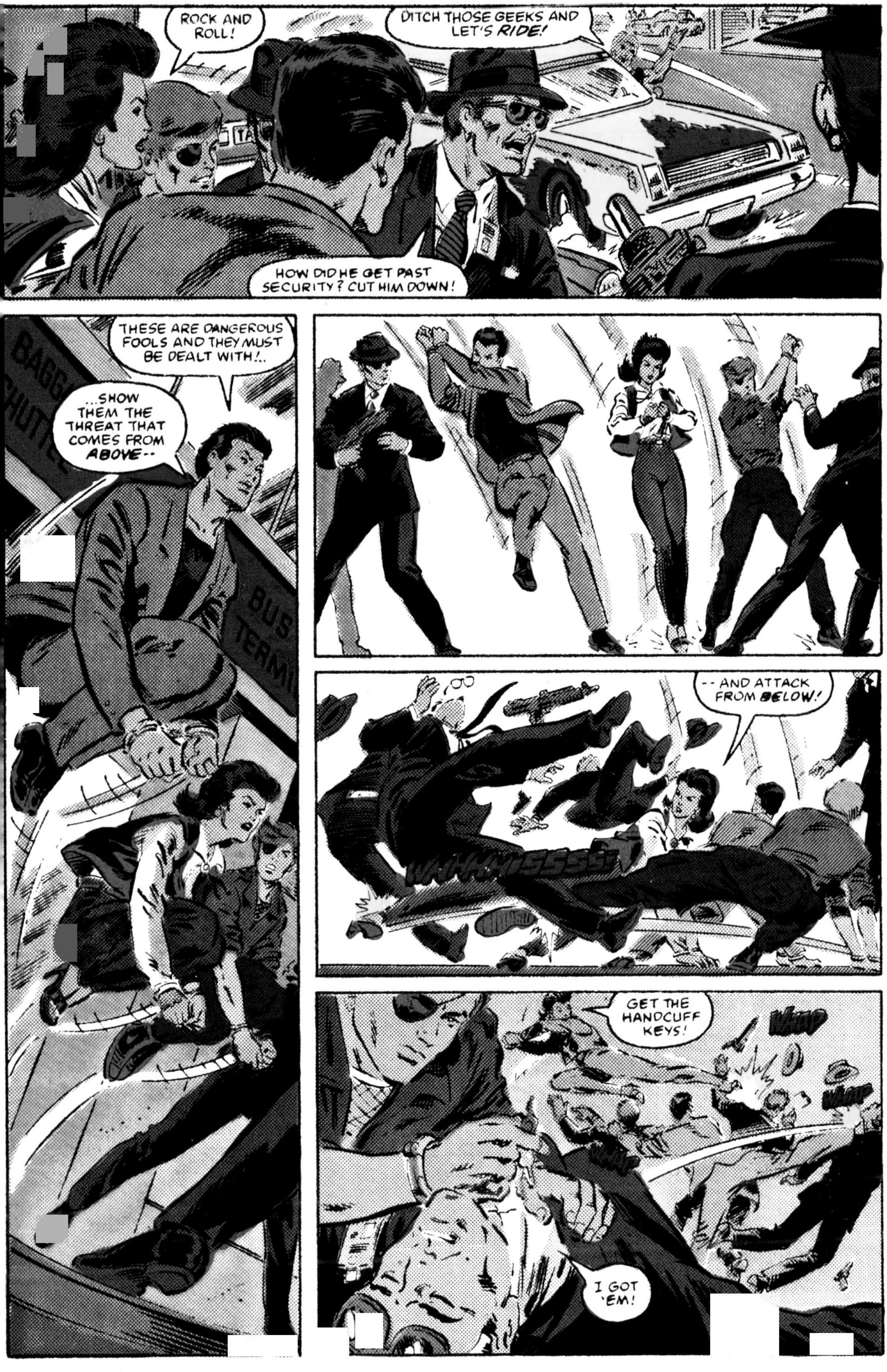

ROCK AND ROLL!
DITCH THOSE GEEKS AND LET'S RIDE!
HOW DID HE GET PAST SECURITY? CUT HIM DOWN!
THESE ARE DANGEROUS FOOLS AND THEY MUST BE DEALT WITH!..
...SHOW THEM THE THREAT THAT COMES FROM ABOVE--
--AND ATTACK FROM BELOW!
GET THE HANDCUFF KEYS!
WHAP
WHAP
I GOT 'EM!

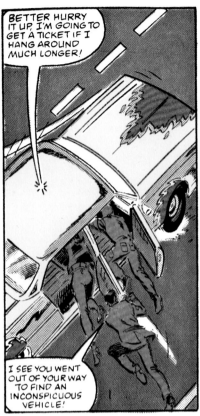

BETTER HURRY IT UP, I'M GOING TO GET A TICKET IF I HANG AROUND MUCH LONGER!

I SEE YOU WENT OUT OF YOUR WAY TO FIND AN INCONSPICUOUS VEHICLE!

WHAT? YOU DON'T LIKE THIS PAINT JOB?

BLOCK THE EXITS! CALL IN FOR MORE BACKUP AND GET THAT CHOPPER TO COVER THE MAIN HIGHWAYS!

SKY-WATCHER-ONE, THIS IS GROUNDLING. YOUR TARGET IS A YELLOW, LATE MODEL CHEVY WITH RED FLAMES ON HOOD AND FENDERS. SUBJECTS ARE DANGEROUS. YOU HAVE AN OPEN SANCTION...

YOU LOST THEM! I'M GOING TO HAVE YOU KNOCKED BACK TO A GS-NOTHING OVER THIS! GENERAL MALTHUS IS GOING TO BE ABSOLUTELY... LIVID!

OH, LIGHTEN UP, WILL YOU? A BRIGHT YELLOW CHEVY WITH RED FLAMES ISN'T THE EASIEST THING IN THE WORLD TO HIDE IN BROAD DAYLIGHT!

THANK YOU. I FEEL MUCH CALMER NOW.

THIS IS NO TIME TO GET THE CAR WASHED, ROCK & ROLL!

CAN'T THINK OF A BETTER TIME!

HEY! THAT'LL BE $4.98 PLUS TAX... AND THAT'S WITHOUT THE HOT WAX!

CAR WASH

SKREEEE

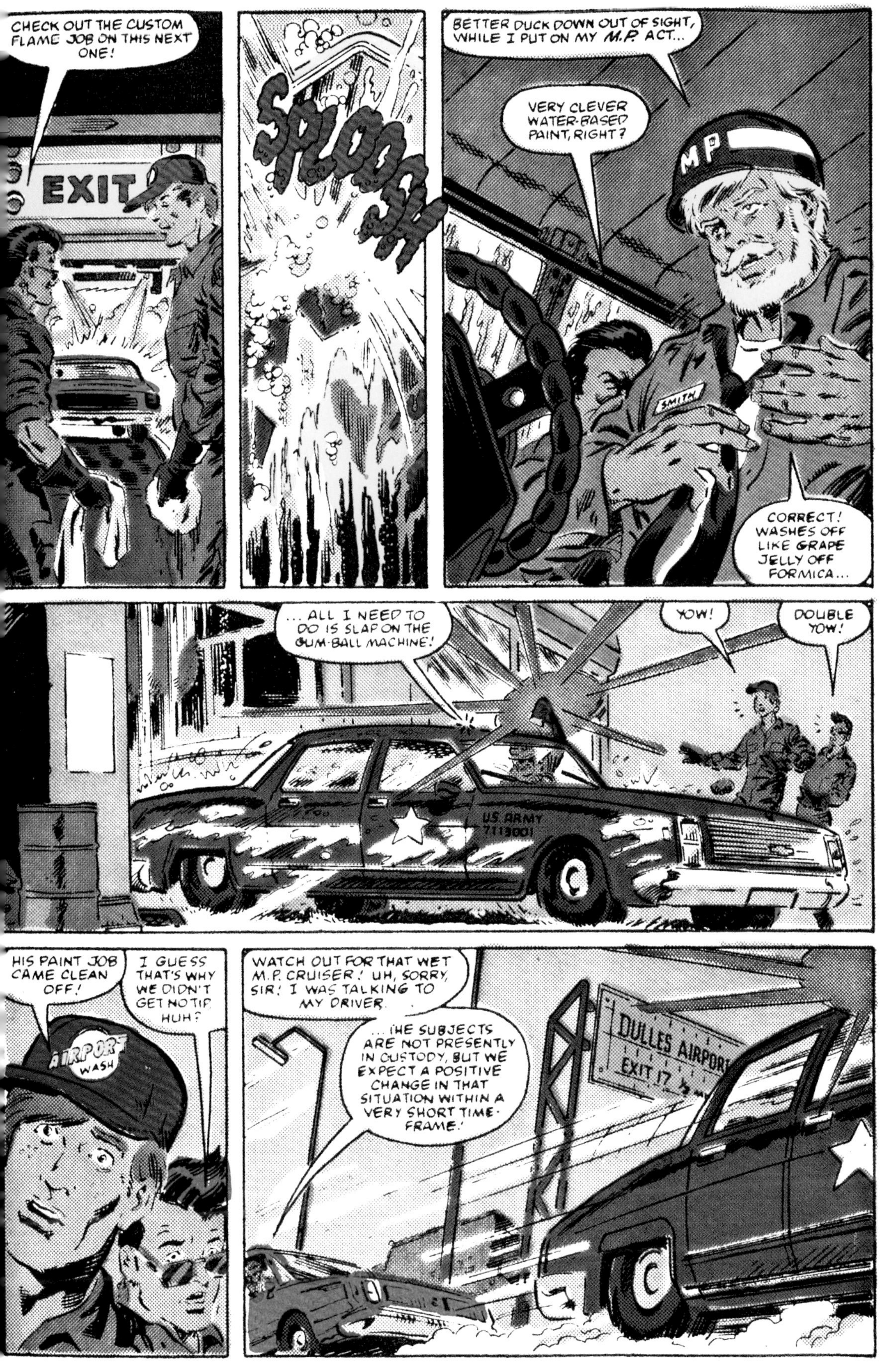
CHECK OUT THE CUSTOM FLAME JOB ON THIS NEXT ONE!
EXIT
SPLOOOSH
BETTER DUCK DOWN OUT OF SIGHT, WHILE I PUT ON MY M.P. ACT...
VERY CLEVER WATER-BASED PAINT, RIGHT?
MP
SMITH
CORRECT! WASHES OFF LIKE GRAPE JELLY OFF FORMICA...
...ALL I NEED TO DO IS SLAP ON THE GUM-BALL MACHINE!
YOW!
DOUBLE YOW!
U.S. ARMY 7113001
HIS PAINT JOB CAME CLEAN OFF!
I GUESS THAT'S WHY WE DIDN'T GET NO TIP, HUH?
AIRPORT WASH
WATCH OUT FOR THAT WET M.P. CRUISER! UH, SORRY, SIR! I WAS TALKING TO MY DRIVER.
...THE SUBJECTS ARE NOT PRESENTLY IN CUSTODY, BUT WE EXPECT A POSITIVE CHANGE IN THAT SITUATION WITHIN A VERY SHORT TIME-FRAME!
DULLES AIRPORT
EXIT 17

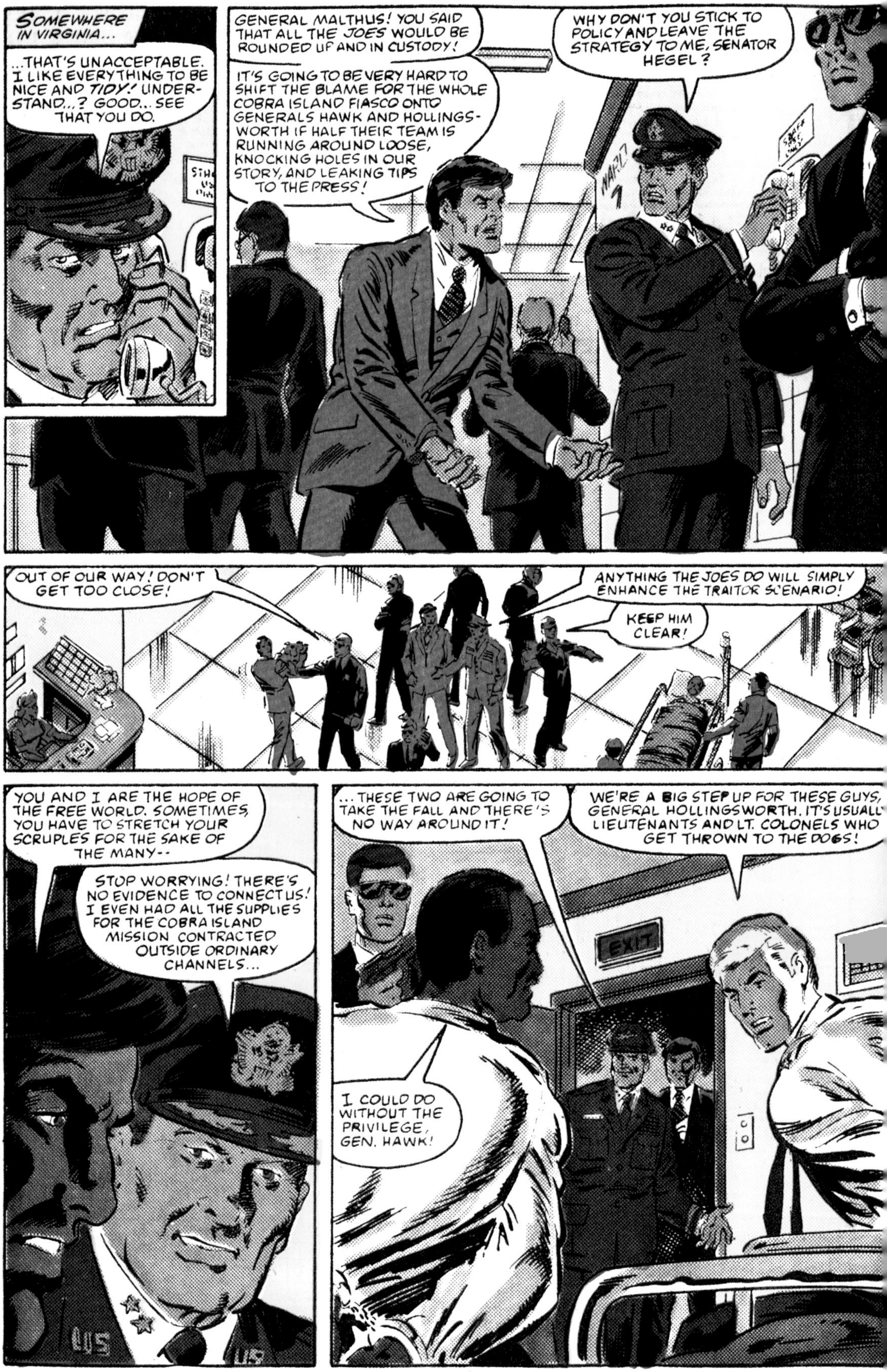
SOMEWHERE IN VIRGINIA...
...THAT'S UNACCEPTABLE. I LIKE EVERYTHING TO BE NICE AND TIDY! UNDERSTAND...? GOOD... SEE THAT YOU DO.
GENERAL MALTHUS! YOU SAID THAT ALL THE JOES WOULD BE ROUNDED UP AND IN CUSTODY!
IT'S GOING TO BE VERY HARD TO SHIFT THE BLAME FOR THE WHOLE COBRA ISLAND FIASCO ONTO GENERALS HAWK AND HOLLINGSWORTH IF HALF THEIR TEAM IS RUNNING AROUND LOOSE, KNOCKING HOLES IN OUR STORY, AND LEAKING TIPS TO THE PRESS!
WHY DON'T YOU STICK TO POLICY AND LEAVE THE STRATEGY TO ME, SENATOR HEGEL?
OUT OF OUR WAY! DON'T GET TOO CLOSE!
ANYTHING THE JOES DO WILL SIMPLY ENHANCE THE TRAITOR SCENARIO!
KEEP HIM CLEAR!
YOU AND I ARE THE HOPE OF THE FREE WORLD. SOMETIMES, YOU HAVE TO STRETCH YOUR SCRUPLES FOR THE SAKE OF THE MANY--
STOP WORRYING! THERE'S NO EVIDENCE TO CONNECT US! I EVEN HAD ALL THE SUPPLIES FOR THE COBRA ISLAND MISSION CONTRACTED OUTSIDE ORDINARY CHANNELS...
...THESE TWO ARE GOING TO TAKE THE FALL AND THERE'S NO WAY AROUND IT!
WE'RE A BIG STEP UP FOR THESE GUYS, GENERAL HOLLINGSWORTH. IT'S USUALLY LIEUTENANTS AND LT. COLONELS WHO GET THROWN TO THE DOGS!
EXIT
I COULD DO WITHOUT THE PRIVILEGE, GEN. HAWK!

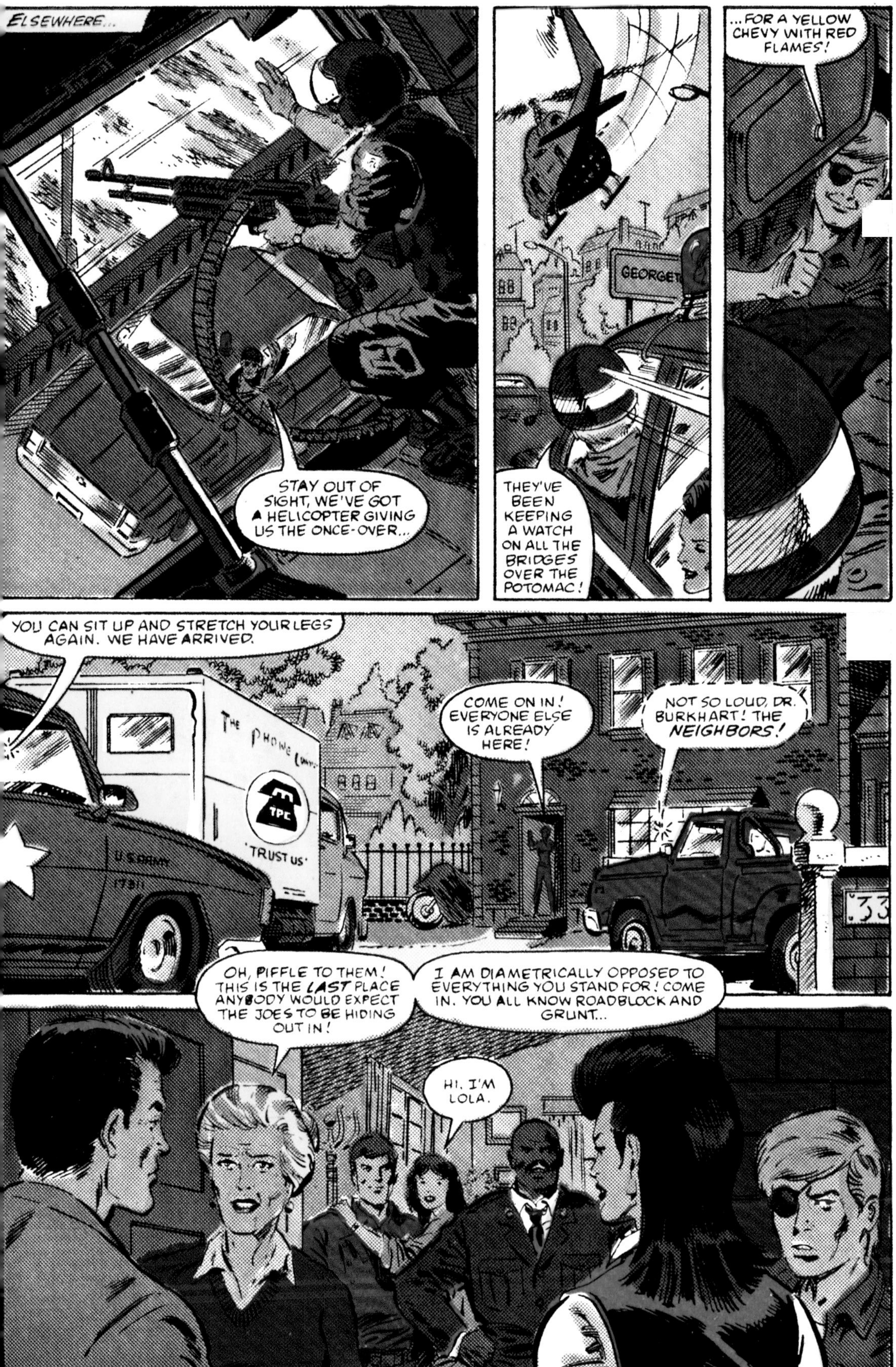
ELSEWHERE...
STAY OUT OF SIGHT, WE'VE GOT A HELICOPTER GIVING US THE ONCE-OVER...
GEORGET
THEY'VE BEEN KEEPING A WATCH ON ALL THE BRIDGES OVER THE POTOMAC!
...FOR A YELLOW CHEVY WITH RED FLAMES!
YOU CAN SIT UP AND STRETCH YOUR LEGS AGAIN. WE HAVE ARRIVED.
THE PHONE COMPANY
TPC
'TRUST US'
U.S. ARMY
17811
COME ON IN! EVERYONE ELSE IS ALREADY HERE!
NOT SO LOUD, DR. BURKHART! THE NEIGHBORS!
OH, PIFFLE TO THEM! THIS IS THE LAST PLACE ANYBODY WOULD EXPECT THE JOES TO BE HIDING OUT IN!
I AM DIAMETRICALLY OPPOSED TO EVERYTHING YOU STAND FOR! COME IN. YOU ALL KNOW ROADBLOCK AND GRUNT...
HI. I'M LOLA.

IN THE ATLANTIC...

I DON'T UNDER-STAND WHY YOU WANT TO GET INVOLVED IN THIS, DESTRO...

...ISN'T IT TO YOUR ADVANTAGE IF THE JOES GET DISCREDITED AND DISBANDED?

JUST PLOT ME A COURSE TO WASHINGTON, BARONESS. THE NEWS BROADCAST MAY EX-PLAIN MY MOTIVATIONS...

...THE JOES ACTED INDEPENDENTLY. IT WAS JUST ANOTHER EXAMPLE OF SPECIAL UNITS HAVING TOO MUCH AUTONOMY!

THE RUMORS THAT THE ORDERS FOR THE COBRA ISLAND OPERATION CAME FROM HIGHER-UPS ARE TOTALLY FALSE! THERE IS NO COVER-UP!

NEWSDAY 7

GENERAL HOLLINGSWORTH AND HAWK COOKED UP THE WHOLE PLOT AS A POWER PLAY. THEY EVEN LIED TO THE MEN IN THEIR COM-MAND, TRYING TO PIN THE BLAME ON ME AND SENATOR HEGEL!

NEWSDAY 7

GEN. MALTHUS

THAT SCABROUS POLTROON, GENERAL MALTHUS IRKS ME NO END!

SONY

IS *HE* THE REASON WE'RE GOING TO WASHINGTON?

CERTAINLY *NOT!* HAWK IS THE REASON. SOMETIMES, THE SOLDIERS YOU RESPECT THE MOST ARE ON THE WRONG SIDE!

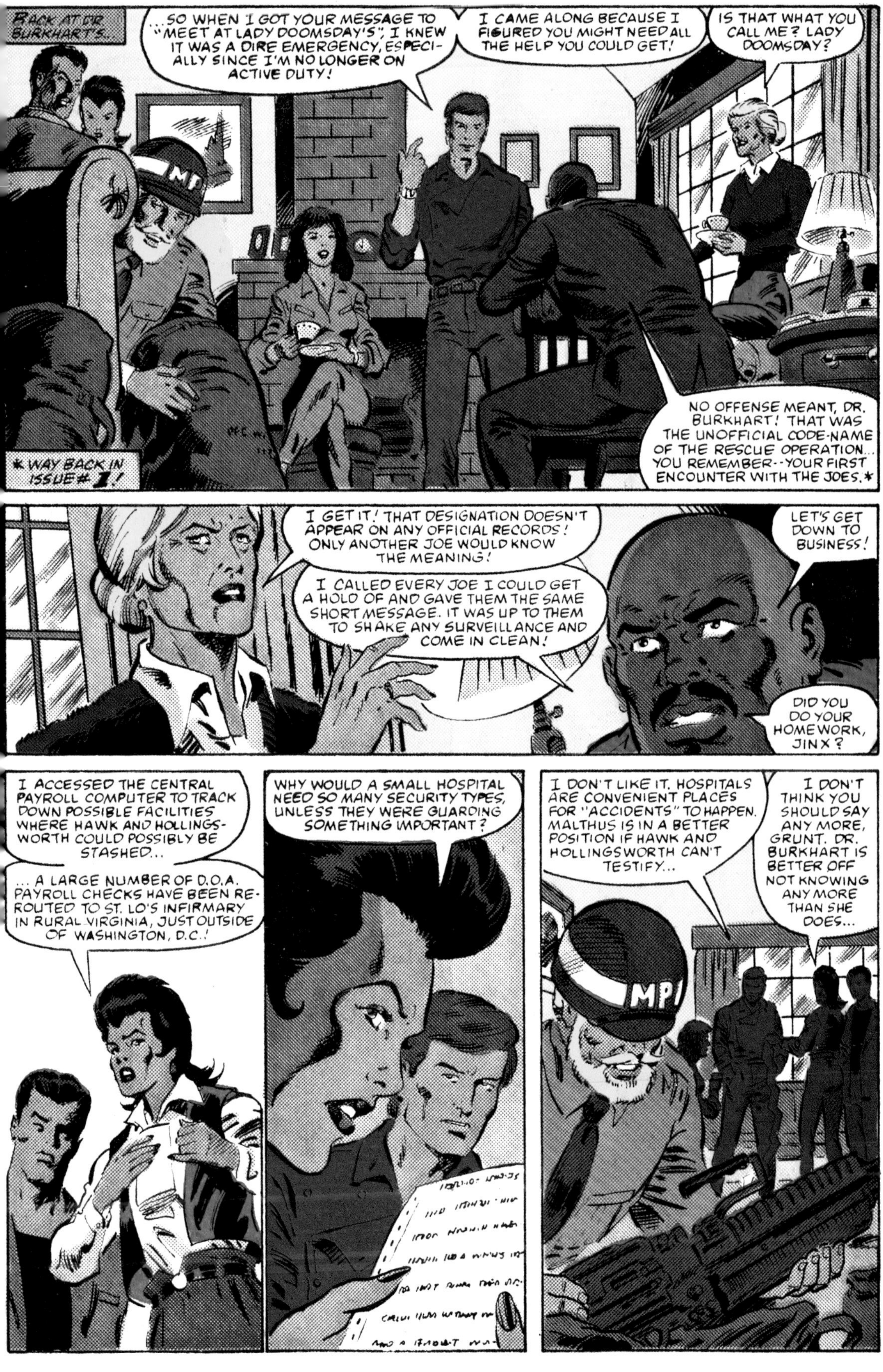
BACK AT DR. BURKHART'S...
...SO WHEN I GOT YOUR MESSAGE TO "MEET AT LADY DOOMSDAY'S", I KNEW IT WAS A DIRE EMERGENCY, ESPECIALLY SINCE I'M NO LONGER ON ACTIVE DUTY!
I CAME ALONG BECAUSE I FIGURED YOU MIGHT NEED ALL THE HELP YOU COULD GET!
IS THAT WHAT YOU CALL ME? LADY DOOMSDAY?
NO OFFENSE MEANT, DR. BURKHART! THAT WAS THE UNOFFICIAL CODE-NAME OF THE RESCUE OPERATION... YOU REMEMBER--YOUR FIRST ENCOUNTER WITH THE JOES.*
* WAY BACK IN ISSUE #1!
I GET IT! THAT DESIGNATION DOESN'T APPEAR ON ANY OFFICIAL RECORDS! ONLY ANOTHER JOE WOULD KNOW THE MEANING!
I CALLED EVERY JOE I COULD GET A HOLD OF AND GAVE THEM THE SAME SHORT MESSAGE. IT WAS UP TO THEM TO SHAKE ANY SURVEILLANCE AND COME IN CLEAN!
LET'S GET DOWN TO BUSINESS!
DID YOU DO YOUR HOMEWORK, JINX?
I ACCESSED THE CENTRAL PAYROLL COMPUTER TO TRACK DOWN POSSIBLE FACILITIES WHERE HAWK AND HOLLINGSWORTH COULD POSSIBLY BE STASHED...
... A LARGE NUMBER OF D.O.A. PAYROLL CHECKS HAVE BEEN REROUTED TO ST. LO'S INFIRMARY IN RURAL VIRGINIA, JUST OUTSIDE OF WASHINGTON, D.C.!
WHY WOULD A SMALL HOSPITAL NEED SO MANY SECURITY TYPES, UNLESS THEY WERE GUARDING SOMETHING IMPORTANT?
I DON'T LIKE IT. HOSPITALS ARE CONVENIENT PLACES FOR "ACCIDENTS" TO HAPPEN. MALTHUS IS IN A BETTER POSITION IF HAWK AND HOLLINGSWORTH CAN'T TESTIFY...
I DON'T THINK YOU SHOULD SAY ANY MORE, GRUNT. DR. BURKHART IS BETTER OFF NOT KNOWING ANY MORE THAN SHE DOES...

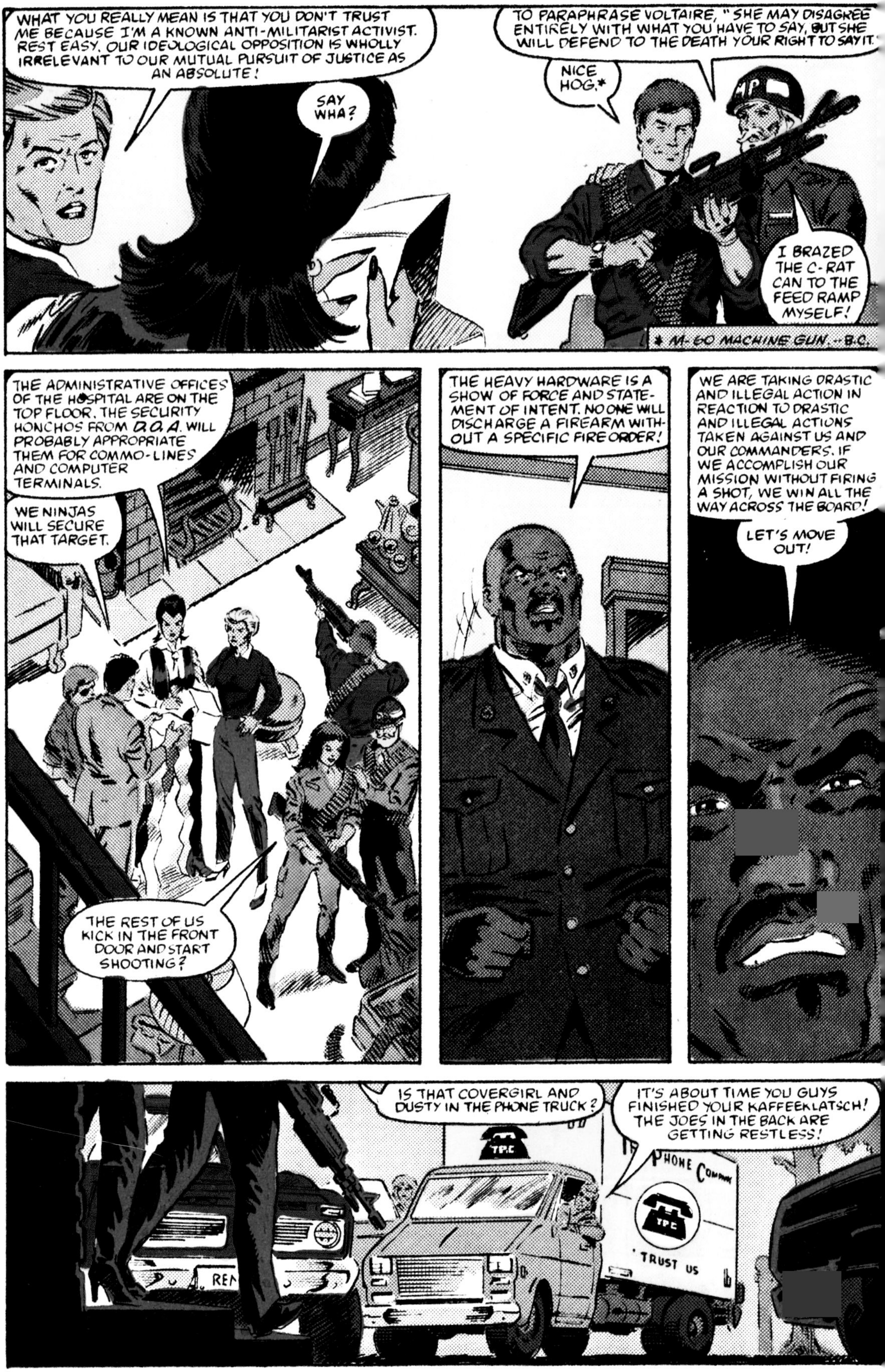
WHAT YOU REALLY MEAN IS THAT YOU DON'T TRUST ME BECAUSE I'M A KNOWN ANTI-MILITARIST ACTIVIST. REST EASY. OUR IDEOLOGICAL OPPOSITION IS WHOLLY IRRELEVANT TO OUR MUTUAL PURSUIT OF JUSTICE AS AN ABSOLUTE!
SAY WHA?
TO PARAPHRASE VOLTAIRE, "SHE MAY DISAGREE ENTIRELY WITH WHAT YOU HAVE TO SAY, BUT SHE WILL DEFEND TO THE DEATH YOUR RIGHT TO SAY IT."
NICE HOG.*
MP
I BRAZED THE C-RAT CAN TO THE FEED RAMP MYSELF!
* M-60 MACHINE GUN. --B.C.
THE ADMINISTRATIVE OFFICES OF THE HOSPITAL ARE ON THE TOP FLOOR. THE SECURITY HONCHOS FROM D.O.A. WILL PROBABLY APPROPRIATE THEM FOR COMMO-LINES AND COMPUTER TERMINALS.
WE NINJAS WILL SECURE THAT TARGET.
THE REST OF US KICK IN THE FRONT DOOR AND START SHOOTING?
THE HEAVY HARDWARE IS A SHOW OF FORCE AND STATEMENT OF INTENT. NO ONE WILL DISCHARGE A FIREARM WITHOUT A SPECIFIC FIRE ORDER!
WE ARE TAKING DRASTIC AND ILLEGAL ACTION IN REACTION TO DRASTIC AND ILLEGAL ACTIONS TAKEN AGAINST US AND OUR COMMANDERS. IF WE ACCOMPLISH OUR MISSION WITHOUT FIRING A SHOT, WE WIN ALL THE WAY ACROSS THE BOARD!
LET'S MOVE OUT!
IS THAT COVERGIRL AND DUSTY IN THE PHONE TRUCK?
IT'S ABOUT TIME YOU GUYS FINISHED YOUR KAFFEEKLATSCH! THE JOES IN THE BACK ARE GETTING RESTLESS!
TPC
PHONE COMPANY
TPC
TRUST US

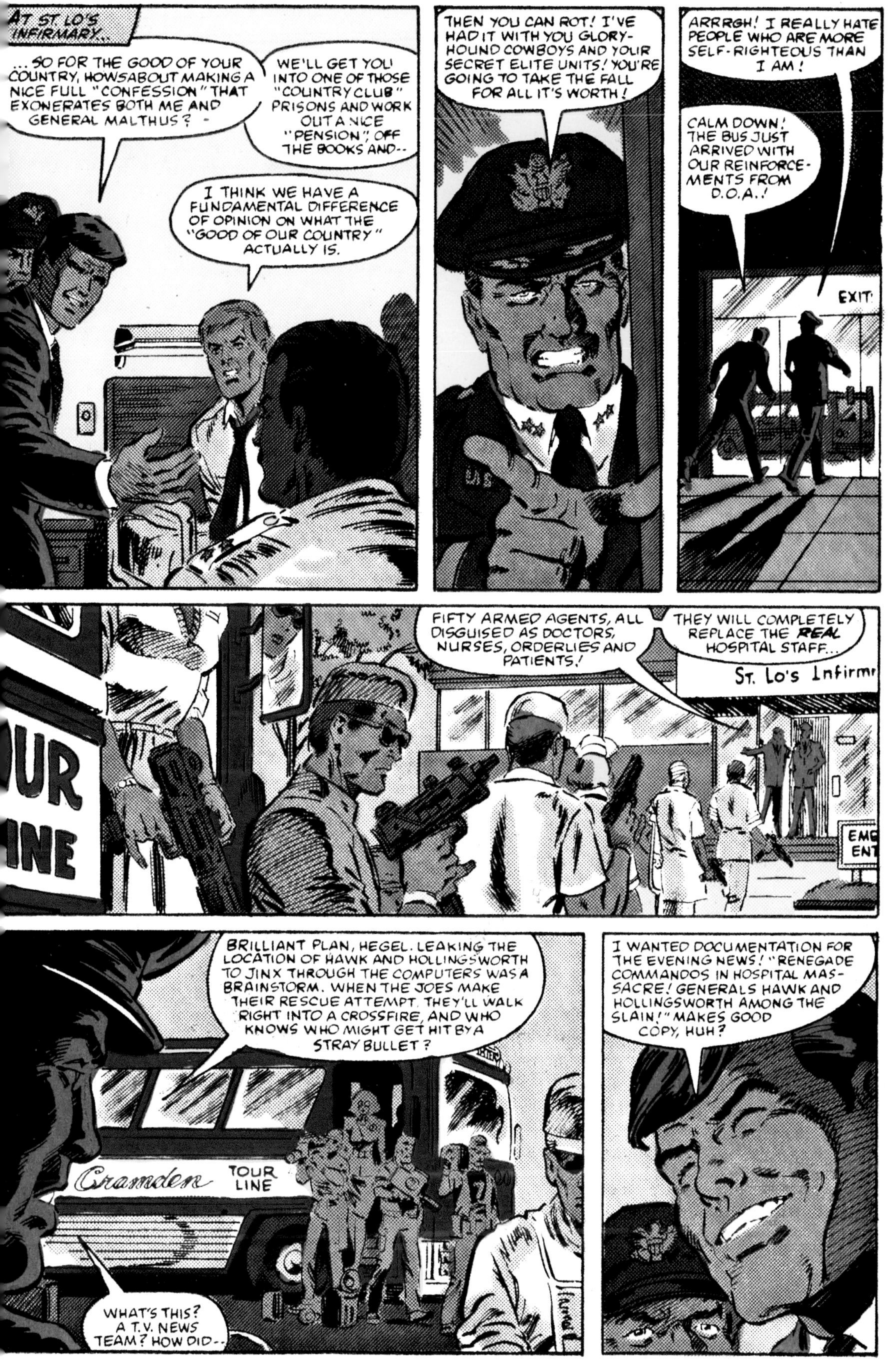

AT ST. LO'S INFIRMARY...
...SO FOR THE GOOD OF YOUR COUNTRY, HOWSABOUT MAKING A NICE FULL "CONFESSION" THAT EXONERATES BOTH ME AND GENERAL MALTHUS? -
WE'LL GET YOU INTO ONE OF THOSE "COUNTRY CLUB" PRISONS AND WORK OUT A NICE "PENSION", OFF THE BOOKS AND--
I THINK WE HAVE A FUNDAMENTAL DIFFERENCE OF OPINION ON WHAT THE "GOOD OF OUR COUNTRY" ACTUALLY IS.
THEN YOU CAN ROT! I'VE HAD IT WITH YOU GLORY-HOUND COWBOYS AND YOUR SECRET ELITE UNITS! YOU'RE GOING TO TAKE THE FALL FOR ALL IT'S WORTH!
ARRRGH! I REALLY HATE PEOPLE WHO ARE MORE SELF-RIGHTEOUS THAN I AM!
CALM DOWN! THE BUS JUST ARRIVED WITH OUR REINFORCE-MENTS FROM D.O.A.!
EXIT
FIFTY ARMED AGENTS, ALL DISGUISED AS DOCTORS, NURSES, ORDERLIES AND PATIENTS!
THEY WILL COMPLETELY REPLACE THE REAL HOSPITAL STAFF...
St. Lo's Infirm
UR
INE
BRILLIANT PLAN, HEGEL. LEAKING THE LOCATION OF HAWK AND HOLLINGSWORTH TO JINX THROUGH THE COMPUTERS WAS A BRAINSTORM. WHEN THE JOES MAKE THEIR RESCUE ATTEMPT, THEY'LL WALK RIGHT INTO A CROSSFIRE, AND WHO KNOWS WHO MIGHT GET HIT BY A STRAY BULLET?
Cramden TOUR LINE
WHAT'S THIS? A T.V. NEWS TEAM? HOW DID--
I WANTED DOCUMENTATION FOR THE EVENING NEWS! "RENEGADE COMMANDOS IN HOSPITAL MAS-SACRE! GENERALS HAWK AND HOLLINGSWORTH AMONG THE SLAIN!" MAKES GOOD COPY, HUH?

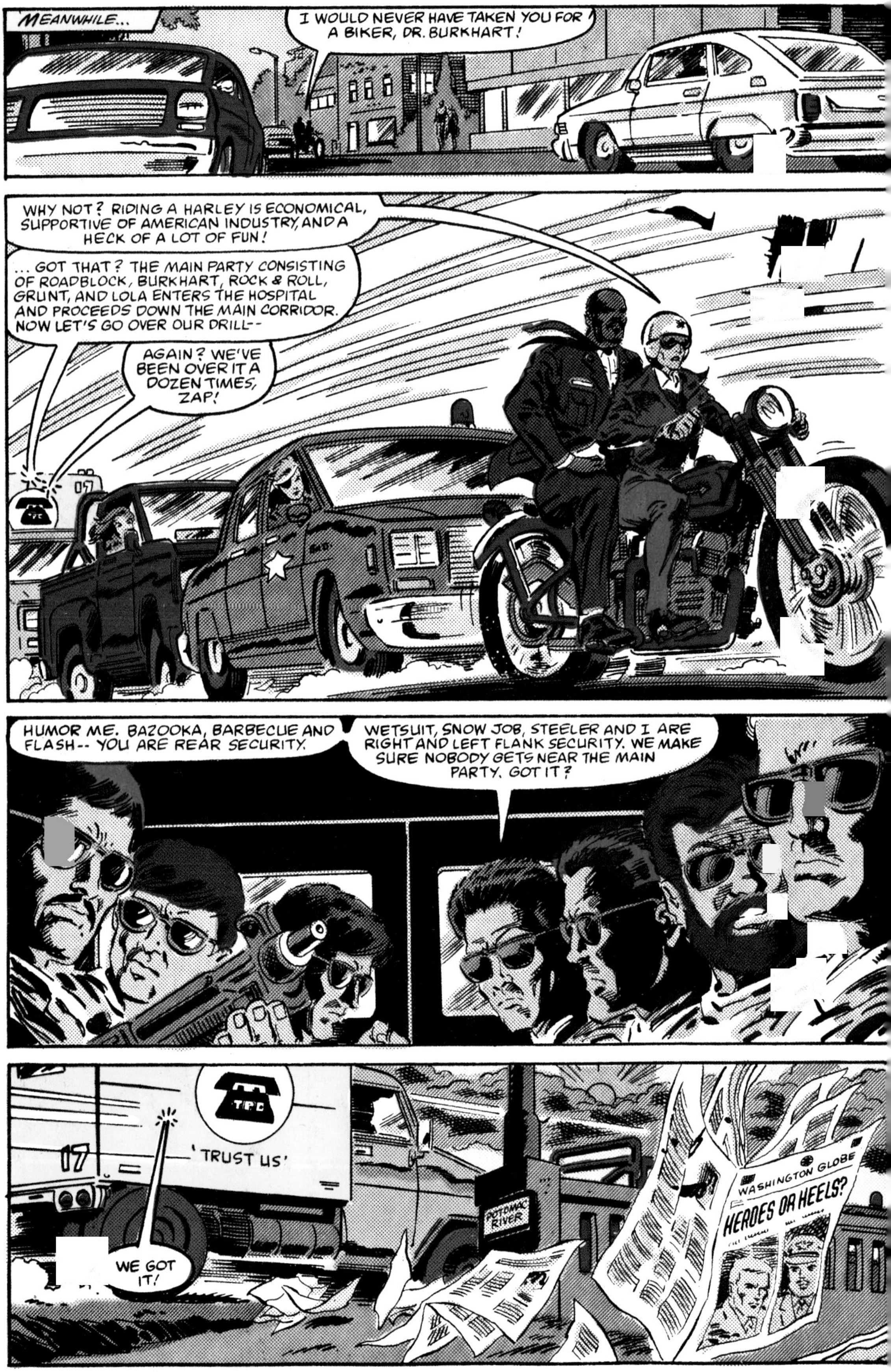

MEANWHILE...
I WOULD NEVER HAVE TAKEN YOU FOR A BIKER, DR. BURKHART!
WHY NOT? RIDING A HARLEY IS ECONOMICAL, SUPPORTIVE OF AMERICAN INDUSTRY, AND A HECK OF A LOT OF FUN!
... GOT THAT? THE MAIN PARTY CONSISTING OF ROADBLOCK, BURKHART, ROCK & ROLL, GRUNT, AND LOLA ENTERS THE HOSPITAL AND PROCEEDS DOWN THE MAIN CORRIDOR. NOW LET'S GO OVER OUR DRILL--
AGAIN? WE'VE BEEN OVER IT A DOZEN TIMES, ZAP!
HUMOR ME. BAZOOKA, BARBECUE AND FLASH-- YOU ARE REAR SECURITY.
WETSUIT, SNOW JOB, STEELER AND I ARE RIGHT AND LEFT FLANK SECURITY. WE MAKE SURE NOBODY GETS NEAR THE MAIN PARTY. GOT IT?
TPC
'TRUST US'
17
WE GOT IT!
POTOMAC RIVER
WASHINGTON GLOBE
HEROES OR HEELS?

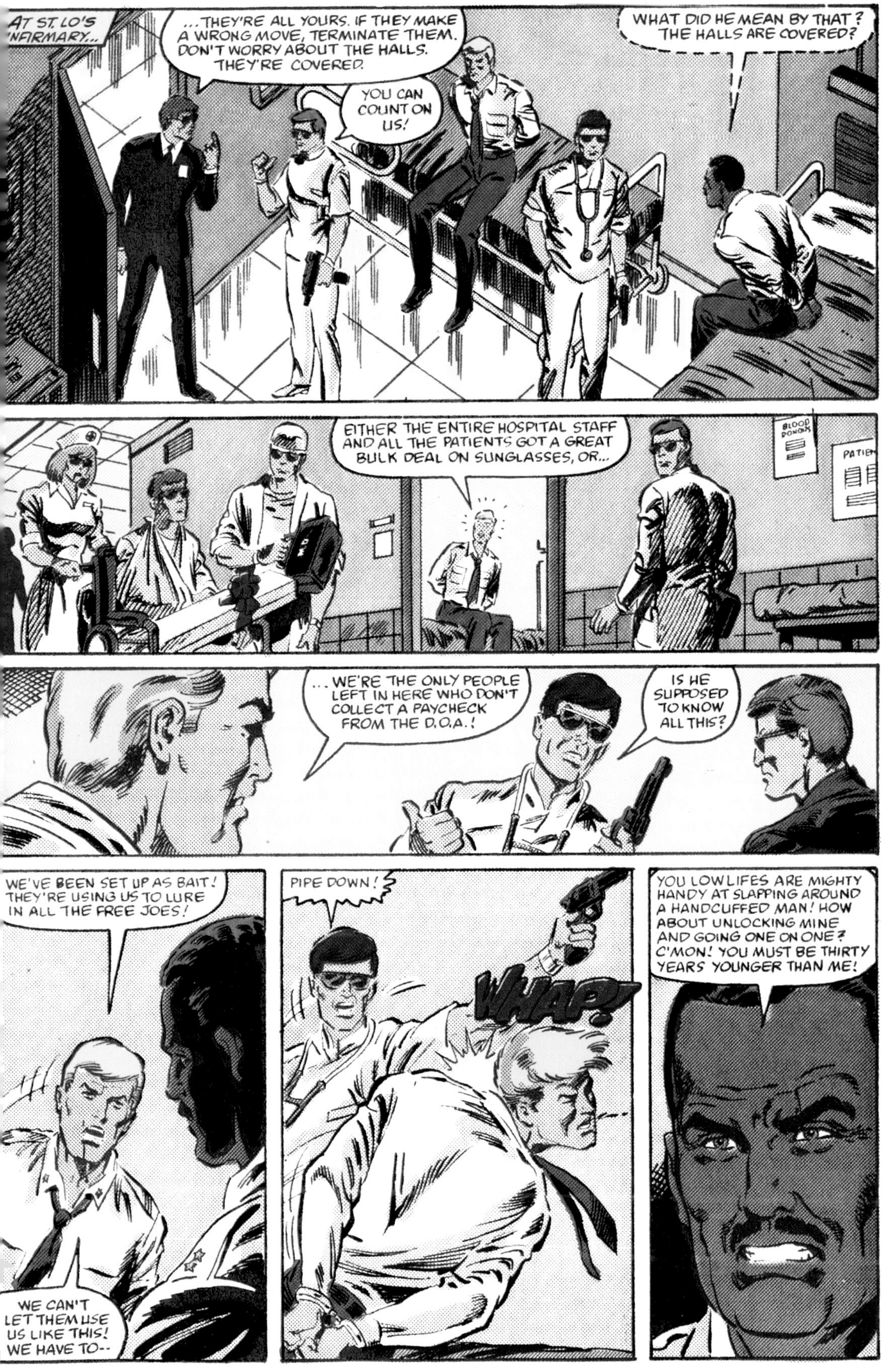

AT ST. LO'S INFIRMARY...
...THEY'RE ALL YOURS. IF THEY MAKE A WRONG MOVE, TERMINATE THEM. DON'T WORRY ABOUT THE HALLS. THEY'RE COVERED.
YOU CAN COUNT ON US!
WHAT DID HE MEAN BY THAT? THE HALLS ARE COVERED?
EITHER THE ENTIRE HOSPITAL STAFF AND ALL THE PATIENTS GOT A GREAT BULK DEAL ON SUNGLASSES, OR...
BLOOD DONORS
...WE'RE THE ONLY PEOPLE LEFT IN HERE WHO DON'T COLLECT A PAYCHECK FROM THE D.O.A.!
IS HE SUPPOSED TO KNOW ALL THIS?
WE'VE BEEN SET UP AS BAIT! THEY'RE USING US TO LURE IN ALL THE FREE JOES!
WE CAN'T LET THEM USE US LIKE THIS! WE HAVE TO--
PIPE DOWN!
WHAP!
YOU LOWLIFES ARE MIGHTY HANDY AT SLAPPING AROUND A HANDCUFFED MAN! HOW ABOUT UNLOCKING MINE AND GOING ONE ON ONE? C'MON! YOU MUST BE THIRTY YEARS YOUNGER THAN ME!

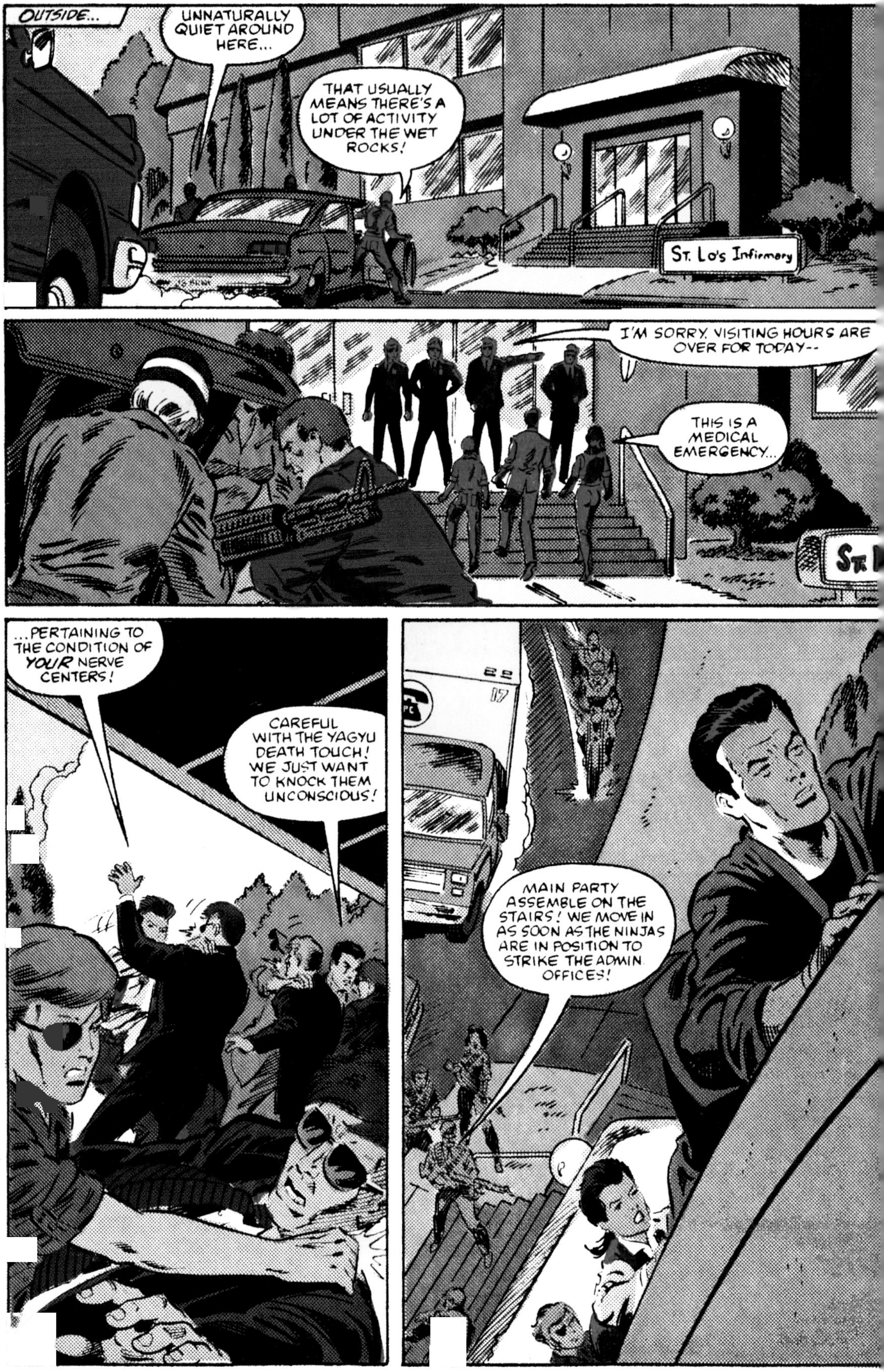
OUTSIDE...
UNNATURALLY QUIET AROUND HERE...
THAT USUALLY MEANS THERE'S A LOT OF ACTIVITY UNDER THE WET ROCKS!
St. Lo's Infirmary
I'M SORRY. VISITING HOURS ARE OVER FOR TODAY--
THIS IS A MEDICAL EMERGENCY...
...PERTAINING TO THE CONDITION OF YOUR NERVE CENTERS!
CAREFUL WITH THE YAGYU DEATH TOUCH! WE JUST WANT TO KNOCK THEM UNCONSCIOUS!
MAIN PARTY ASSEMBLE ON THE STAIRS! WE MOVE IN AS SOON AS THE NINJAS ARE IN POSITION TO STRIKE THE ADMIN OFFICES!

HOW DO YOU CARRY THIS MA-DEUCE? TWO OF US CAN BARELY LIFT IT!

CLEAN LIVING AND HIGH PAIN TOLERANCE!

I DON'T SUPPOSE YOU NEED A WEAPON, DR. BURKHART?

THE PRESS IS WAITING INSIDE. THE ONLY ARMAMENT I NEED IS MY BRIEFCASE AND MY REPUTATION!

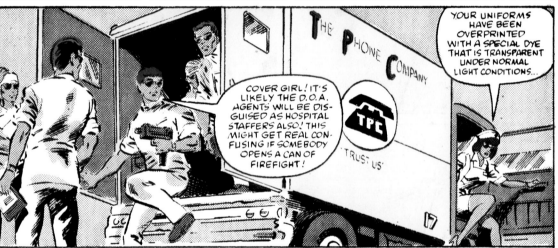

COVER GIRL! IT'S LIKELY THE D.O.A. AGENTS WILL BE DISGUISED AS HOSPITAL STAFFERS ALSO! THIS MIGHT GET REAL CONFUSING IF SOMEBODY OPENS A CAN OF FIREFIGHT!

THE PHONE COMPANY

TPC

"TRUST US"

YOUR UNIFORMS HAVE BEEN OVERPRINTED WITH A SPECIAL DYE THAT IS TRANSPARENT UNDER NORMAL LIGHT CONDITIONS...

THE "SHADES" YOU WILL BE WEARING ARE FITTED WITH POLARIZED FILTERS--

--WHICH MAKE THAT DYE VISIBLE TO YOU ALONE! YOU CAN REALLY TELL WHO YOUR FRIENDS ARE!

REMEMBER TO SMILE NICELY WHEN THE CAMERA IS POINTED YOUR WAY!

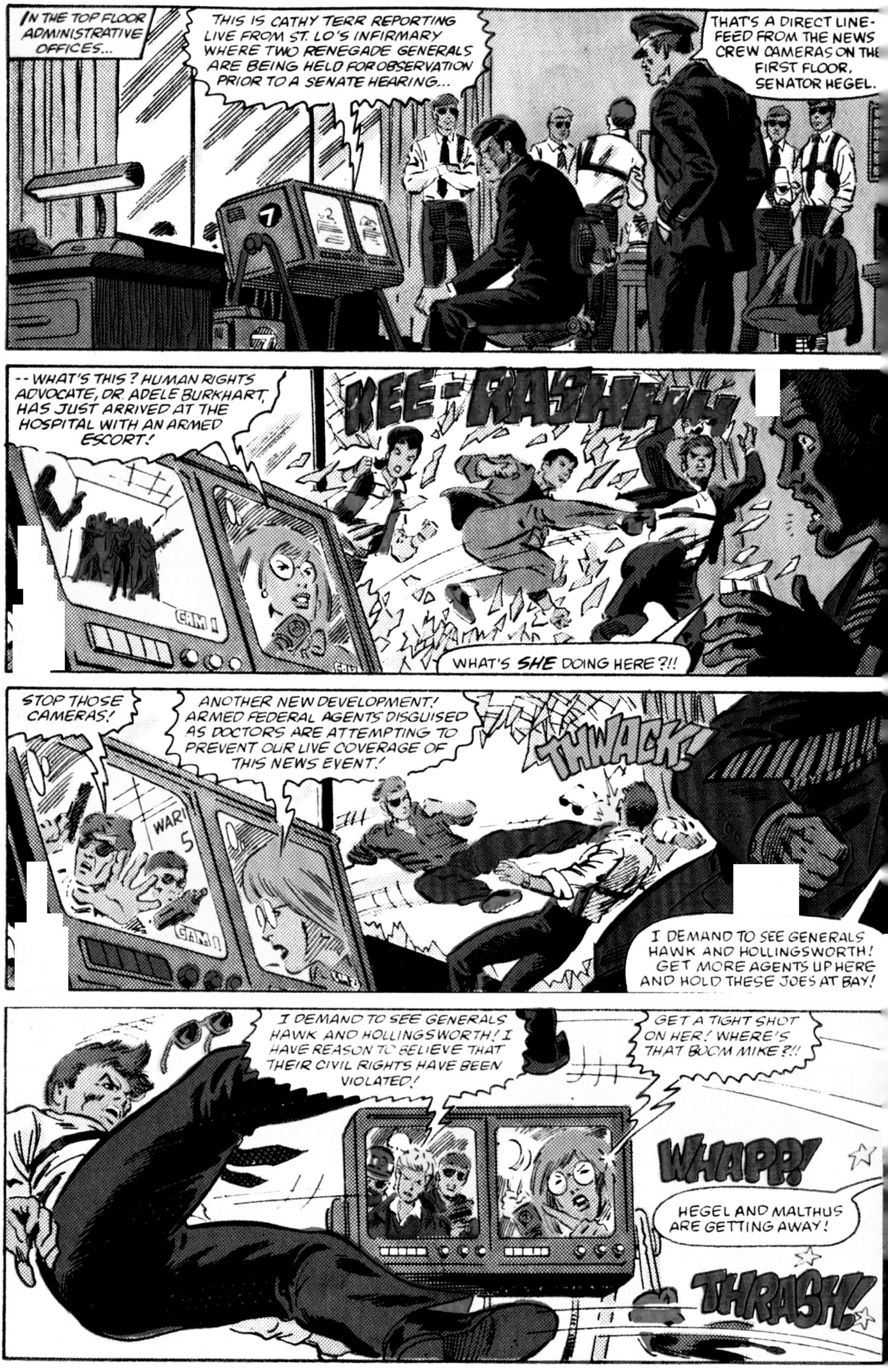
IN THE TOP FLOOR ADMINISTRATIVE OFFICES...
THIS IS CATHY TERR REPORTING LIVE FROM ST. LO'S INFIRMARY WHERE TWO RENEGADE GENERALS ARE BEING HELD FOR OBSERVATION PRIOR TO A SENATE HEARING...
THAT'S A DIRECT LINE-FEED FROM THE NEWS CREW CAMERAS ON THE FIRST FLOOR, SENATOR HEGEL.
-- WHAT'S THIS? HUMAN RIGHTS ADVOCATE, DR. ADELE BURKHART, HAS JUST ARRIVED AT THE HOSPITAL WITH AN ARMED ESCORT!
KEE-RASHHH
CAM 1
WHAT'S SHE DOING HERE?!!
STOP THOSE CAMERAS!
ANOTHER NEW DEVELOPMENT! ARMED FEDERAL AGENTS DISGUISED AS DOCTORS ARE ATTEMPTING TO PREVENT OUR LIVE COVERAGE OF THIS NEWS EVENT!
THWACK!
WARD 5
CAM 1
I DEMAND TO SEE GENERALS HAWK AND HOLLINGSWORTH! GET MORE AGENTS UP HERE AND HOLD THESE JOES AT BAY!
I DEMAND TO SEE GENERALS HAWK AND HOLLINGSWORTH! I HAVE REASON TO BELIEVE THAT THEIR CIVIL RIGHTS HAVE BEEN VIOLATED!
GET A TIGHT SHOT ON HER! WHERE'S THAT BOOM MIKE?!!
WHAPP!
HEGEL AND MALTHUS ARE GETTING AWAY!
THRASH!

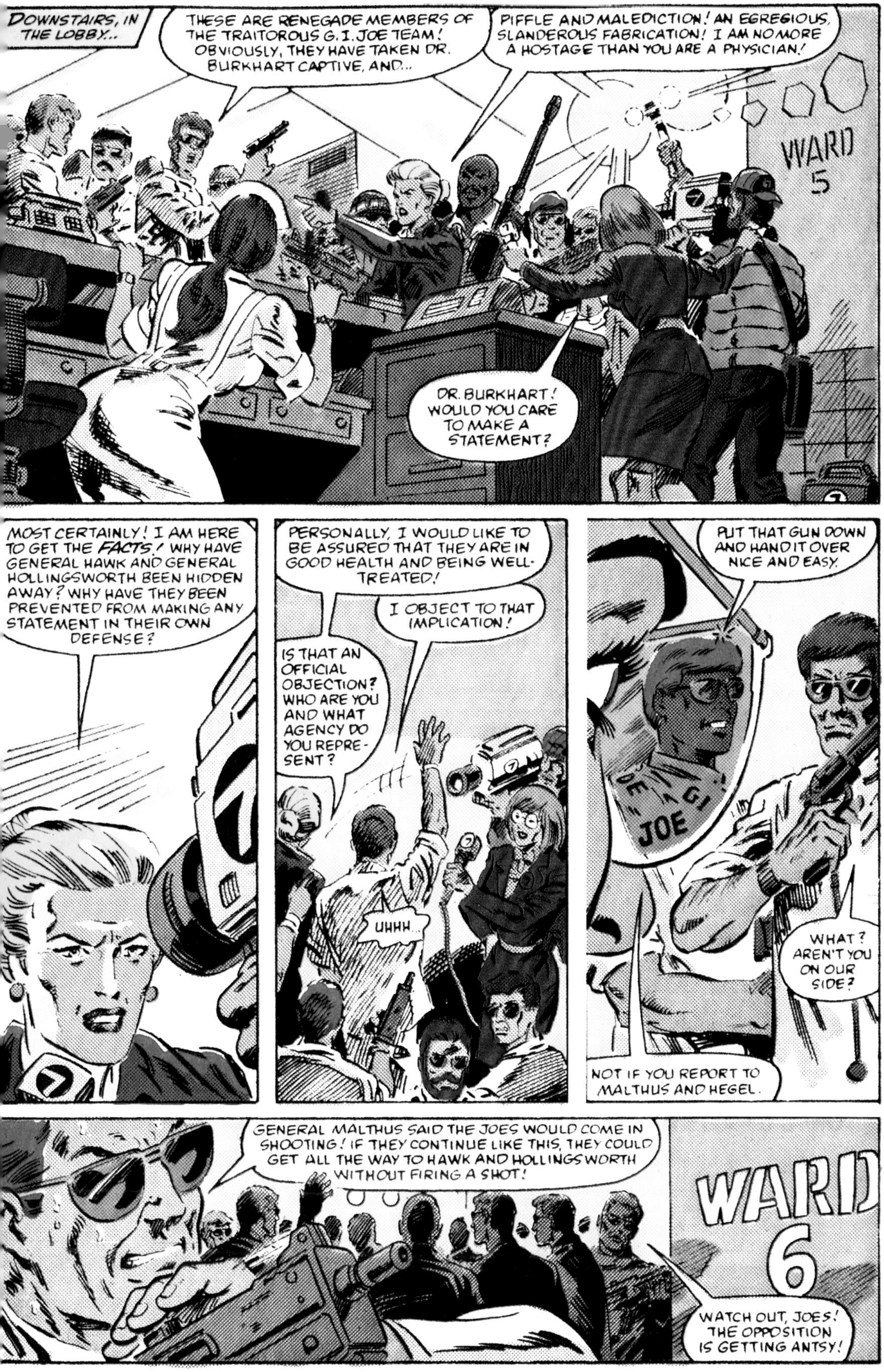

DOWNSTAIRS, IN THE LOBBY...
THESE ARE RENEGADE MEMBERS OF THE TRAITOROUS G.I. JOE TEAM! OBVIOUSLY, THEY HAVE TAKEN DR. BURKHART CAPTIVE, AND...
PIFFLE AND MALEDICTION! AN EGREGIOUS, SLANDEROUS FABRICATION! I AM NO MORE A HOSTAGE THAN YOU ARE A PHYSICIAN!
WARD 5
DR. BURKHART! WOULD YOU CARE TO MAKE A STATEMENT?
MOST CERTAINLY! I AM HERE TO GET THE FACTS! WHY HAVE GENERAL HAWK AND GENERAL HOLLINGSWORTH BEEN HIDDEN AWAY? WHY HAVE THEY BEEN PREVENTED FROM MAKING ANY STATEMENT IN THEIR OWN DEFENSE?
PERSONALLY, I WOULD LIKE TO BE ASSURED THAT THEY ARE IN GOOD HEALTH AND BEING WELL-TREATED!
I OBJECT TO THAT IMPLICATION!
IS THAT AN OFFICIAL OBJECTION? WHO ARE YOU AND WHAT AGENCY DO YOU REPRESENT?
UHHH...
PUT THAT GUN DOWN AND HAND IT OVER NICE AND EASY.
JOE
WHAT? AREN'T YOU ON OUR SIDE?
NOT IF YOU REPORT TO MALTHUS AND HEGEL.
GENERAL MALTHUS SAID THE JOES WOULD COME IN SHOOTING! IF THEY CONTINUE LIKE THIS, THEY COULD GET ALL THE WAY TO HAWK AND HOLLINGSWORTH WITHOUT FIRING A SHOT!
WARD 6
WATCH OUT, JOES! THE OPPOSITION IS GETTING ANTSY!

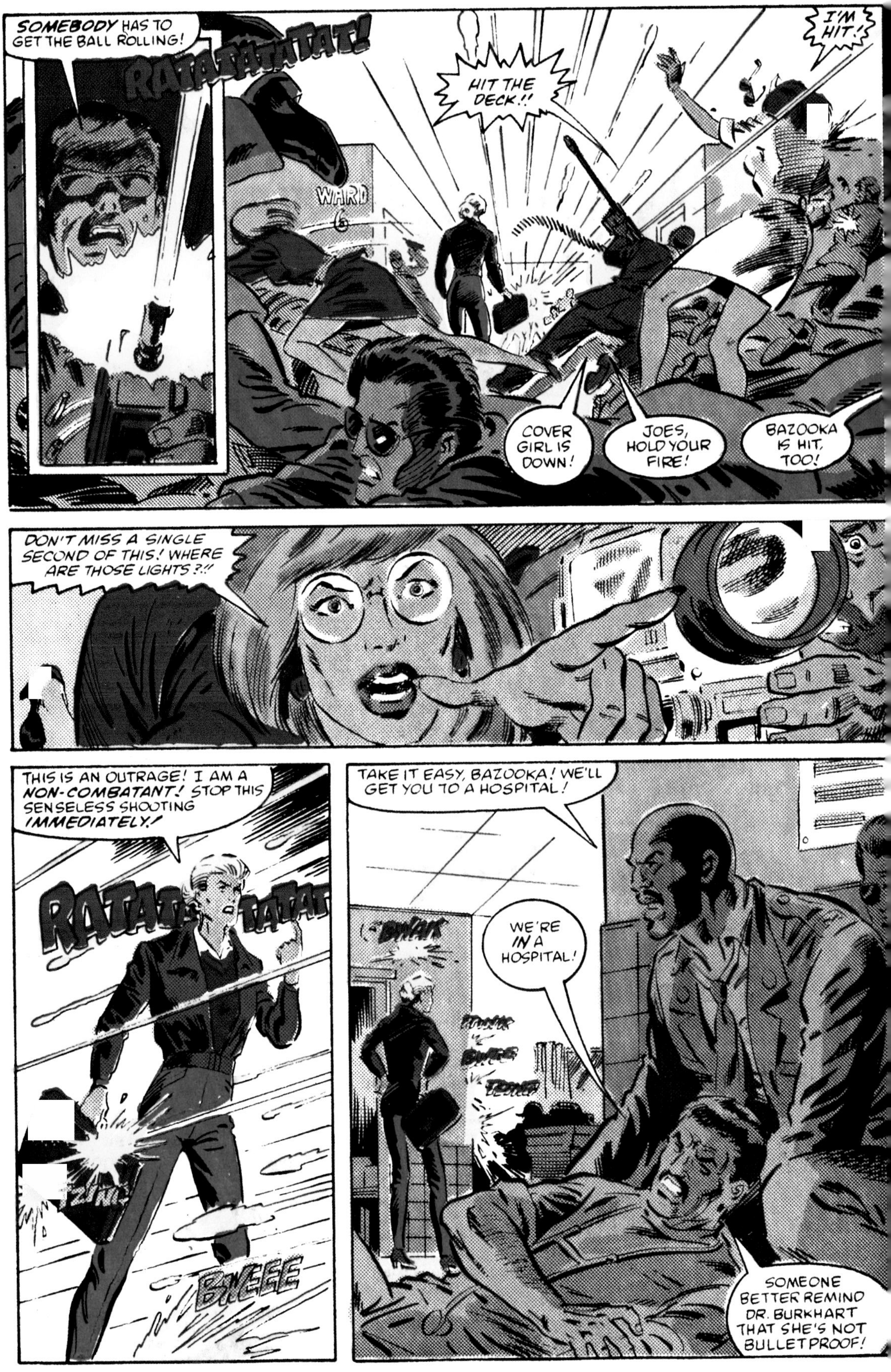

SOMEBODY HAS TO GET THE BALL ROLLING!
RATATATATATAT!
HIT THE DECK!!
I'M HIT!
WHAP
COVER GIRL IS DOWN!
JOES, HOLD YOUR FIRE!
BAZOOKA IS HIT, TOO!
DON'T MISS A SINGLE SECOND OF THIS! WHERE ARE THOSE LIGHTS?!!
THIS IS AN OUTRAGE! I AM A NON-COMBATANT! STOP THIS SENSELESS SHOOTING IMMEDIATELY!
BWEEE
TAKE IT EASY, BAZOOKA! WE'LL GET YOU TO A HOSPITAL!
WE'RE IN A HOSPITAL!
SOMEONE BETTER REMIND DR. BURKHART THAT SHE'S NOT BULLETPROOF!

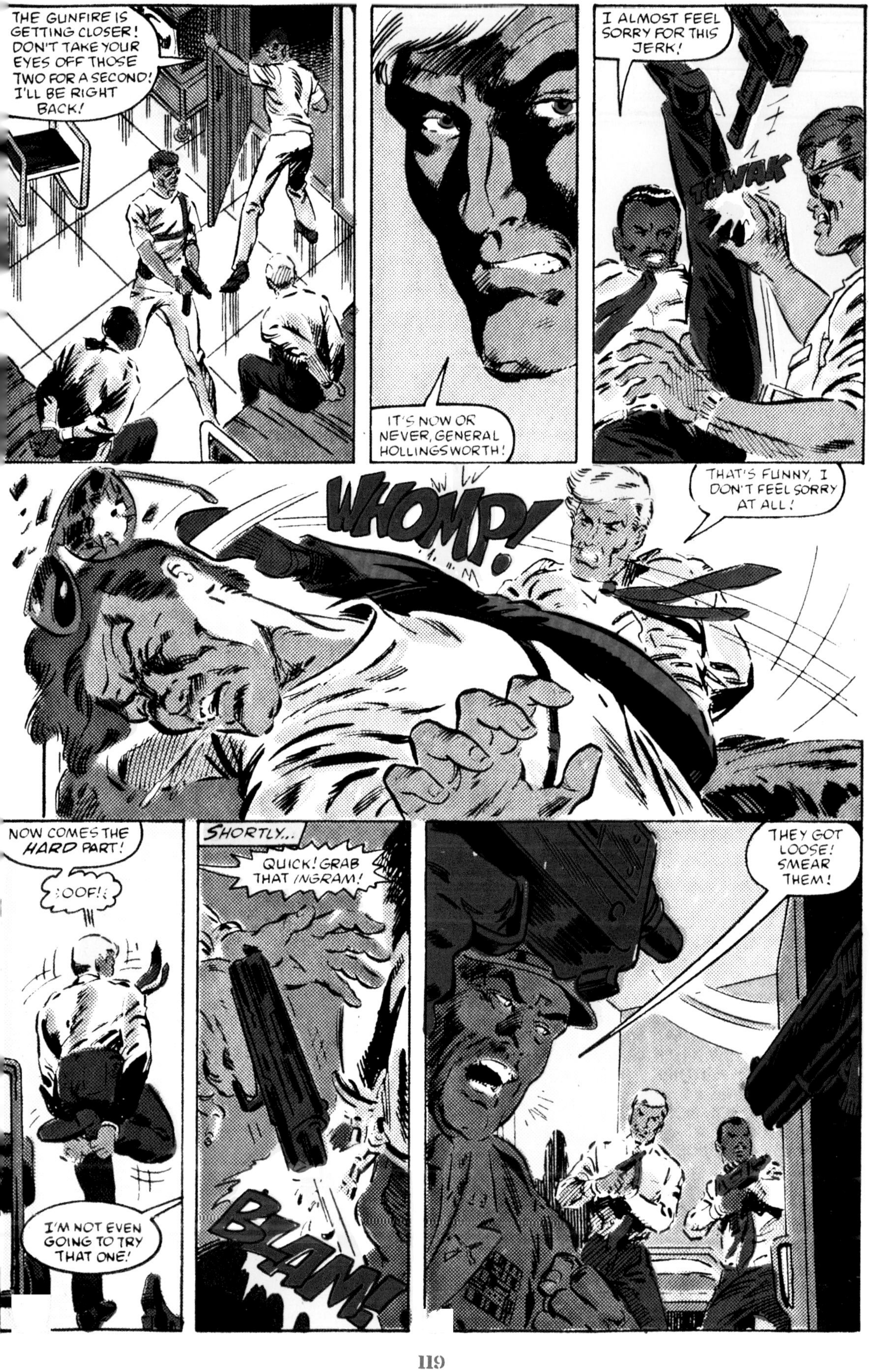
THE GUNFIRE IS GETTING CLOSER! DON'T TAKE YOUR EYES OFF THOSE TWO FOR A SECOND! I'LL BE RIGHT BACK!
IT'S NOW OR NEVER, GENERAL HOLLINGSWORTH!
I ALMOST FEEL SORRY FOR THIS JERK!
THWAK
WHOMP!
THAT'S FUNNY, I DON'T FEEL SORRY AT ALL!
NOW COMES THE HARD PART!
OOF!
I'M NOT EVEN GOING TO TRY THAT ONE!
SHORTLY...
QUICK! GRAB THAT INGRAM!
BLAM!
THEY GOT LOOSE! SMEAR THEM!

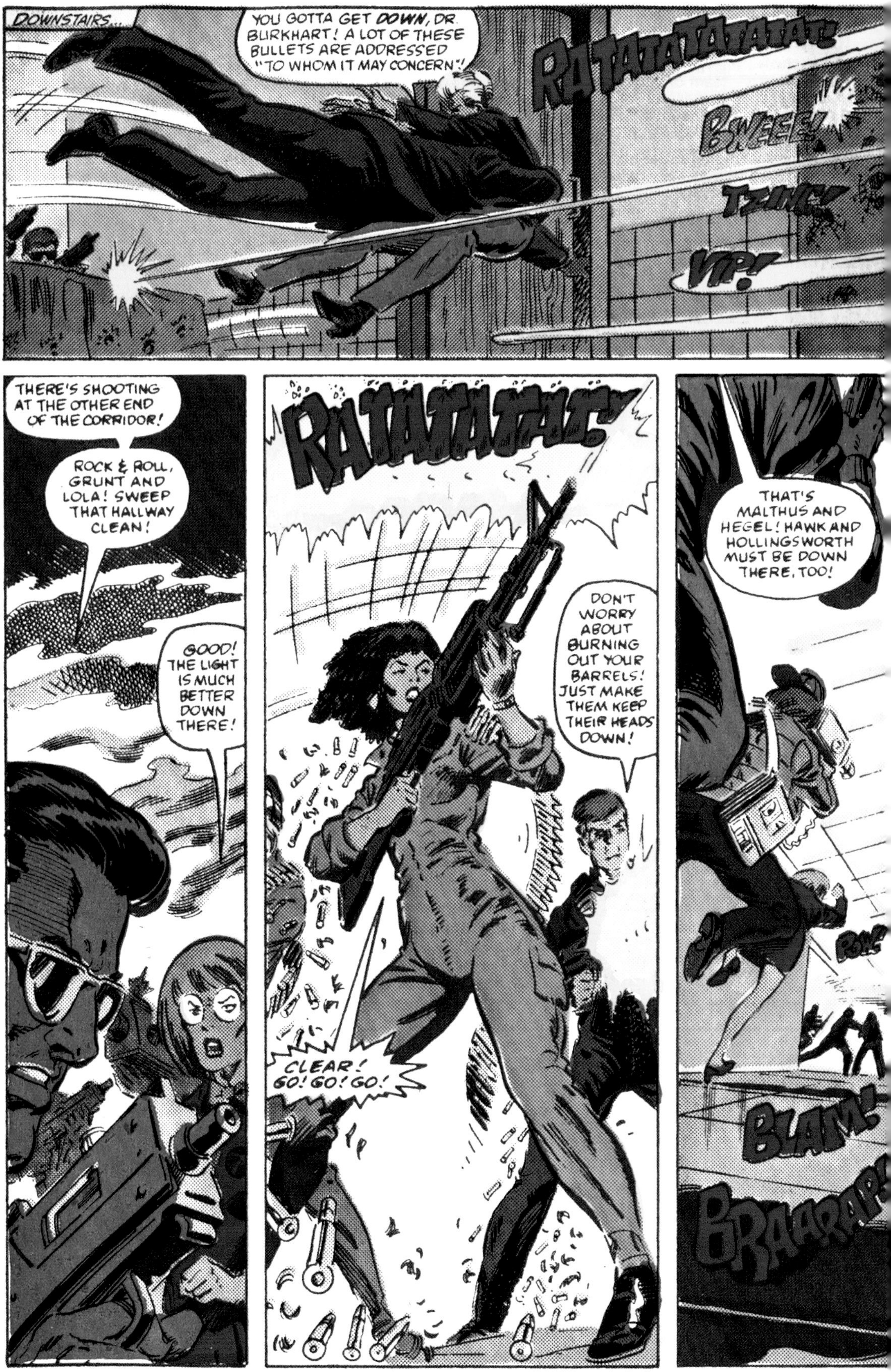

DOWNSTAIRS...
YOU GOTTA GET DOWN, DR. BURKHART! A LOT OF THESE BULLETS ARE ADDRESSED "TO WHOM IT MAY CONCERN"!
RATATATATATAT!
BWEEE!
TZING!
VIP!
THERE'S SHOOTING AT THE OTHER END OF THE CORRIDOR!
ROCK & ROLL, GRUNT AND LOLA! SWEEP THAT HALLWAY CLEAN!
GOOD! THE LIGHT IS MUCH BETTER DOWN THERE!
RATATATATAT!
DON'T WORRY ABOUT BURNING OUT YOUR BARRELS! JUST MAKE THEM KEEP THEIR HEADS DOWN!
CLEAR! GO! GO! GO!
THAT'S MALTHUS AND HEGEL! HAWK AND HOLLINGSWORTH MUST BE DOWN THERE, TOO!
BLAM!

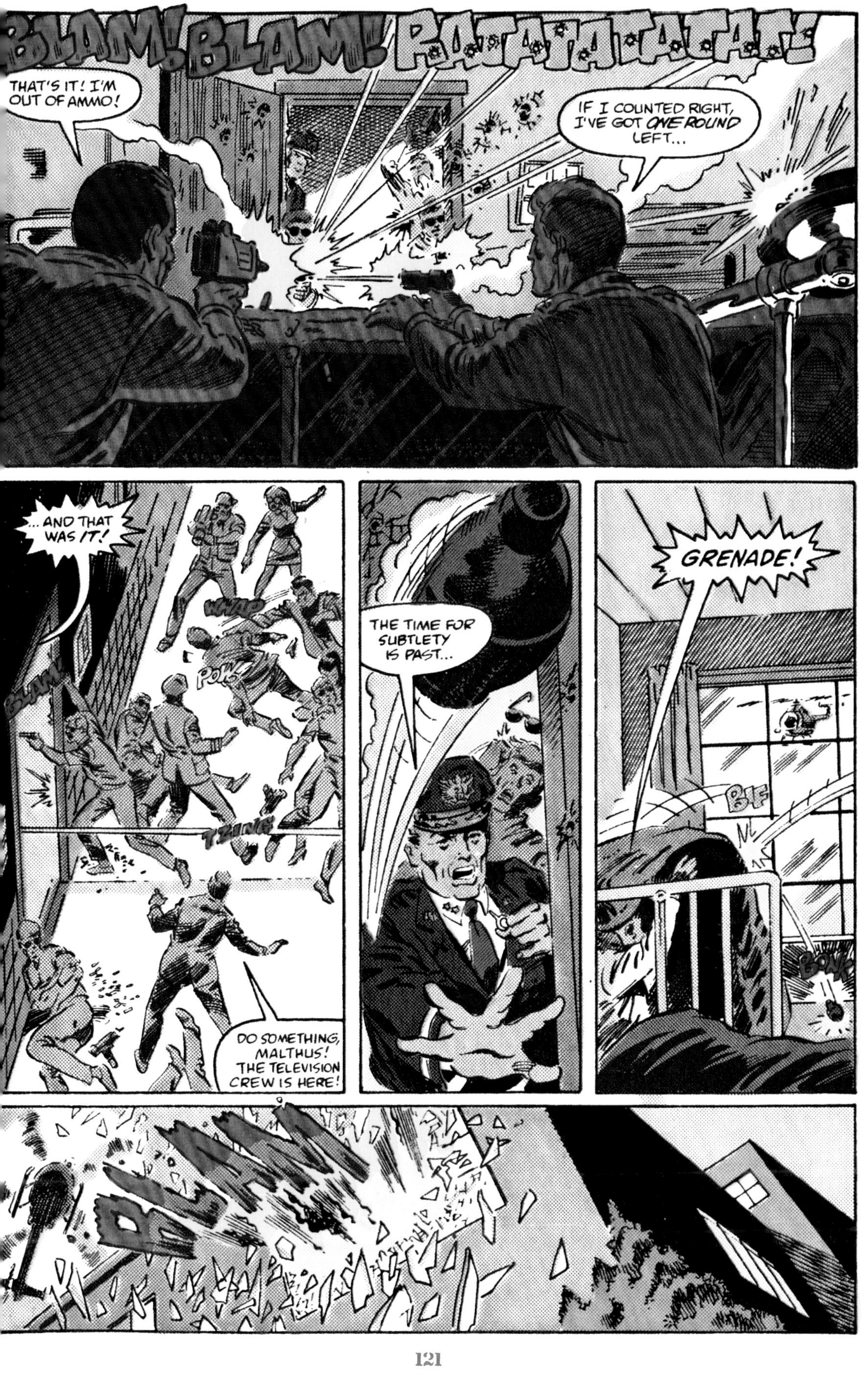
BLAM! BLAM! RATATATATAT!
THAT'S IT! I'M OUT OF AMMO!
IF I COUNTED RIGHT, I'VE GOT ONE ROUND LEFT...
...AND THAT WAS IT!
WHAP
POW
DO SOMETHING, MALTHUS! THE TELEVISION CREW IS HERE!
THE TIME FOR SUBTLETY IS PAST...
GRENADE!
BONK

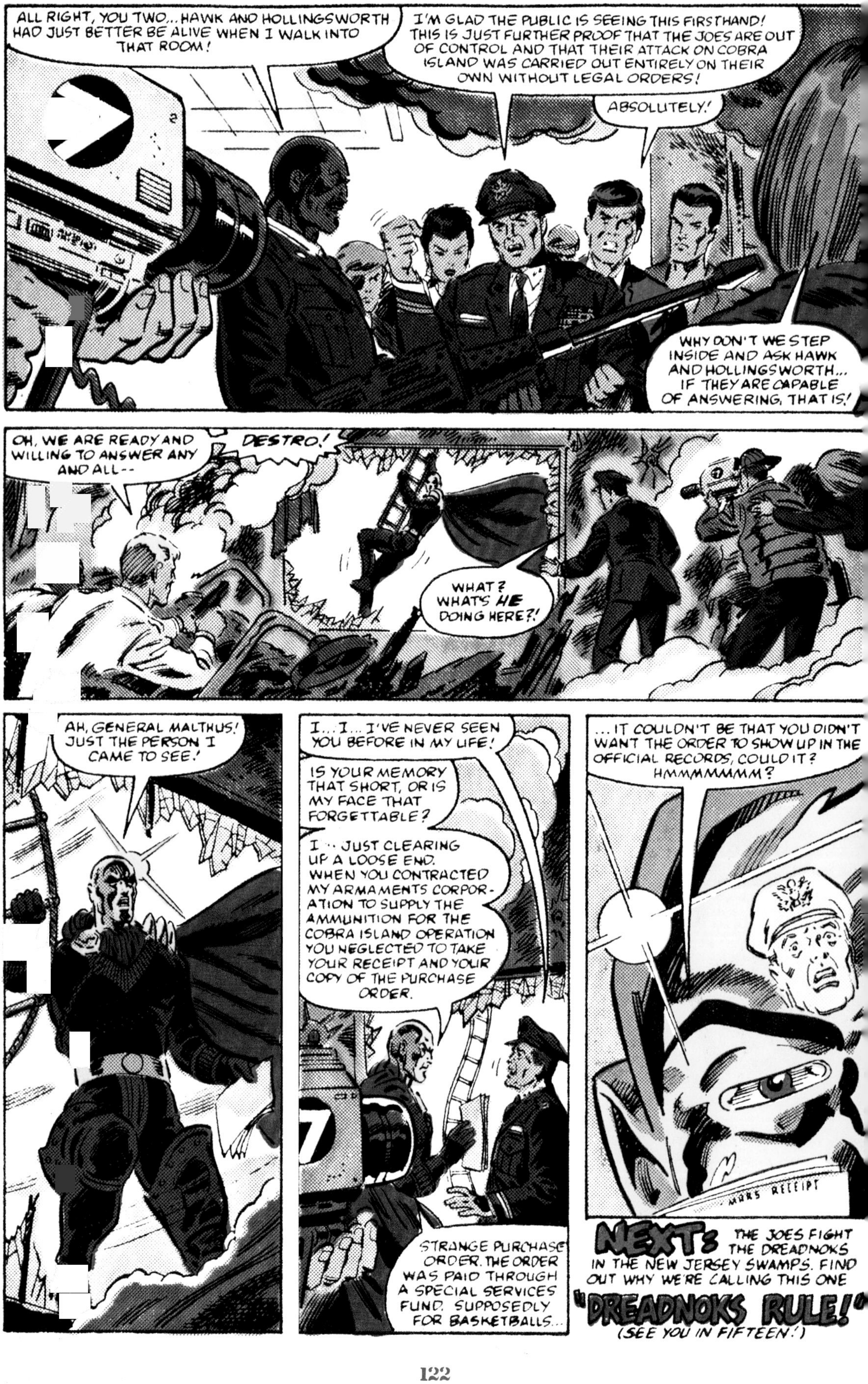
ALL RIGHT, YOU TWO... HAWK AND HOLLINGSWORTH HAD JUST BETTER BE ALIVE WHEN I WALK INTO THAT ROOM!
I'M GLAD THE PUBLIC IS SEEING THIS FIRSTHAND! THIS IS JUST FURTHER PROOF THAT THE JOES ARE OUT OF CONTROL AND THAT THEIR ATTACK ON COBRA ISLAND WAS CARRIED OUT ENTIRELY ON THEIR OWN WITHOUT LEGAL ORDERS!
ABSOLUTELY!
WHY DON'T WE STEP INSIDE AND ASK HAWK AND HOLLINGSWORTH... IF THEY ARE CAPABLE OF ANSWERING, THAT IS!
OH, WE ARE READY AND WILLING TO ANSWER ANY AND ALL--
DESTRO!
WHAT? WHAT'S HE DOING HERE?!
AH, GENERAL MALTHUS! JUST THE PERSON I CAME TO SEE!
I... I... I'VE NEVER SEEN YOU BEFORE IN MY LIFE!
IS YOUR MEMORY THAT SHORT, OR IS MY FACE THAT FORGETTABLE?
I'M JUST CLEARING UP A LOOSE END. WHEN YOU CONTRACTED MY ARMAMENTS CORPORATION TO SUPPLY THE AMMUNITION FOR THE COBRA ISLAND OPERATION YOU NEGLECTED TO TAKE YOUR RECEIPT AND YOUR COPY OF THE PURCHASE ORDER.
STRANGE PURCHASE ORDER. THE ORDER WAS PAID THROUGH A SPECIAL SERVICES FUND. SUPPOSEDLY FOR BASKETBALLS...
...IT COULDN'T BE THAT YOU DIDN'T WANT THE ORDER TO SHOW UP IN THE OFFICIAL RECORDS, COULD IT? HMMMMMMM?
RECEIPT
NEXT: THE JOES FIGHT THE DREADNOKS IN THE NEW JERSEY SWAMPS. FIND OUT WHY WE'RE CALLING THIS ONE "DREADNOKS RULE!"
(SEE YOU IN FIFTEEN!)

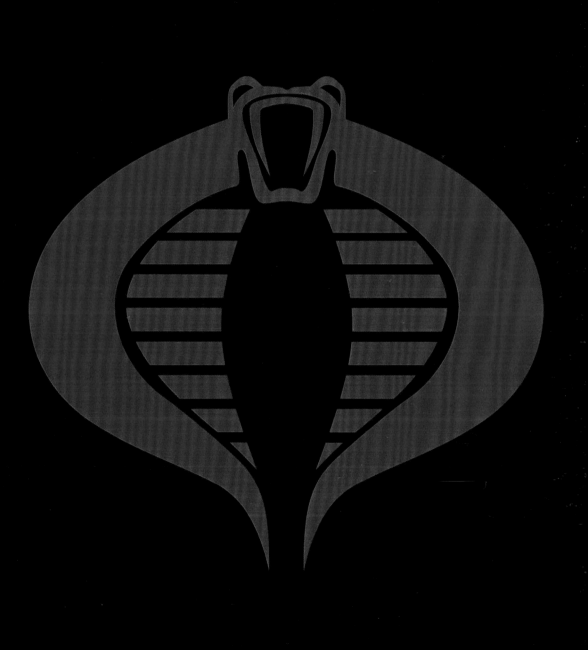

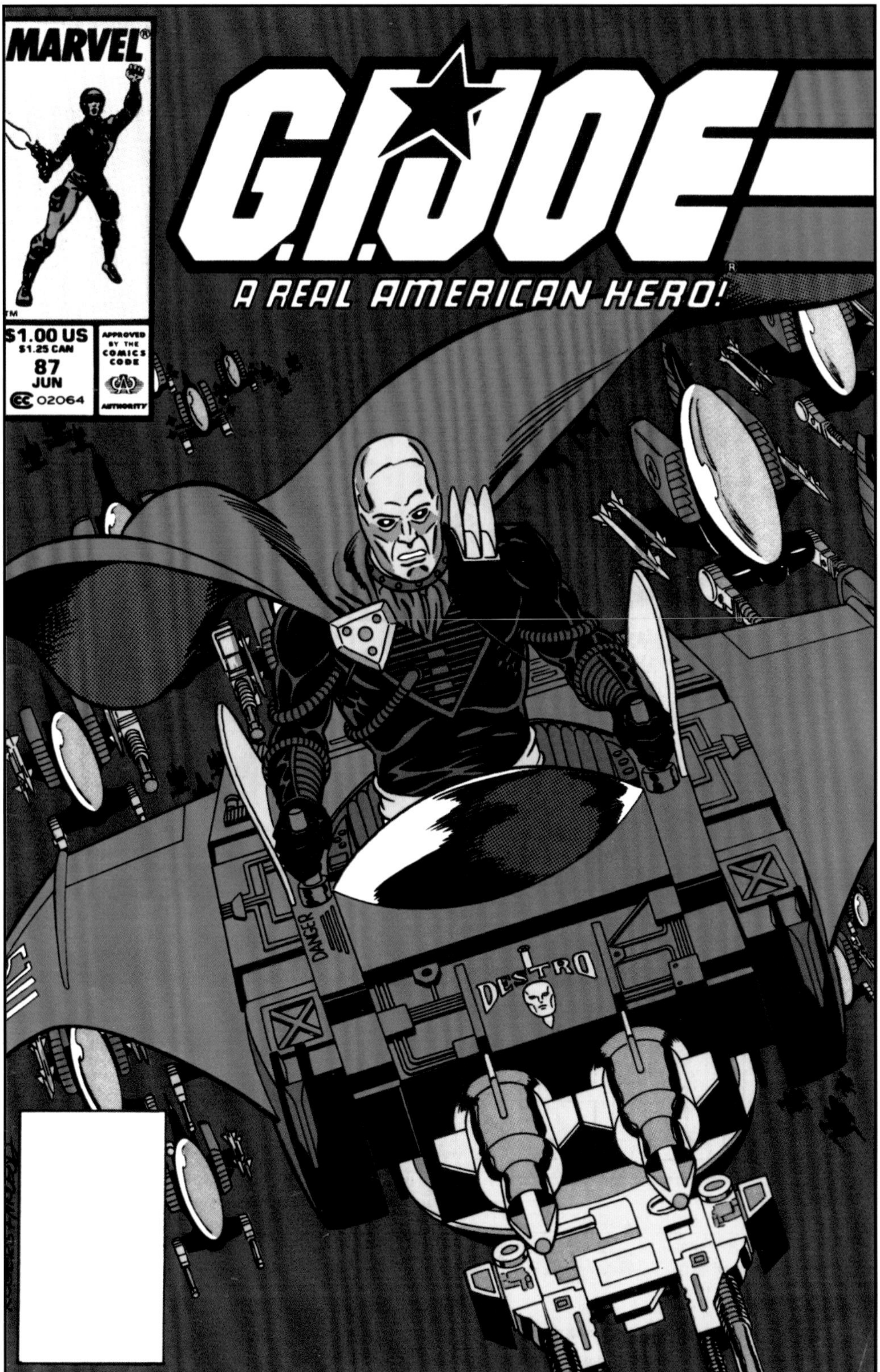
MARVEL
G.I. JOE
A REAL AMERICAN HERO!
$1.00 US
$1.25 CAN
87
JUN
02064
APPROVED BY THE COMICS CODE AUTHORITY
DANGER
DESTRO

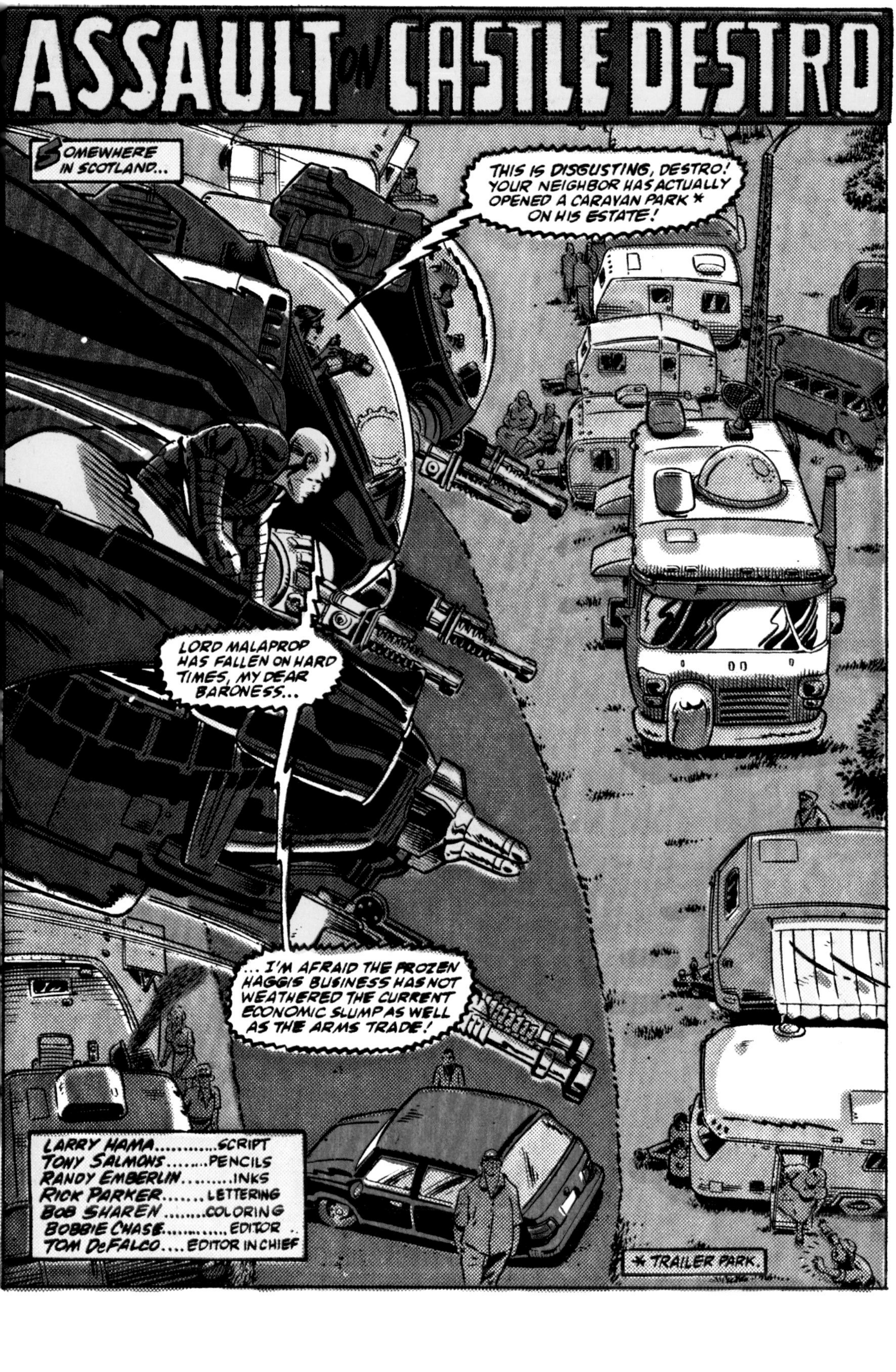
ASSAULT ON CASTLE DESTRO
SOMEWHERE IN SCOTLAND...
THIS IS DISGUSTING, DESTRO! YOUR NEIGHBOR HAS ACTUALLY OPENED A CARAVAN PARK * ON HIS ESTATE!
LORD MALAPROP HAS FALLEN ON HARD TIMES, MY DEAR BARONESS...
...I'M AFRAID THE FROZEN HAGGIS BUSINESS HAS NOT WEATHERED THE CURRENT ECONOMIC SLUMP AS WELL AS THE ARMS TRADE!
LARRY HAMA...........SCRIPT
TONY SALMONS........PENCILS
RANDY EMBERLIN........INKS
RICK PARKER.......LETTERING
BOB SHAREN........COLORING
BOBBIE CHASE..........EDITOR
TOM DEFALCO....EDITOR IN CHIEF
* TRAILER PARK.

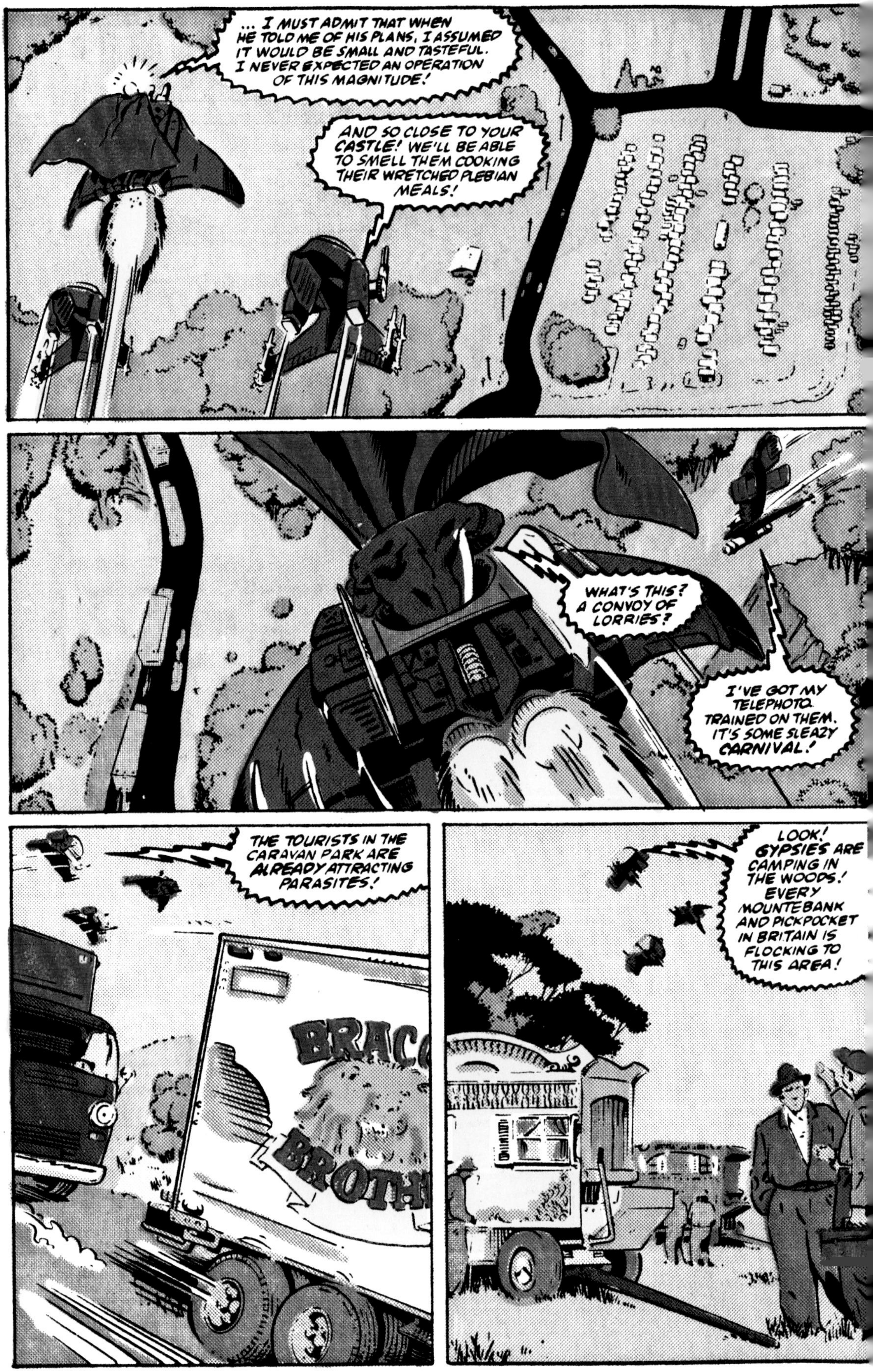
... I MUST ADMIT THAT WHEN HE TOLD ME OF HIS PLANS, I ASSUMED IT WOULD BE SMALL AND TASTEFUL. I NEVER EXPECTED AN OPERATION OF THIS MAGNITUDE!
AND SO CLOSE TO YOUR CASTLE! WE'LL BE ABLE TO SMELL THEM COOKING THEIR WRETCHED PLEBIAN MEALS!
WHAT'S THIS? A CONVOY OF LORRIES?
I'VE GOT MY TELEPHOTO TRAINED ON THEM. IT'S SOME SLEAZY CARNIVAL!
THE TOURISTS IN THE CARAVAN PARK ARE ALREADY ATTRACTING PARASITES!
BRACC
BROTH
LOOK! GYPSIES ARE CAMPING IN THE WOODS! EVERY MOUNTEBANK AND PICKPOCKET IN BRITAIN IS FLOCKING TO THIS AREA!

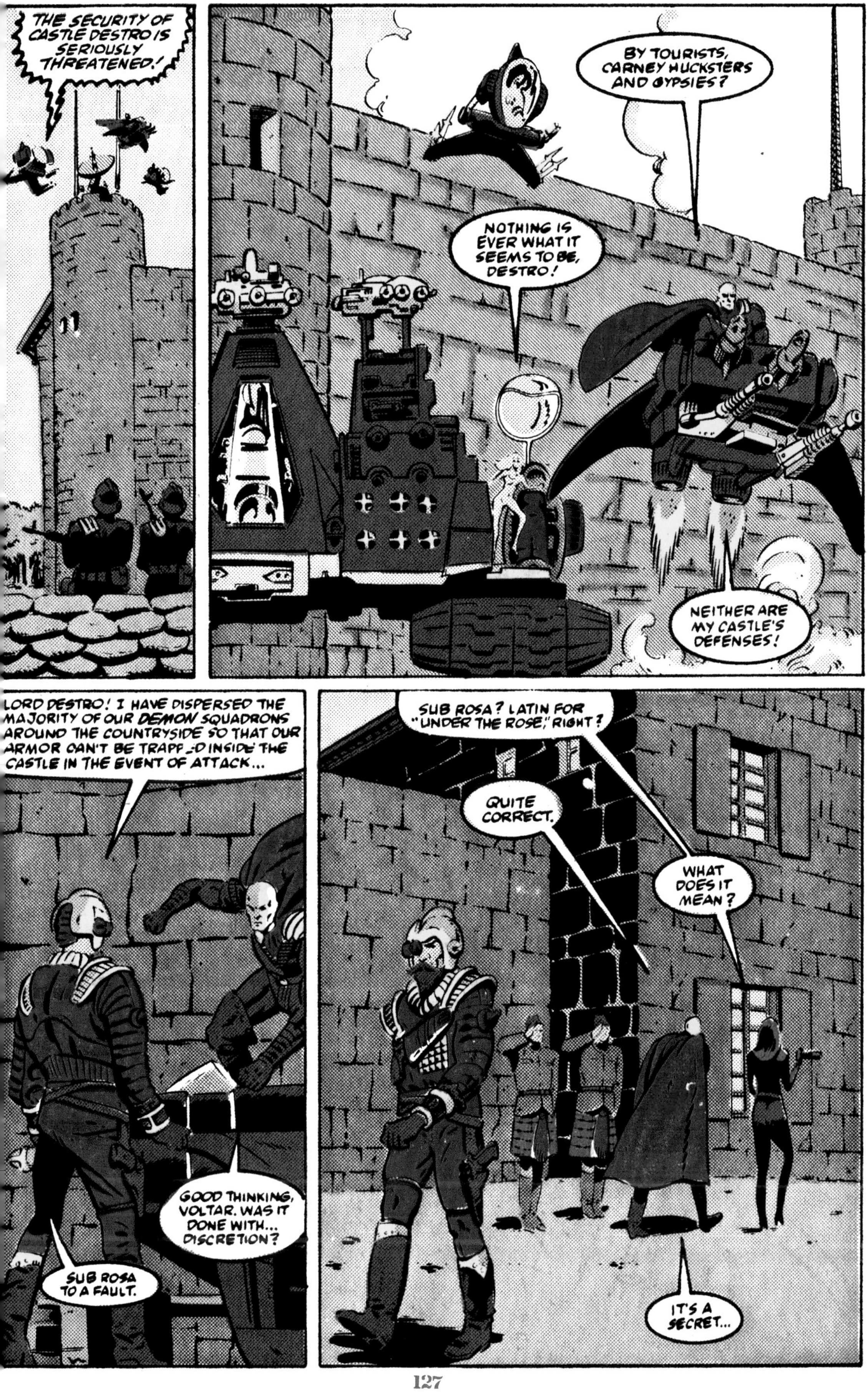
THE SECURITY OF CASTLE DESTRO IS SERIOUSLY THREATENED!
BY TOURISTS, CARNEY HUCKSTERS AND GYPSIES?
NOTHING IS EVER WHAT IT SEEMS TO BE, DESTRO!
NEITHER ARE MY CASTLE'S DEFENSES!
LORD DESTRO! I HAVE DISPERSED THE MAJORITY OF OUR DEMON SQUADRONS AROUND THE COUNTRYSIDE SO THAT OUR ARMOR CAN'T BE TRAPPED INSIDE THE CASTLE IN THE EVENT OF ATTACK...
GOOD THINKING, VOLTAR. WAS IT DONE WITH... DISCRETION?
SUB ROSA TO A FAULT.
SUB ROSA? LATIN FOR "UNDER THE ROSE," RIGHT?
QUITE CORRECT.
WHAT DOES IT MEAN?
IT'S A SECRET...

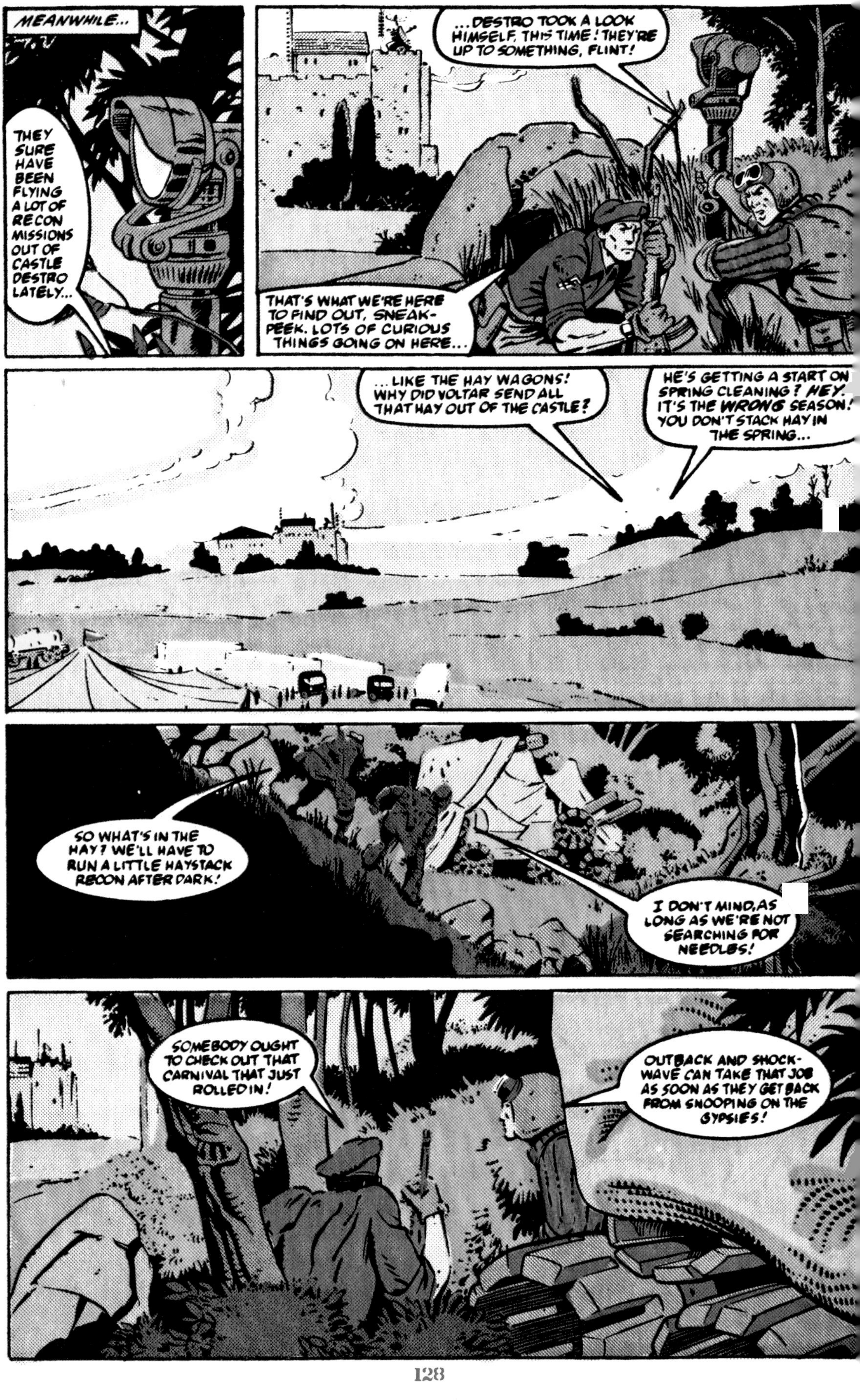
MEANWHILE...
THEY SURE HAVE BEEN FLYING A LOT OF RECON MISSIONS OUT OF CASTLE DESTRO LATELY...
...DESTRO TOOK A LOOK HIMSELF, THIS TIME! THEY'RE UP TO SOMETHING, FLINT!
THAT'S WHAT WE'RE HERE TO FIND OUT, SNEAK-PEEK. LOTS OF CURIOUS THINGS GOING ON HERE...
...LIKE THE HAY WAGONS! WHY DID VOLTAR SEND ALL THAT HAY OUT OF THE CASTLE?
HE'S GETTING A START ON SPRING CLEANING? HEY. IT'S THE WRONG SEASON! YOU DON'T STACK HAY IN THE SPRING...
SO WHAT'S IN THE HAY? WE'LL HAVE TO RUN A LITTLE HAYSTACK RECON AFTER DARK!
I DON'T MIND, AS LONG AS WE'RE NOT SEARCHING FOR NEEDLES!
SOMEBODY OUGHT TO CHECK OUT THAT CARNIVAL THAT JUST ROLLED IN!
OUTBACK AND SHOCK-WAVE CAN TAKE THAT JOB AS SOON AS THEY GET BACK FROM SNOOPING ON THE GYPSIES!

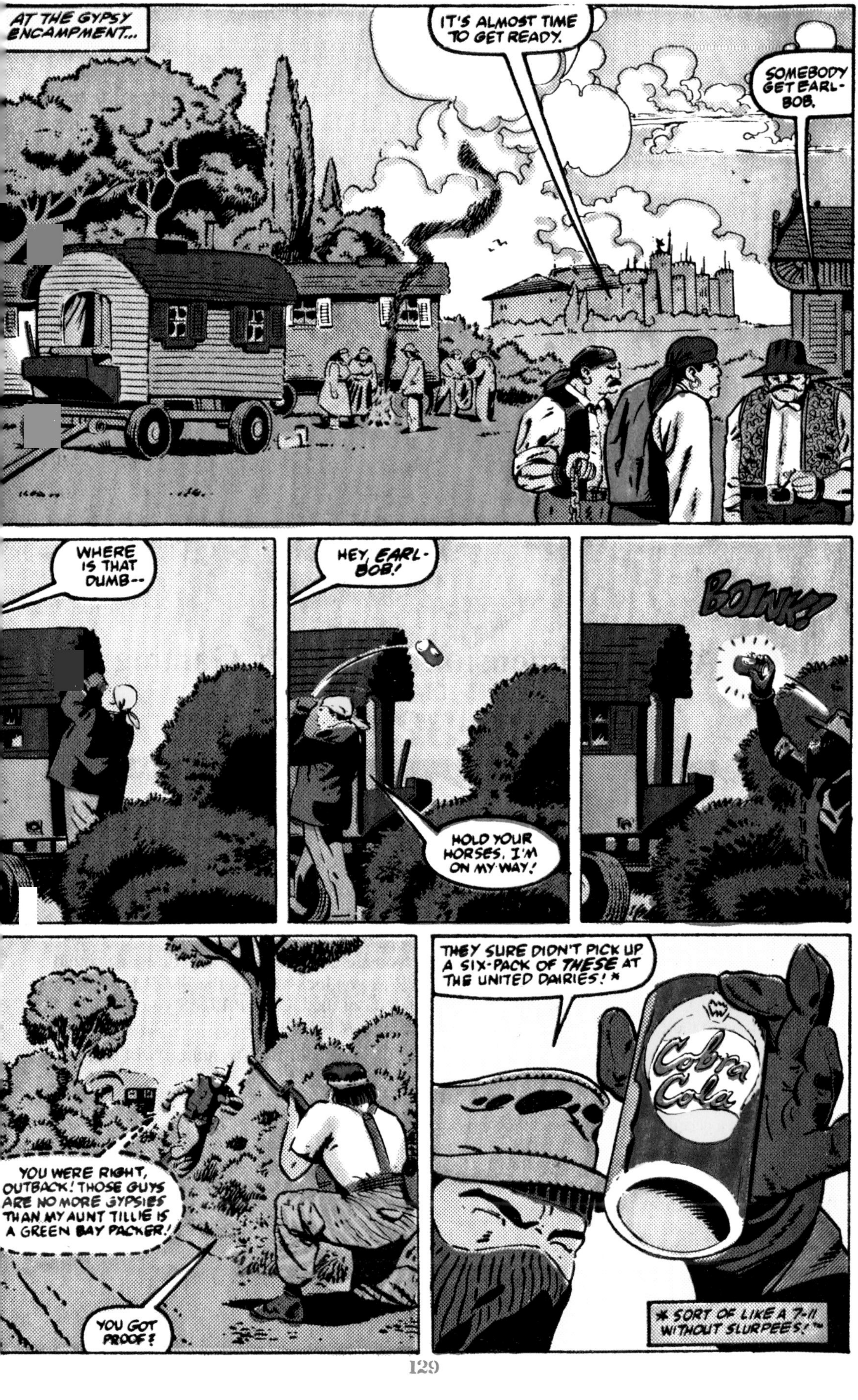

AT THE GYPSY ENCAMPMENT...
IT'S ALMOST TIME TO GET READY.
SOMEBODY GET EARL-BOB.
WHERE IS THAT DUMB--
HEY, EARL-BOB!
HOLD YOUR HORSES, I'M ON MY WAY!
BOINK!
YOU WERE RIGHT, OUTBACK! THOSE GUYS ARE NO MORE GYPSIES THAN MY AUNT TILLIE IS A GREEN BAY PACKER!
YOU GOT PROOF?
THEY SURE DIDN'T PICK UP A SIX-PACK OF THESE AT THE UNITED DAIRIES! *
Cobra Cola
* SORT OF LIKE A 7-11 WITHOUT SLURPEES! ™

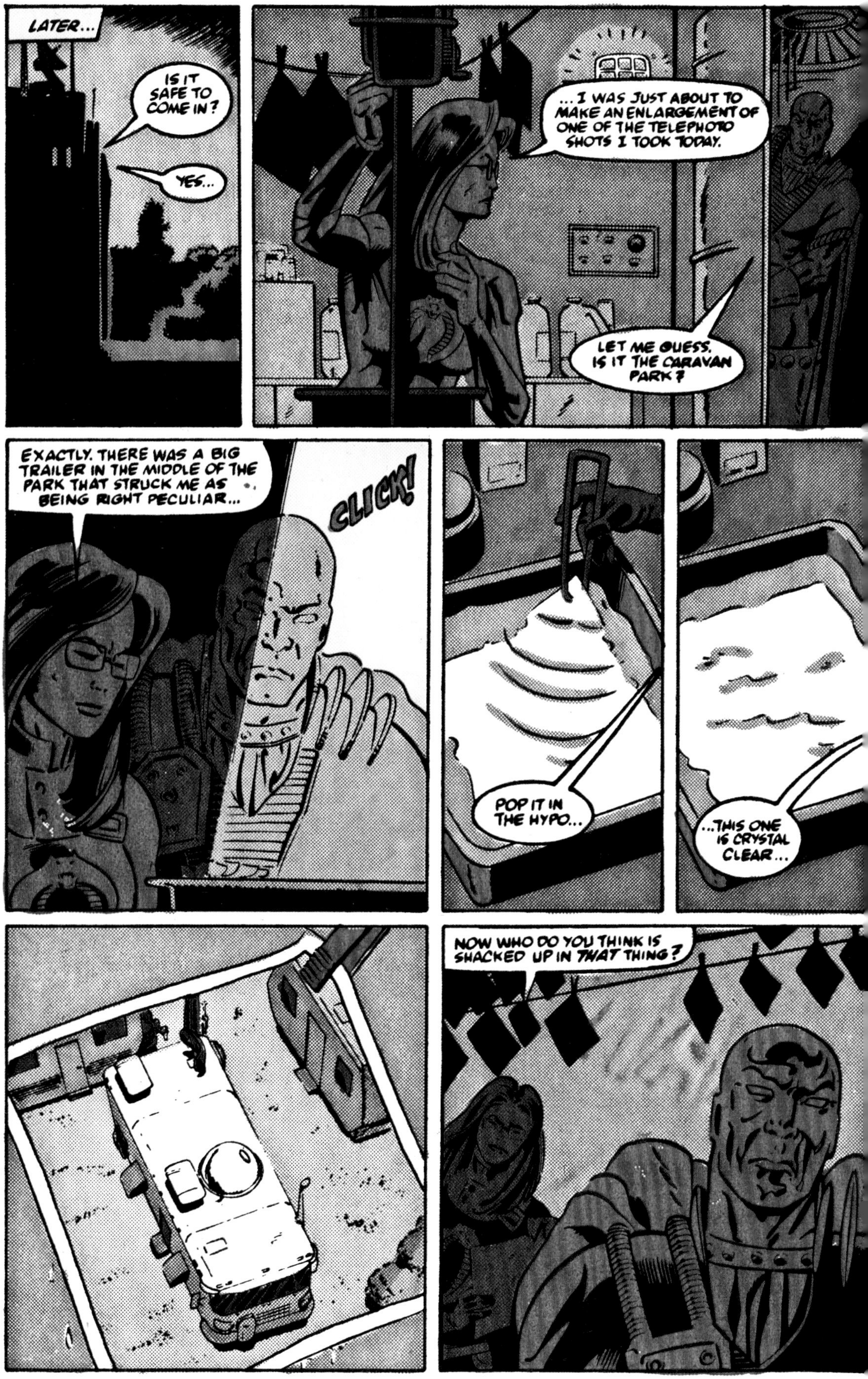
LATER...
IS IT SAFE TO COME IN?
YES...
... I WAS JUST ABOUT TO MAKE AN ENLARGEMENT OF ONE OF THE TELEPHOTO SHOTS I TOOK TODAY.
LET ME GUESS. IS IT THE CARAVAN PARK?
EXACTLY. THERE WAS A BIG TRAILER IN THE MIDDLE OF THE PARK THAT STRUCK ME AS BEING RIGHT PECULIAR...
CLICK!
POP IT IN THE HYPO...
...THIS ONE IS CRYSTAL CLEAR...
NOW WHO DO YOU THINK IS SHACKED UP IN THAT THING?

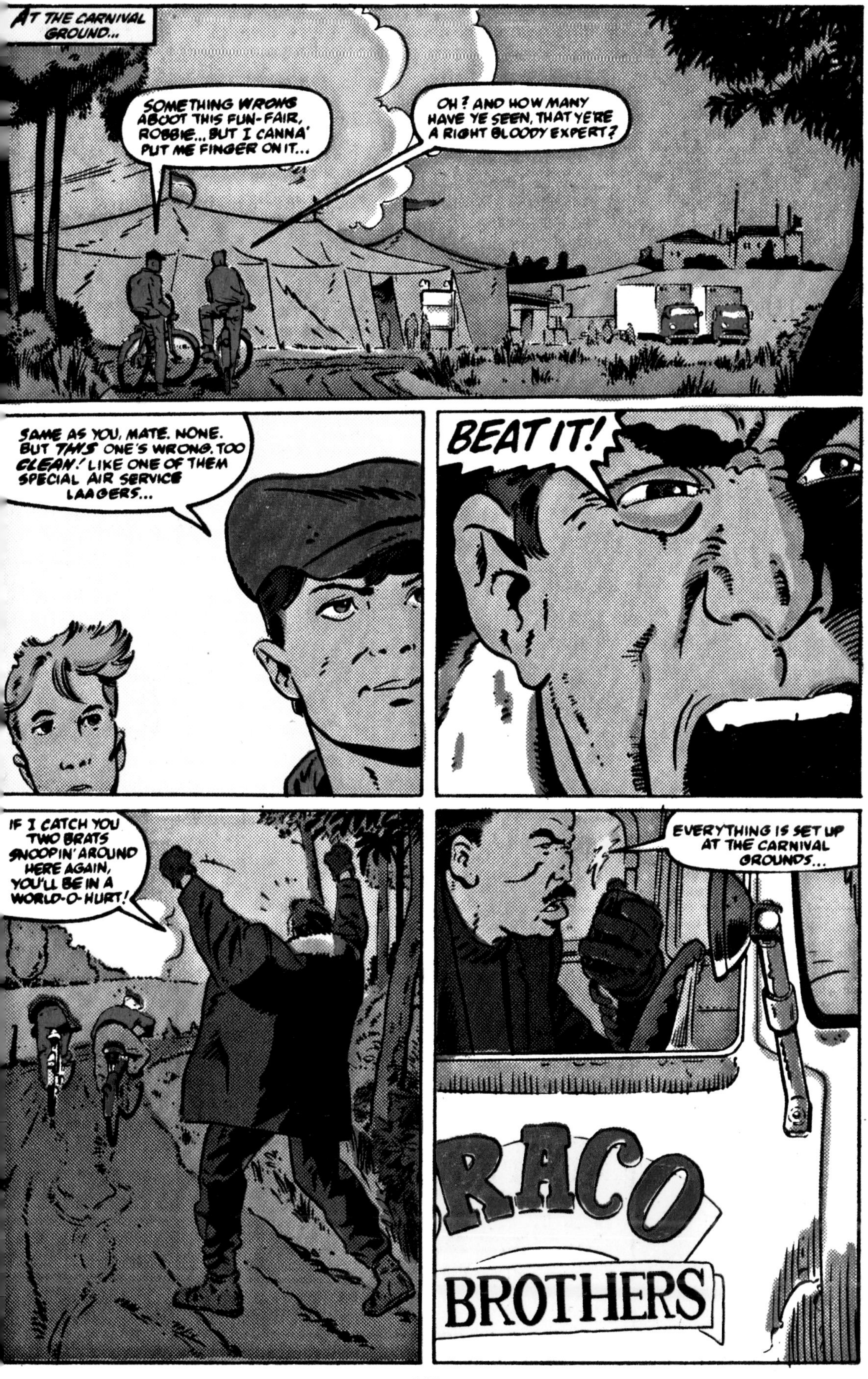
AT THE CARNIVAL GROUND...
SOMETHING WRONG ABOOT THIS FUN-FAIR, ROBBIE... BUT I CANNA' PUT ME FINGER ON IT...
OH? AND HOW MANY HAVE YE SEEN, THAT YE'RE A RIGHT BLOODY EXPERT?
SAME AS YOU, MATE. NONE. BUT THIS ONE'S WRONG. TOO CLEAN! LIKE ONE OF THEM SPECIAL AIR SERVICE LAAGERS...
BEAT IT!
IF I CATCH YOU TWO BRATS SNOOPIN' AROUND HERE AGAIN, YOU'LL BE IN A WORLD-O-HURT!
EVERYTHING IS SET UP AT THE CARNIVAL GROUNDS...
RACO
BROTHERS

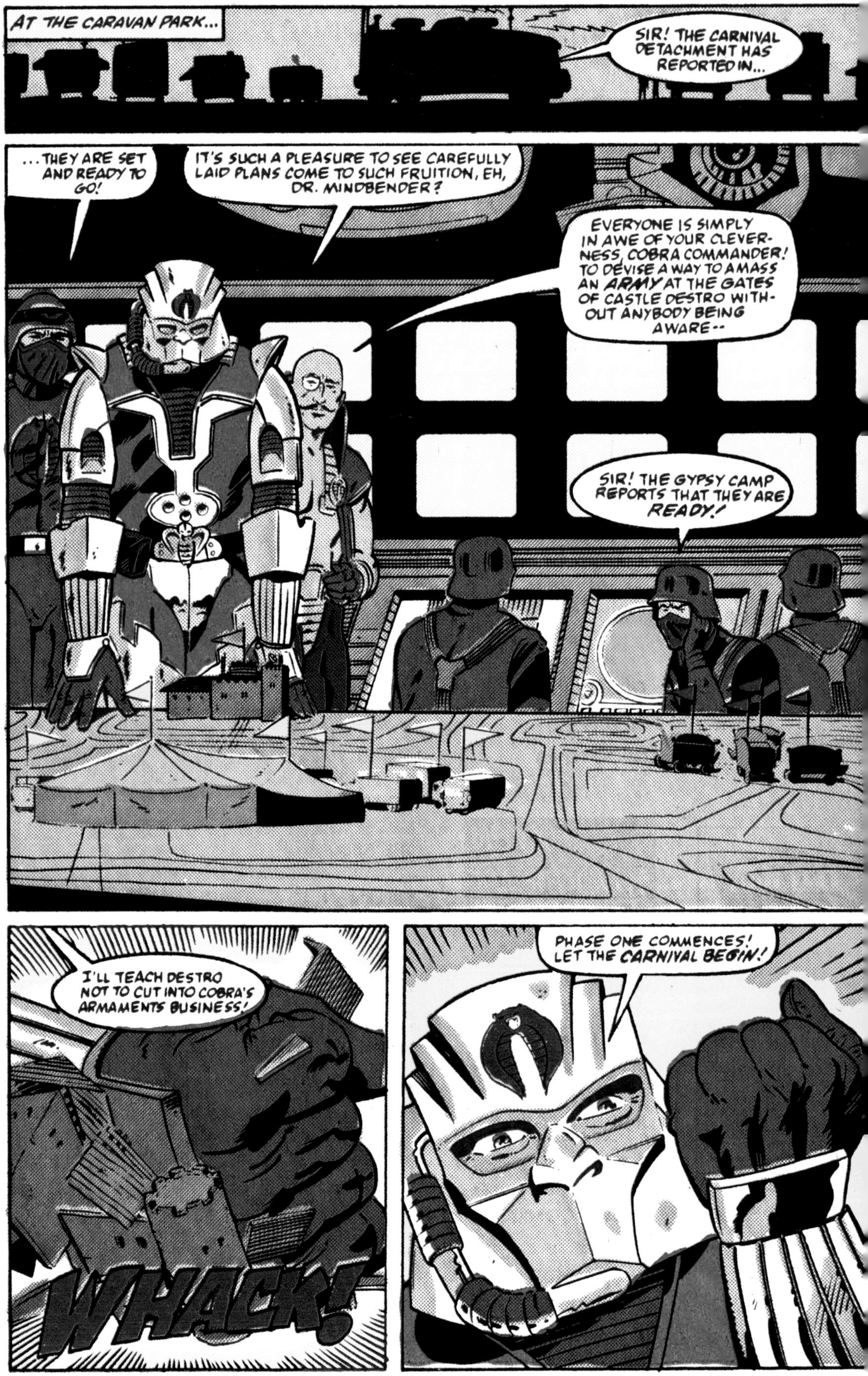

AT THE CARAVAN PARK...
SIR! THE CARNIVAL DETACHMENT HAS REPORTED IN...
...THEY ARE SET AND READY TO GO!
IT'S SUCH A PLEASURE TO SEE CAREFULLY LAID PLANS COME TO SUCH FRUITION, EH, DR. MINDBENDER?
EVERYONE IS SIMPLY IN AWE OF YOUR CLEVERNESS, COBRA COMMANDER! TO DEVISE A WAY TO AMASS AN ARMY AT THE GATES OF CASTLE DESTRO WITHOUT ANYBODY BEING AWARE--
SIR! THE GYPSY CAMP REPORTS THAT THEY ARE READY!
I'LL TEACH DESTRO NOT TO CUT INTO COBRA'S ARMAMENTS BUSINESS!
WHACK!
PHASE ONE COMMENCES! LET THE CARNIVAL BEGIN!

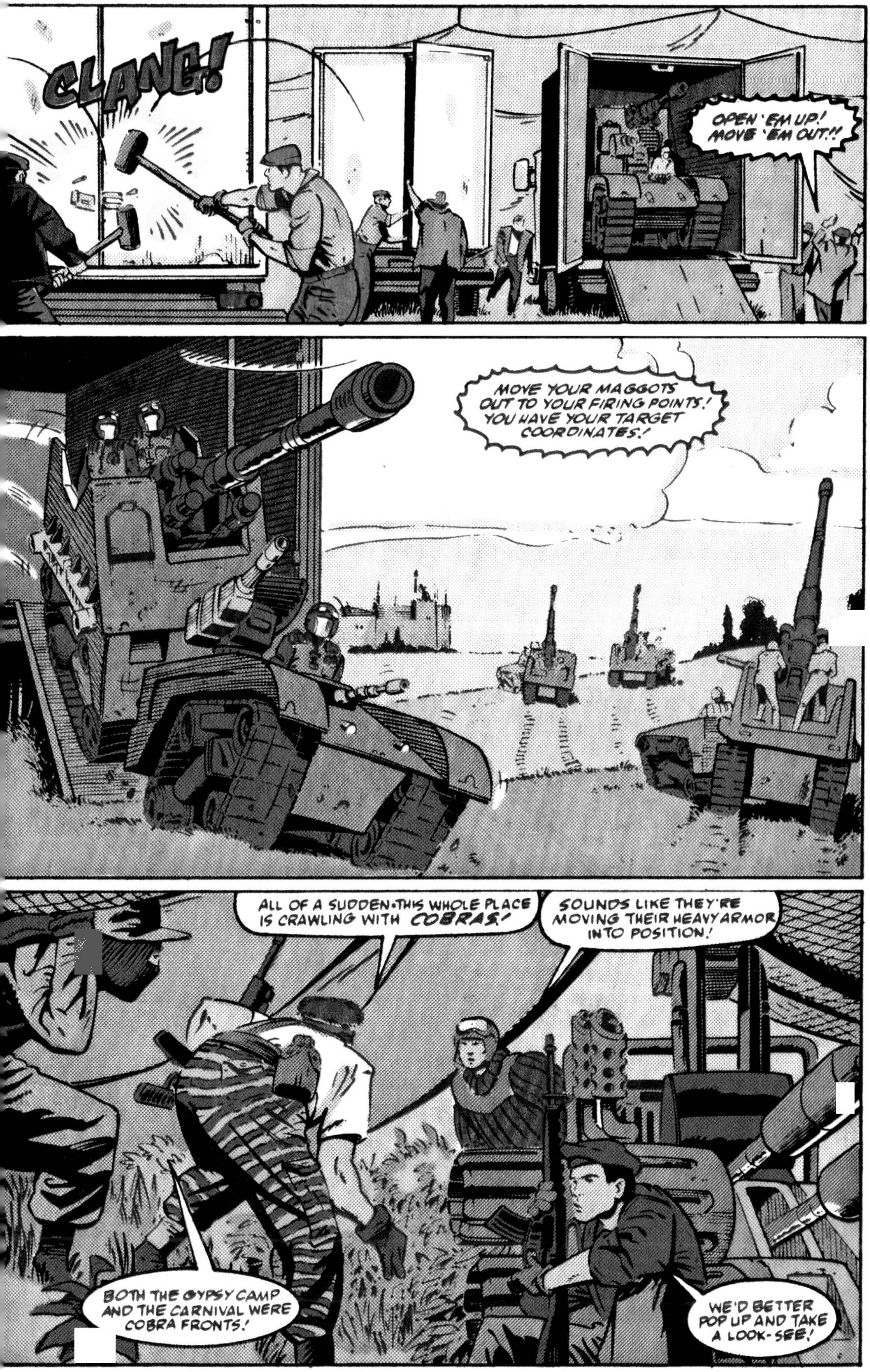
CLANG!
OPEN 'EM UP! MOVE 'EM OUT!!
MOVE YOUR MAGGOTS OUT TO YOUR FIRING POINTS! YOU HAVE YOUR TARGET COORDINATES!
ALL OF A SUDDEN THIS WHOLE PLACE IS CRAWLING WITH COBRAS!
SOUNDS LIKE THEY'RE MOVING THEIR HEAVY ARMOR INTO POSITION!
BOTH THE GYPSY CAMP AND THE CARNIVAL WERE COBRA FRONTS!
WE'D BETTER POP UP AND TAKE A LOOK-SEE!

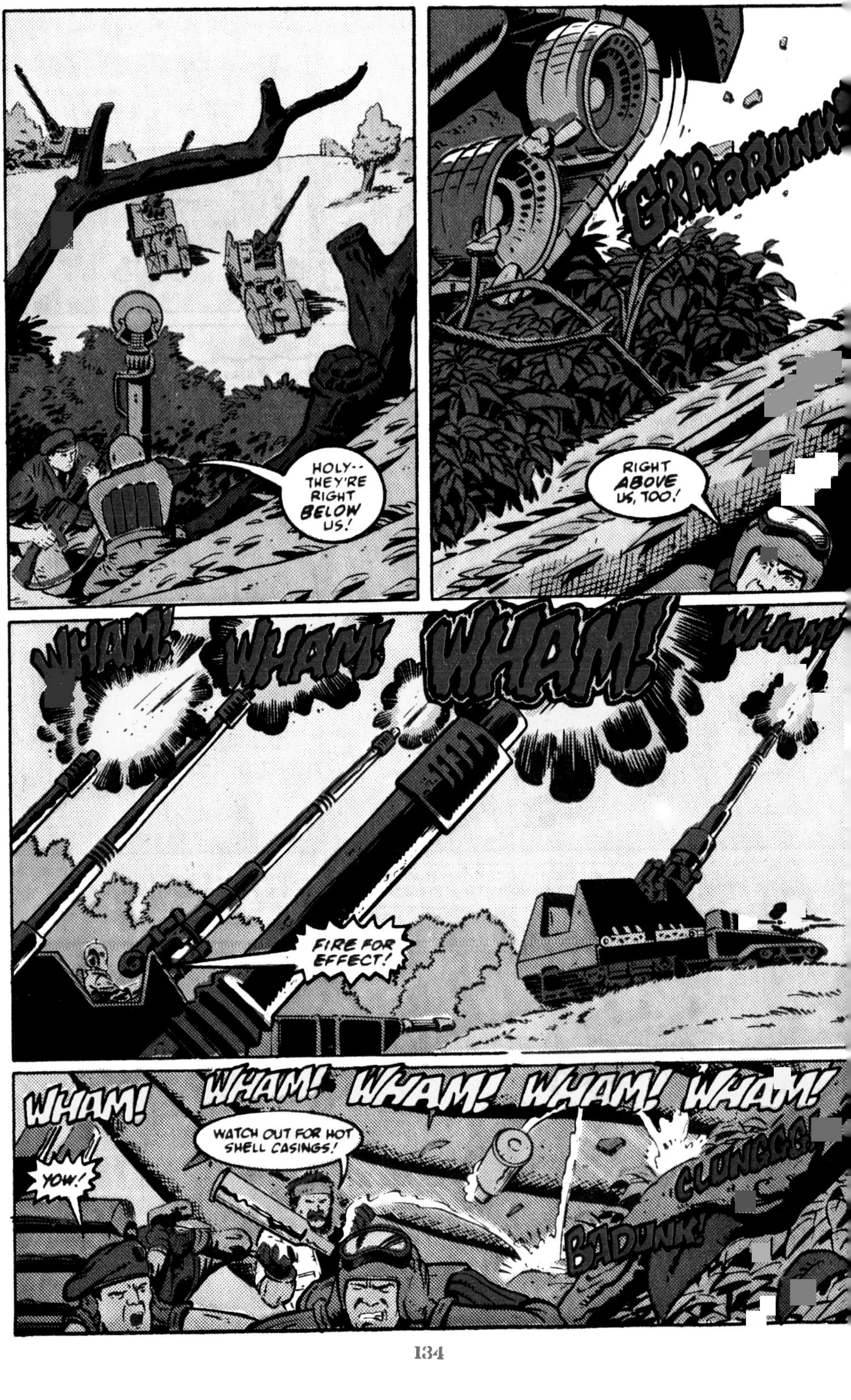
HOLY-- THEY'RE RIGHT BELOW US!
GRRRRUNK!
RIGHT ABOVE US, TOO!
WHAM! WHAM! WHAM! WHAM!
FIRE FOR EFFECT!
WHAM! WHAM! WHAM! WHAM! WHAM!
WATCH OUT FOR HOT SHELL CASINGS!
YOW!
CLUNCCC
BADUNK!

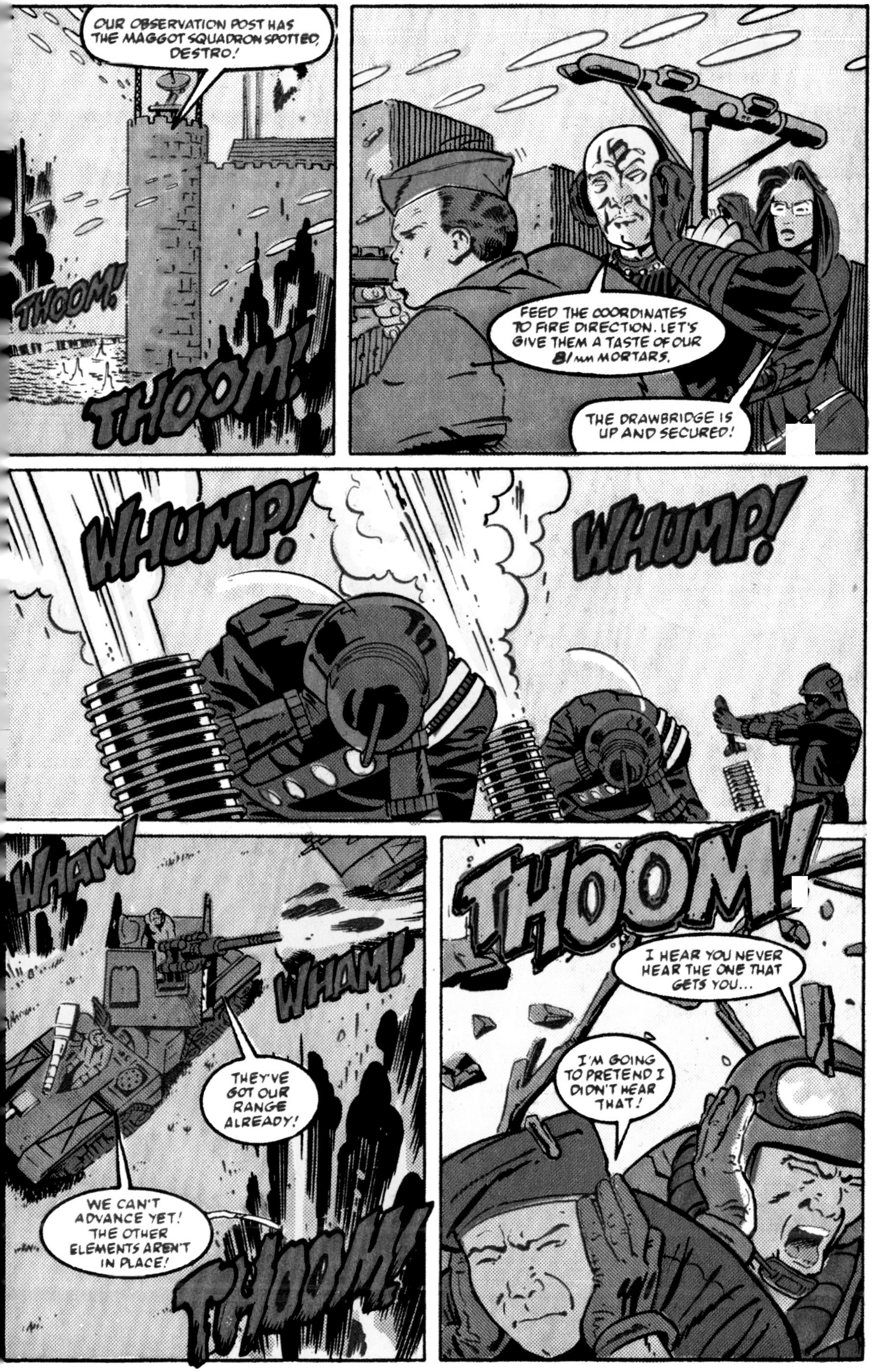
OUR OBSERVATION POST HAS THE MAGGOT SQUADRON SPOTTED, DESTRO!
THOOM!
THOOM!
FEED THE COORDINATES TO FIRE DIRECTION. LET'S GIVE THEM A TASTE OF OUR 81mm MORTARS.
THE DRAWBRIDGE IS UP AND SECURED!
WHUMP!
WHUMP!
WHAM!
WHAM!
THEY'VE GOT OUR RANGE ALREADY!
WE CAN'T ADVANCE YET! THE OTHER ELEMENTS AREN'T IN PLACE!
THOOM!
THOOM!
I HEAR YOU NEVER HEAR THE ONE THAT GETS YOU...
I'M GOING TO PRETEND I DIDN'T HEAR THAT!

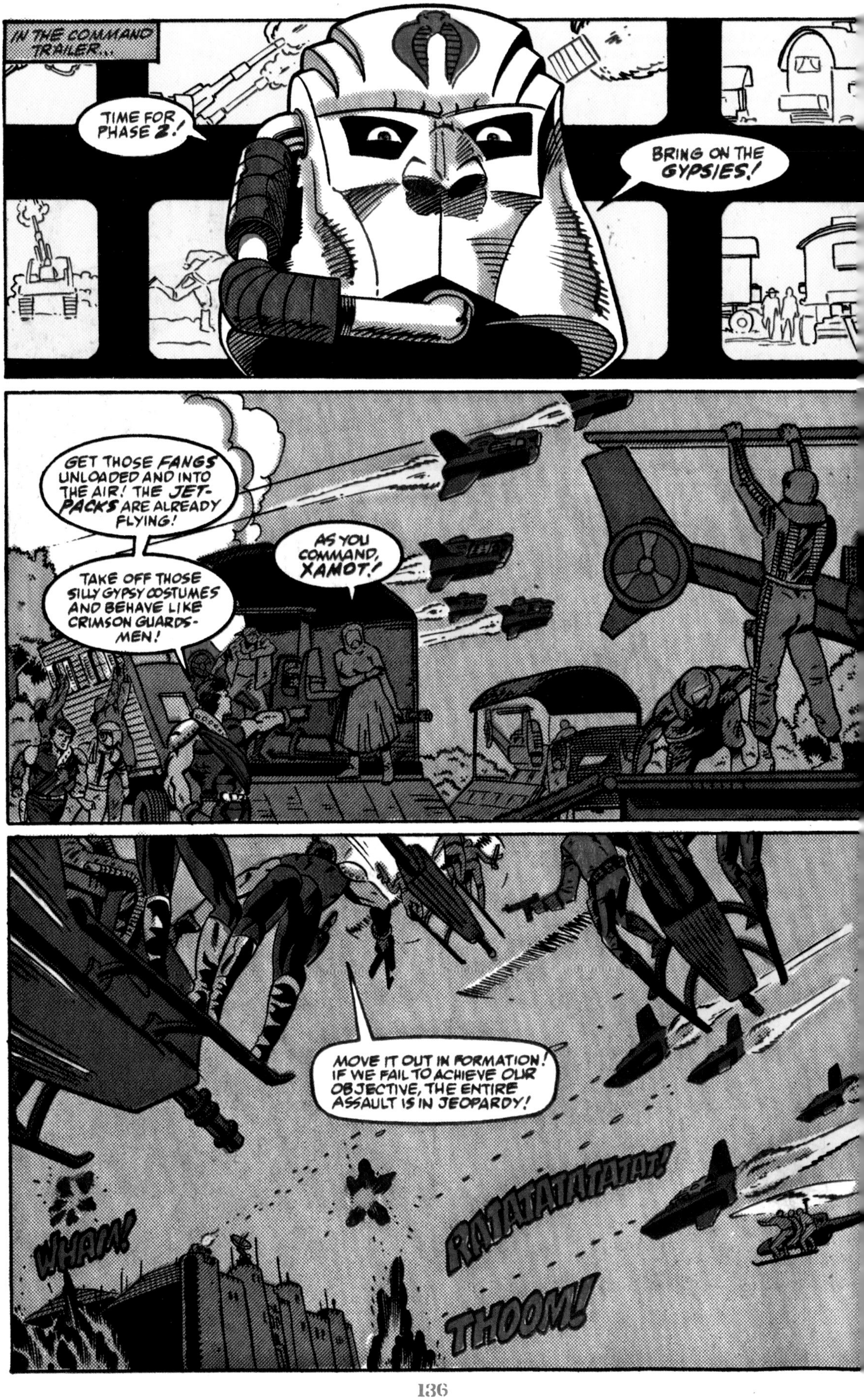
IN THE COMMAND TRAILER...
TIME FOR PHASE 2!
BRING ON THE GYPSIES!
GET THOSE FANGS UNLOADED AND INTO THE AIR! THE JET-PACKS ARE ALREADY FLYING!
TAKE OFF THOSE SILLY GYPSY COSTUMES AND BEHAVE LIKE CRIMSON GUARDS-MEN!
AS YOU COMMAND, XAMOT!
MOVE IT OUT IN FORMATION! IF WE FAIL TO ACHIEVE OUR OBJECTIVE, THE ENTIRE ASSAULT IS IN JEOPARDY!
WHAM!
RATATATATATAT!
THOOM!

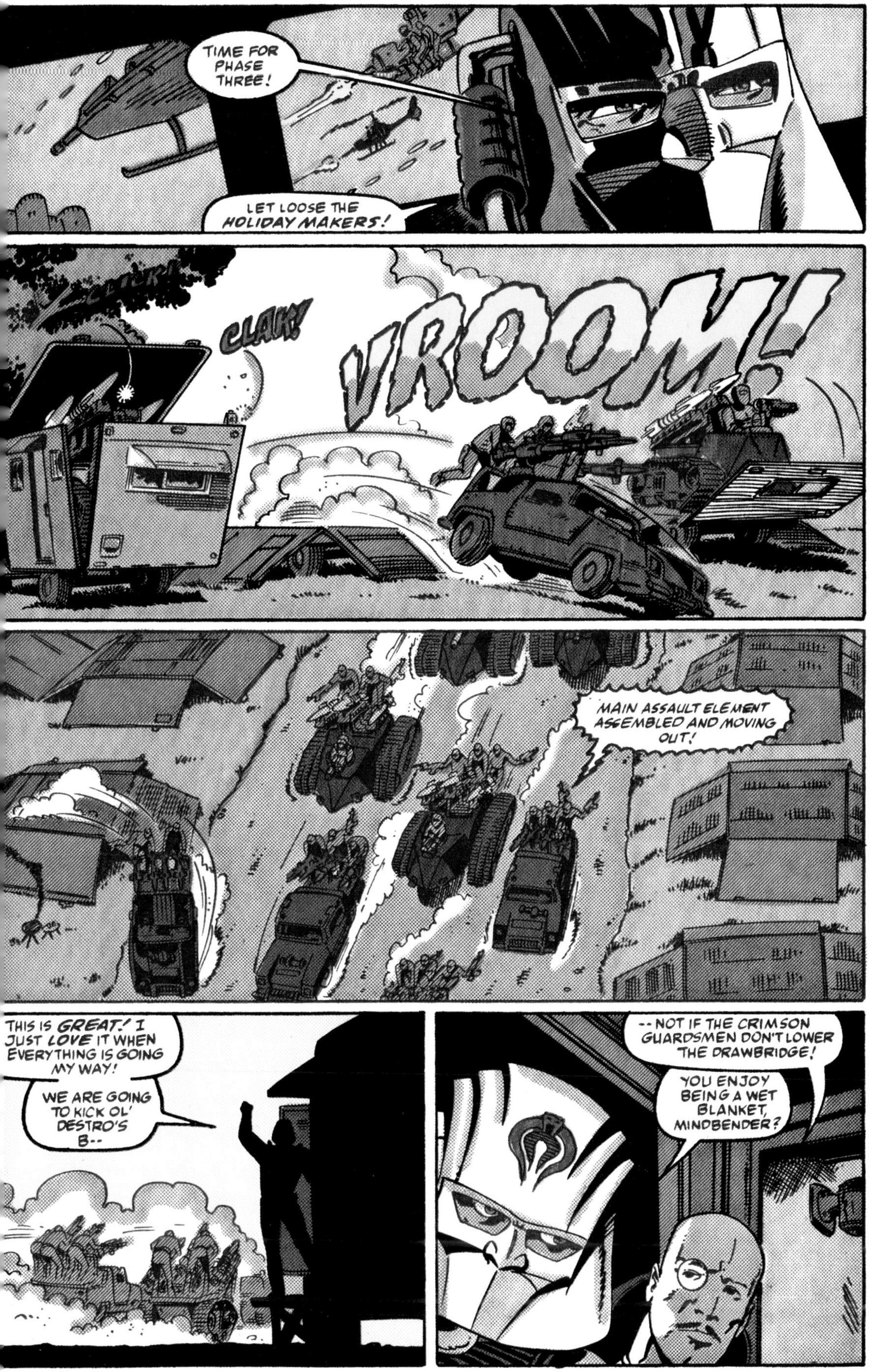
TIME FOR PHASE THREE!
LET LOOSE THE HOLIDAY MAKERS!
CLAK!
VROOM!
MAIN ASSAULT ELEMENT ASSEMBLED AND MOVING OUT!
THIS IS GREAT! I JUST LOVE IT WHEN EVERYTHING IS GOING MY WAY!
WE ARE GOING TO KICK OL' DESTRO'S B--
--NOT IF THE CRIMSON GUARDSMEN DON'T LOWER THE DRAWBRIDGE!
YOU ENJOY BEING A WET BLANKET, MINDBENDER?

RATATATATAT

BLAM!

WHAM!

VIP

B'WEEE!

THE *FANGS* WILL COVER US! GO FOR THE DRAWBRIDGE MACHINERY!

RATATATAT

RIG RAPPELLING LINES!

B'WEE

RATATATAT

LOOKS LIKE DESTRO MODERNIZED THE DRAWBRIDGE AND ELECTRIFIED THE MACHINERY!

JUST SET THE CHARGES!

SOON...

RATATATATAT

CHARGES ARE SET!

WE'LL BE WIRED UP TO THE BLASTING MACHINE IN A SECOND!

FOOOSH!

COBRAAAAA!

FOOOSH!

IF THAT DRAWBRIDGE ISN'T DOWN BY THE TIME WE REACH IT, WE'RE GOING TO BE CUT TO *SHREDS!*

TELL ME!

WHOMP!

WHOMP!

THOOM!

SHALL WE--

--DO IT? BY ALL

...MEANS!

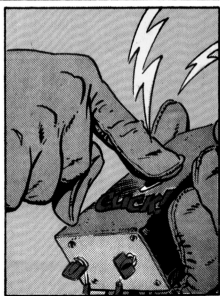

CLICK!

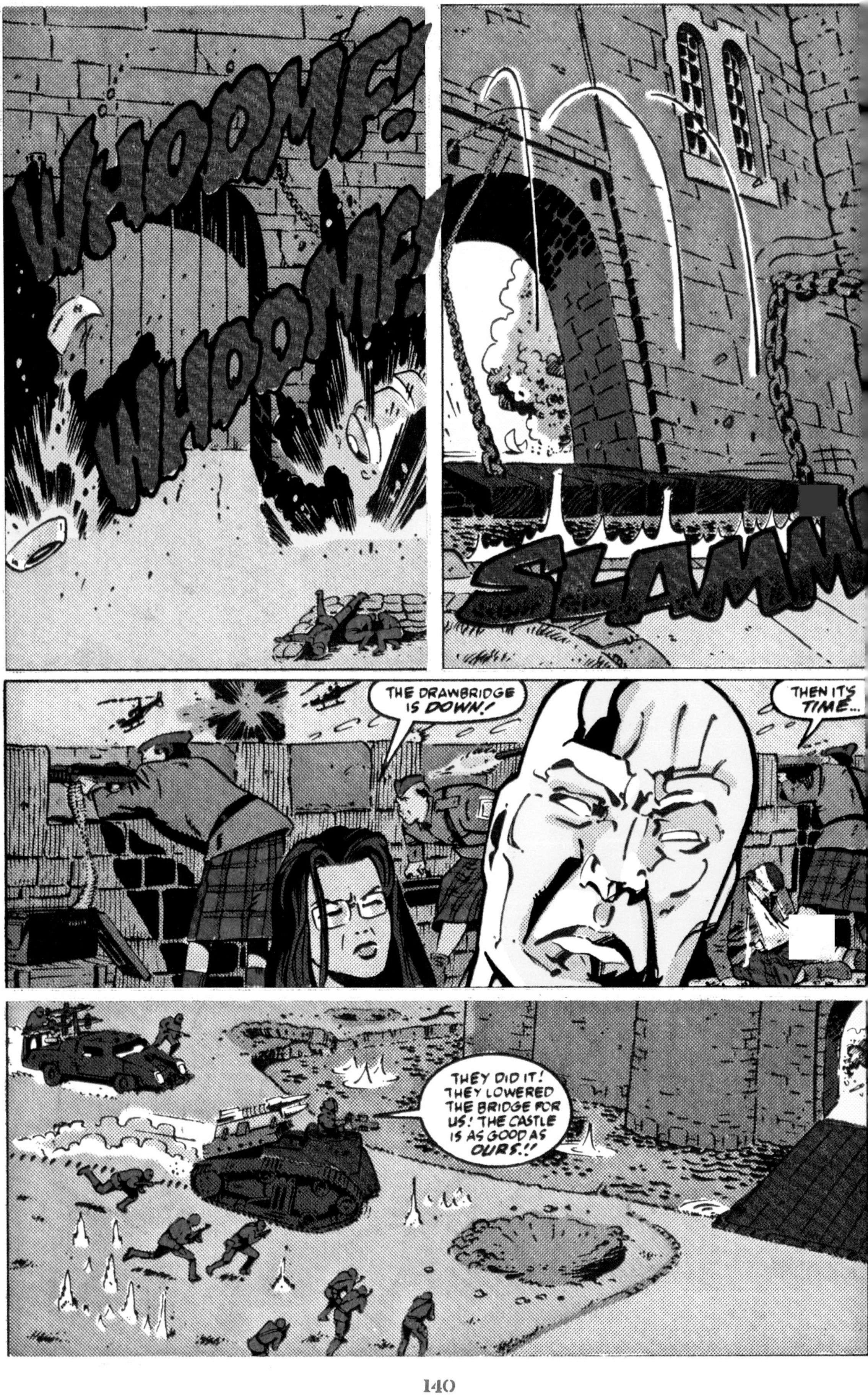
WHOOMF!
WHOOMF!
SLAMM
THE DRAWBRIDGE IS DOWN!
THEN IT'S TIME...
THEY DID IT! THEY LOWERED THE BRIDGE FOR US! THE CASTLE IS AS GOOD AS OURS!!

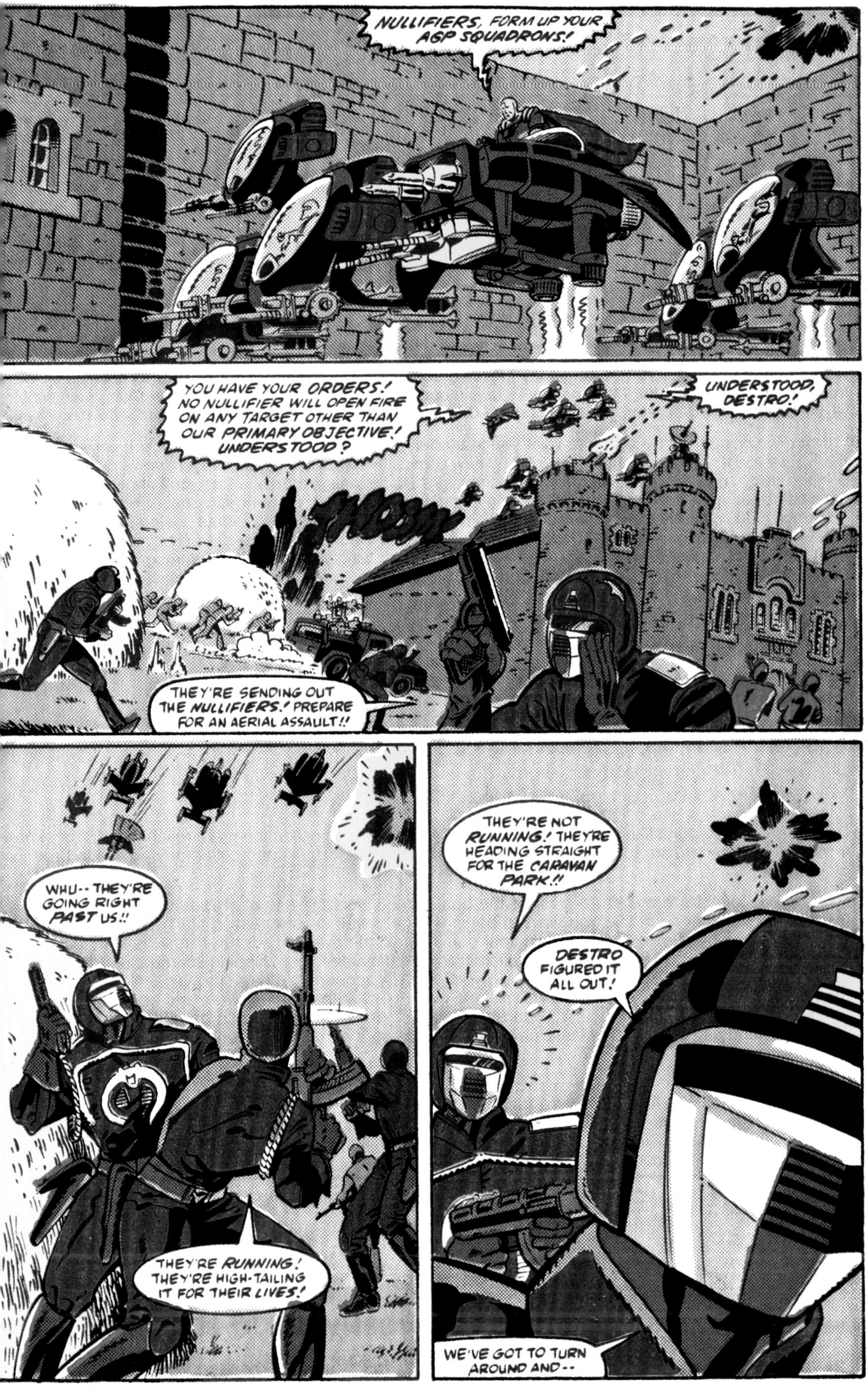
NULLIFIERS, FORM UP YOUR AGP SQUADRONS!
YOU HAVE YOUR ORDERS! NO NULLIFIER WILL OPEN FIRE ON ANY TARGET OTHER THAN OUR PRIMARY OBJECTIVE! UNDERSTOOD?
UNDERSTOOD, DESTRO!
THEY'RE SENDING OUT THE NULLIFIERS! PREPARE FOR AN AERIAL ASSAULT!!
WHU-- THEY'RE GOING RIGHT PAST US!!
THEY'RE RUNNING! THEY'RE HIGH-TAILING IT FOR THEIR LIVES!
THEY'RE NOT RUNNING! THEY'RE HEADING STRAIGHT FOR THE CARAVAN PARK!!
DESTRO FIGURED IT ALL OUT!
WE'VE GOT TO TURN AROUND AND--

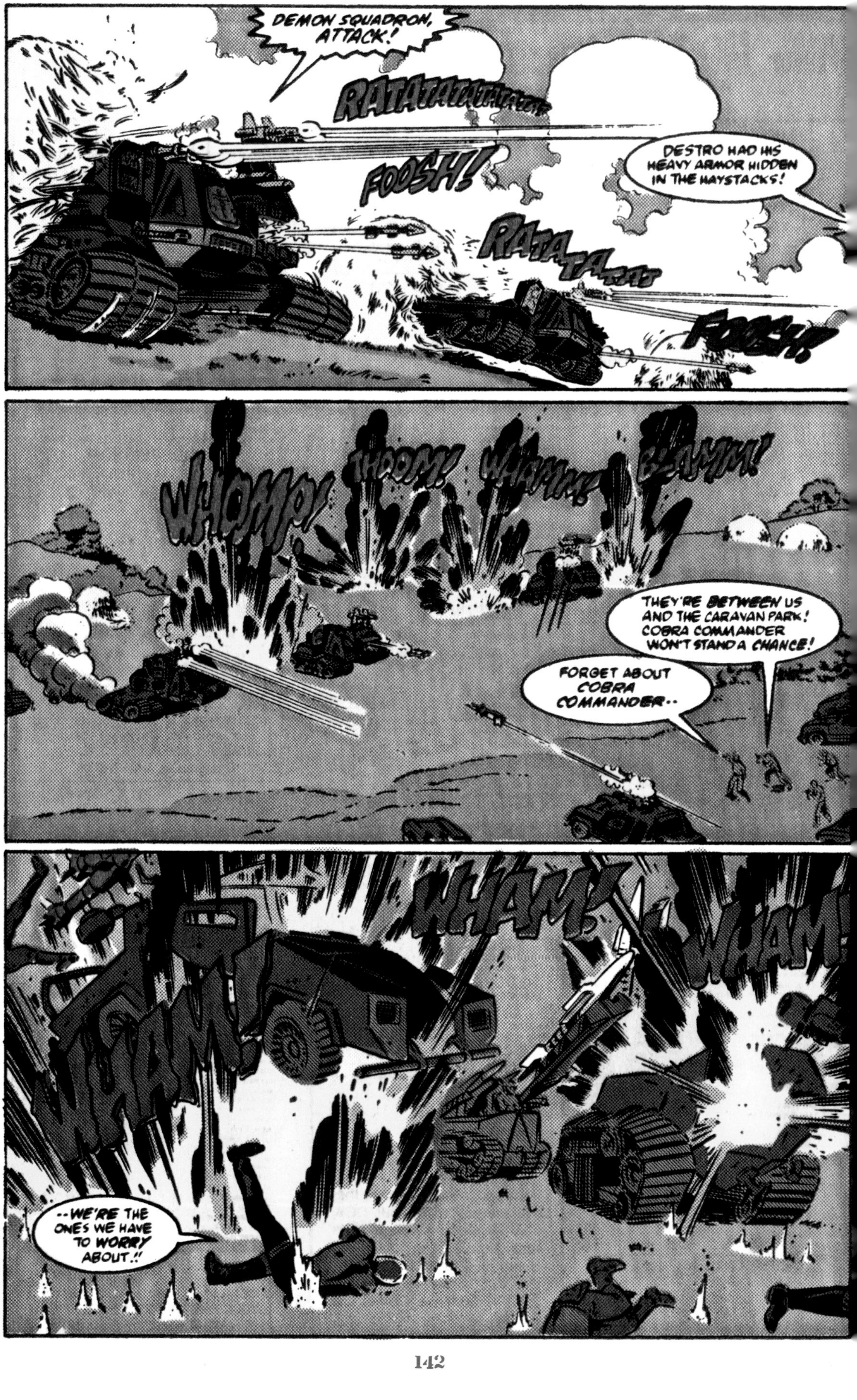
DEMON SQUADRON, ATTACK!
RATATATATATATAT
FOOSH!
DESTRO HAD HIS HEAVY ARMOR HIDDEN IN THE HAYSTACKS!
RATATATAT
FOOSH!
WHOMP!
THOOM!
WHAMM!
BLAMM!
THEY'RE BETWEEN US AND THE CARAVAN PARK! COBRA COMMANDER WON'T STAND A CHANCE!
FORGET ABOUT COBRA COMMANDER..
WHAM!
WHAM!
WHAM!
..WE'RE THE ONES WE HAVE TO WORRY ABOUT.!!

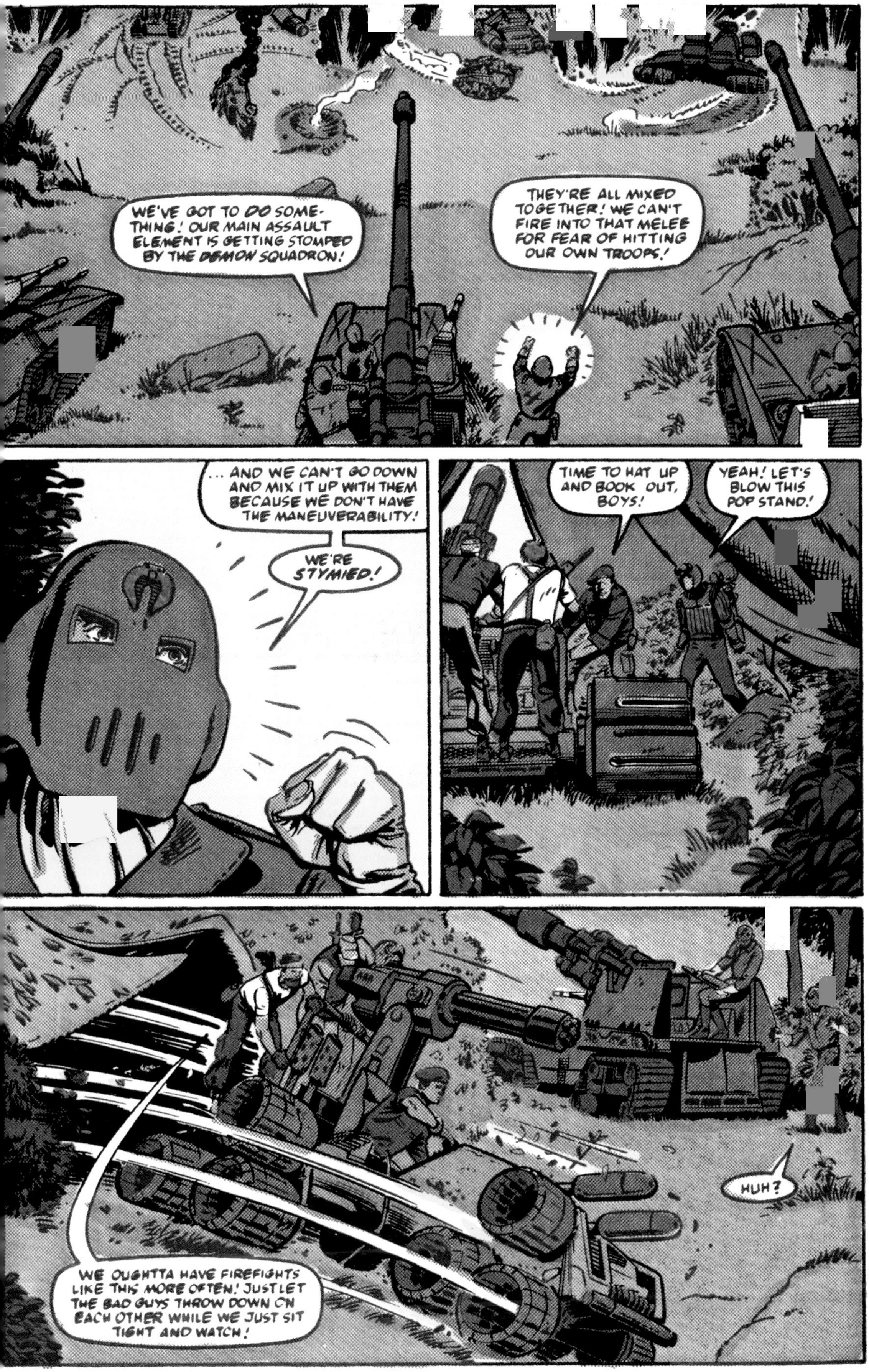

WE'VE GOT TO DO SOME-THING! OUR MAIN ASSAULT ELEMENT IS GETTING STOMPED BY THE DEMON SQUADRON!
THEY'RE ALL MIXED TOGETHER! WE CAN'T FIRE INTO THAT MELEE FOR FEAR OF HITTING OUR OWN TROOPS!
... AND WE CAN'T GO DOWN AND MIX IT UP WITH THEM BECAUSE WE DON'T HAVE THE MANEUVERABILITY!
WE'RE STYMIED!
TIME TO HAT UP AND BOOK OUT, BOYS!
YEAH! LET'S BLOW THIS POP STAND!
HUH?
WE OUGHTTA HAVE FIREFIGHTS LIKE THIS MORE OFTEN! JUST LET THE BAD GUYS THROW DOWN ON EACH OTHER WHILE WE JUST SIT TIGHT AND WATCH!

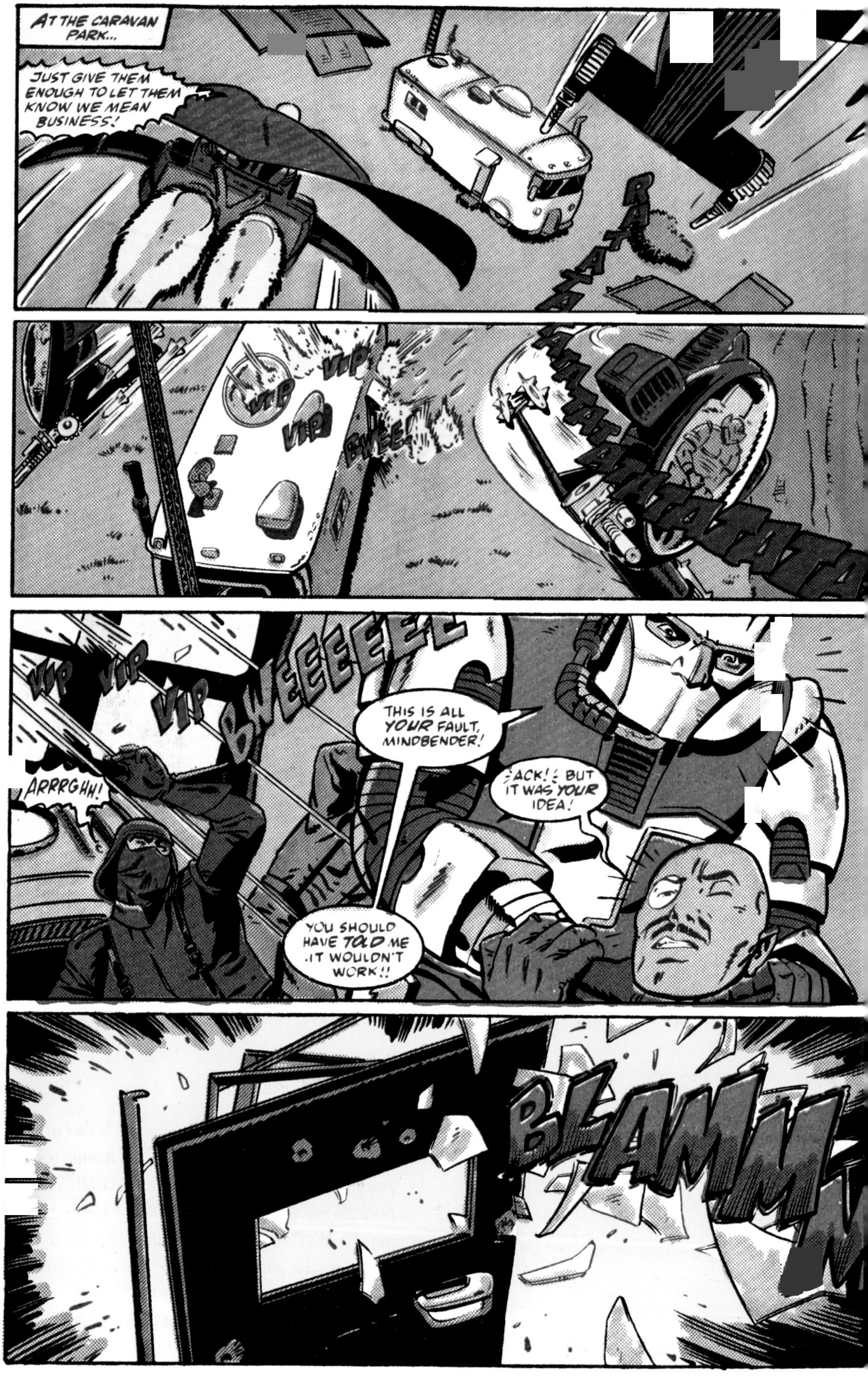

AT THE CARAVAN PARK...
JUST GIVE THEM ENOUGH TO LET THEM KNOW WE MEAN BUSINESS!
VIP VIP VIP
BWEE!
VIP VIP VIP
BWEEEEEEE
THIS IS ALL YOUR FAULT, MINDBENDER!
ARRRGHH!
ACK! BUT IT WAS YOUR IDEA!
YOU SHOULD HAVE TOLD ME IT WOULDN'T WORK!!
BLAMM

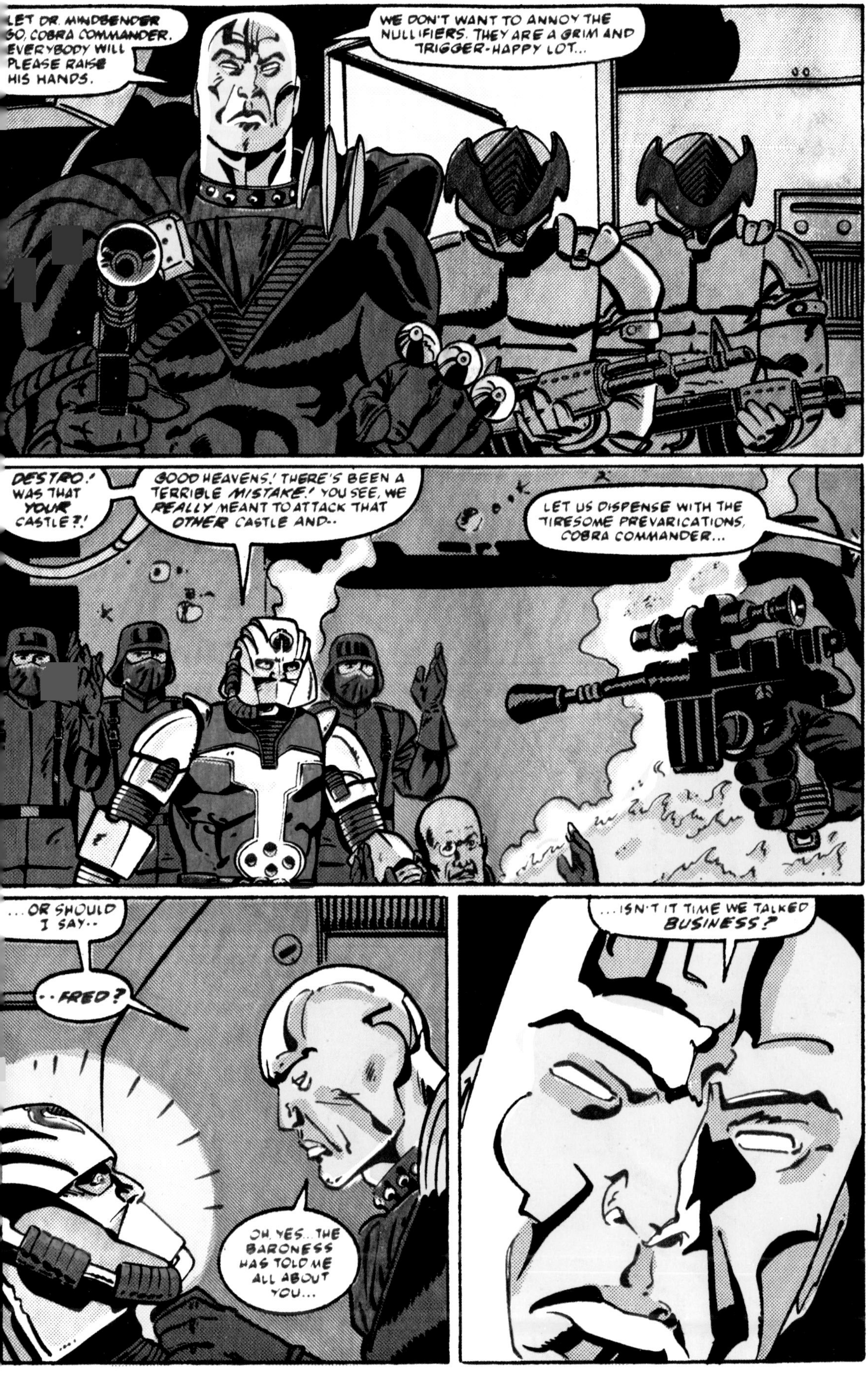
LET DR. MINDBENDER GO, COBRA COMMANDER. EVERYBODY WILL PLEASE RAISE HIS HANDS.
WE DON'T WANT TO ANNOY THE NULLIFIERS. THEY ARE A GRIM AND TRIGGER-HAPPY LOT...
DESTRO.! WAS THAT YOUR CASTLE?!
GOOD HEAVENS! THERE'S BEEN A TERRIBLE MISTAKE! YOU SEE, WE REALLY MEANT TO ATTACK THAT OTHER CASTLE AND--
LET US DISPENSE WITH THE TIRESOME PREVARICATIONS, COBRA COMMANDER...
...OR SHOULD I SAY--
--FRED?
OH, YES... THE BARONESS HAS TOLD ME ALL ABOUT YOU...
...ISN'T IT TIME WE TALKED BUSINESS?

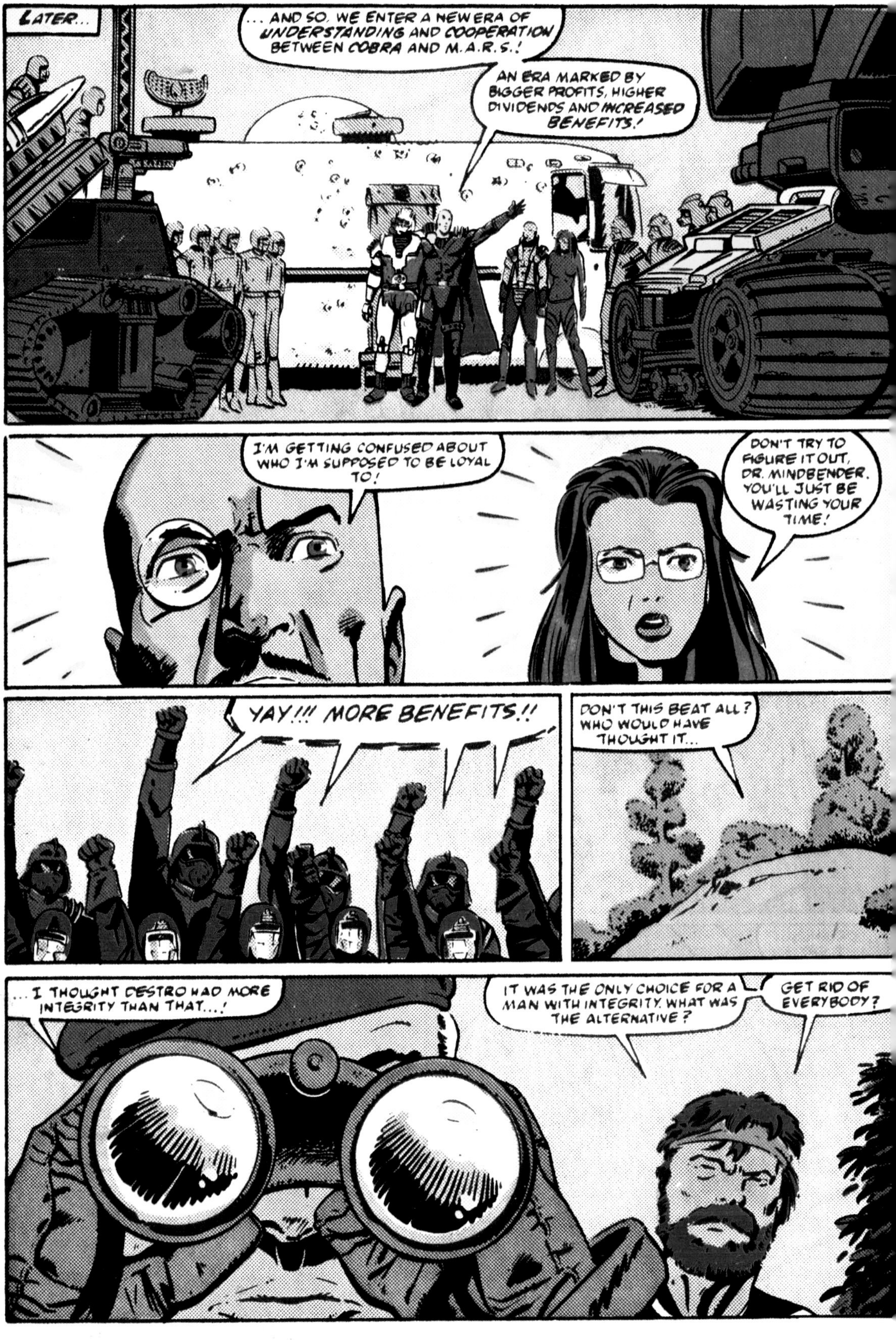
LATER...
...AND SO, WE ENTER A NEW ERA OF UNDERSTANDING AND COOPERATION BETWEEN COBRA AND M.A.R.S.!
AN ERA MARKED BY BIGGER PROFITS, HIGHER DIVIDENDS AND INCREASED BENEFITS!
I'M GETTING CONFUSED ABOUT WHO I'M SUPPOSED TO BE LOYAL TO!
DON'T TRY TO FIGURE IT OUT, DR. MINDBENDER. YOU'LL JUST BE WASTING YOUR TIME!
YAY!!! MORE BENEFITS!!
DON'T THIS BEAT ALL? WHO WOULD HAVE THOUGHT IT...
...I THOUGHT DESTRO HAD MORE INTEGRITY THAN THAT...!
IT WAS THE ONLY CHOICE FOR A MAN WITH INTEGRITY. WHAT WAS THE ALTERNATIVE?
GET RID OF EVERYBODY?

THIS CONCLUDES G.I. JOE BEST OF / WORST DESTRO

MORE VOLUMES AVAILABLE WITH YOUR FAVORITE HEROES AND VILLAINS

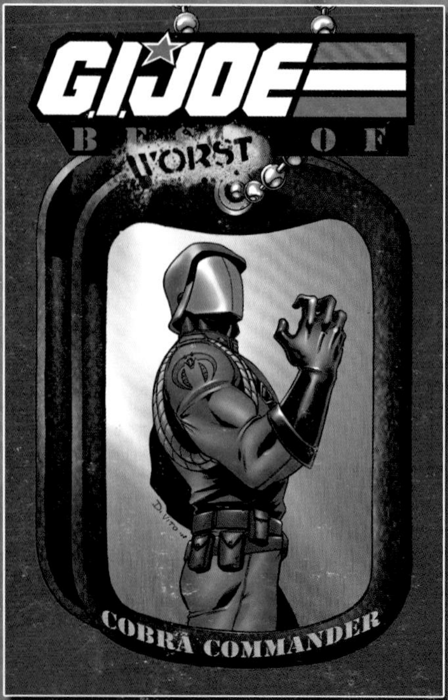
G.I. JOE
BEST OF
WORST
COBRA COMMANDER

THE BEST OF COBRA COMMANDER
ISBN: 978-1-60010-428-2

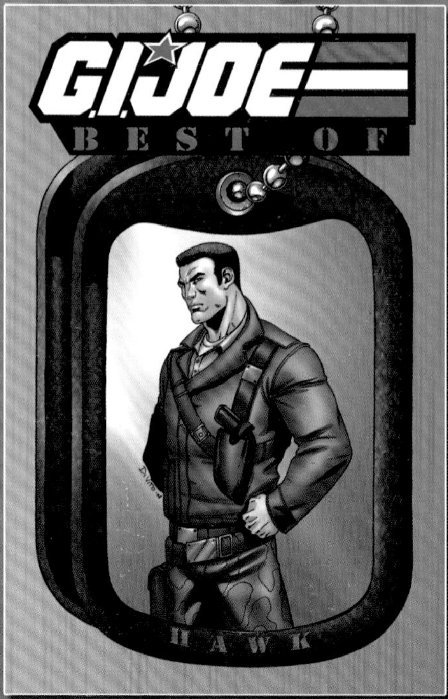
G.I. JOE
BEST OF
HAWK

THE BEST OF HAWK
ISBN: 978-1-60010-427-5

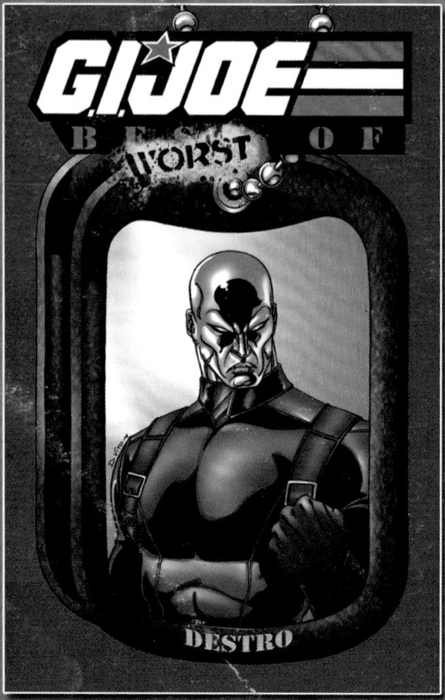
G.I. JOE
BEST OF
WORST
DESTRO

THE BEST OF DESTRO
ISBN: 978-1-60010-448-0

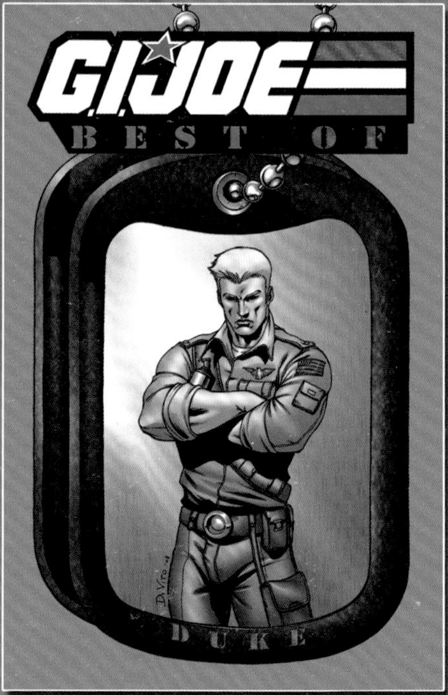
G.I. JOE
BEST OF
DUKE

THE BEST OF DUKE
ISBN: 978-1-60010-447-3

WWW.IDWPUBLISHING.COM

ON SALE NOW!